Freegans

Freegans

Diving into the Wealth of Food Waste in America

Alex V. Barnard

University of Minnesota Press
Minneapolis · London

Chapter 3 was originally published as "Waving the Banana at Capitalism: Political Theater and Social Movement Strategy among New York's 'Freegan' Dumpster Divers," *Ethnography* 12, no. 4 (2011): 419–44.

Published by the University of Minnesota Press
111 Third Avenue South, Suite 290
Minneapolis, MN 55401-2520
http://www.upress.umn.edu

A Cataloging-in-Publication record for this book
is available from the Library of Congress.

ISBN 978-0-8166-9811-0 (hc)
ISBN 978-0-8166-9813-4 (pb)

Printed in the United States of America on acid-free paper

The University of Minnesota is an equal-opportunity educator and employer.

21 20 19 18 17 16   10 9 8 7 6 5 4 3 2 1

This book is dedicated to Janet and Marie

The decay spreads over the State, and the sweet smell is a great sorrow on the land. Men who can graft the trees and make the seed fertile and big can find no way to let the hungry people eat their produce. Men who have created new fruits in the world cannot create a system whereby the fruits may be eaten. . . .

The works of the roots, of the vines, of the trees, must be destroyed to keep up the price, and this is the saddest, bitterest thing of all. Carloads of oranges dumped on the ground. The people came for miles to take the fruit, but this could not be. How would they buy oranges at twenty cents a dozen if they could drive out and pick them up? . . .

There is a crime here that goes beyond denunciation. There is a sorrow here that weeping cannot symbolize. There is a failure here that topples all our success.

—John Steinbeck, *The Grapes of Wrath*

Contents

Preface

In the summer of 2007 I read a *New York Times* article titled "Not Buying It" that explored the ideologies and practices of a new, and supposedly growing, movement of people called "freegans." Freeganism seemed to mean a great many different things, but what stuck with me, and probably most readers, was that freegans ate garbage. More than that: freegans were people with homes and educations and reliable sources of income who ate garbage *voluntarily*.

In retrospect, I was probably in a demographic sliver particularly susceptible to the freegan message. I was an affluent white male attending an exclusive private college. At the same time, I was a recently converted vegan, increasingly attuned to the ethical and political implications of my consumption choices. And, it should be added, I had a six-inch-tall Mohawk. This minor detail hints at an alternative streak that primed me for a "deviant" activity like "dumpster diving"—that is to say, recovering discarded goods (often food) from trash bins outside commercial establishments.[1] Perhaps that hairstyle enabled many freegans to see past my Princeton pedigree and accept me as an authentic activist.

Nevertheless, when I first traveled to Brooklyn from my home in New Jersey to attend one of the public, organized, collective dumpster dives that the website freegan.info called a "trash tour," I was not anticipating any long-term involvement. Slightly concerned about whether freegans would be as welcoming as their online event description suggested, I convinced a friend to join me. I imagined that we would spend a few hours searching out rotten apple cores and potato peelings and come home more or less empty-handed. I'm sure many people embark on their first freegan forays with the same mix of trepidation and low expectations.

What I saw on that night's trash tour—and again, and again, and again as I returned in the ensuing years—was waste on a scale that boggled my mind and defied easy explanation. Or, perhaps, the biggest problem was that what I saw didn't seem like waste at all.

After all, "waste" is supposed to be dirty, rotten, useless, and contaminated; the food we found routinely surpassed in quality what I ate in my school's dining hall. This sharp contrast between what I expected to find in the garbage and what I encountered drove my subsequent involvement in freeganism. The concepts of the ex-commodity and fetish of waste that anchor this book were right in front of me from that first night, even if it took me the better part of a decade to fully articulate them.

I continued to come into New York regularly from 2007 to 2009. I moved from merely attending freegan events to taking part in freegan working groups and organizational meetings. I joined freegans as they participated in protests and actions organized by New York's activist scene. In 2009 I interviewed twenty freegan.info participants, which constituted nearly all the people regularly involved with the group at the time. In 2012 I returned briefly to New York on three occasions and conducted follow-up interviews with seven of the freegans I had interviewed in 2009, some of whom had since left the movement. I supplemented my research by analyzing nearly a decade of freegan.info e-mail Listserv archives and online literature, and I interviewed freegans throughout the United States and in Western Europe, as well as conducting a year of participant-observations of a freegan-affiliated movement, Food Not Bombs, in the East Bay near San Francisco.

Other experiences round out my understanding of freeganism and waste but don't fit neatly under the heading "data collection." I have been involved in a wide range of activism around food for the past decade: as a campaigner for animal rights and veganism in New Jersey and England; as a supporter of social movements against waste in Berkeley and Paris; as a volunteer for a food redistribution charity in Oxford; as a paid employee of a food distribution charity in Arizona. While I never considered myself committed enough to self-identify as a freegan, I gradually incorporated freegan practices of limited consumption and waste reclamation into my daily life. I've recovered nearly all my food for months at a time; I've traveled thousands of miles for free by hitchhiking; I've partaken of the *real* "sharing economy" through couch surfing and freecycle; I've learned how to repair my bike and my clothes. These actions were not taken with scholarly intent, but they inflect this book throughout (as well as hint at some of my biases).

This book is intended as more than a piece of journalistic reporting. Freegan.info has already received ample media attention, and there is no shortage of descriptions of freegans and what they do. There is, however, an absence of serious discussion of the underlying processes that make freeganism possible and the issues that drive them to the dumpster. My goal is to put my close, on-the-ground observations of the freegan.info community in dialogue with social scientific theories about capitalism, waste, and social movements. I make no pretensions to have entered "the field" free from preconceptions. Instead, I sought to challenge and reconstruct these preconceptions, as well as the implicit or explicit social theories that lie behind them, through ethnography. In sociological parlance, this is the approach known as the "extended case" method.[2]

Using "theory" is not an attempt to obfuscate freeganism in a fog of academic jargon. As I argue throughout this book, all of us have "theories" about how markets work, what winds up in the garbage, or what constitutes effective activism. I see engaging with theory, then, as a challenge to how both social scientists and nonacademics view the world. I argue that the study of freeganism illuminates not just one peculiar group of people in New York City but broader truths about the nature of the economic system that most of humanity lives under. That said, I tried to confine the more arcane theoretical references to the endnotes, where they join links to various studies and statistics about issues of concern to the freegans. My ultimate goal has been to write a book that is convincing to sociologists yet compelling and accessible to nonsociologists; the reader will be the judge of my success.

Before diving in, I want to make one crucial caveat explicit. When I conducted my research, freegan.info was the most organized and visible group of self-identified freegans in the world. As they were careful to point out on their website, however, "We do not speak for all freegans worldwide, nor do we claim to have better knowledge than anyone else on what freeganism is."[3] It follows that a book about freegan.info cannot claim to be a book about all "freegans," even though, for convenience, I often use the labels "freegan.info participants" and "freegans" interchangeably.

Even within freegan.info there was no consensus about what freeganism meant or who freegans were. People active in the group before I arrived or after I left might find some of the participants

Introduction

A Brief History of a Tomato

On a cold night in December 2008, a slightly overripe tomato sits inside a black plastic trash bag on a sidewalk outside a D'Agostino supermarket in Murray Hill, a wealthy residential district east of midtown Manhattan. A sticker on its side, "Grown in Mexico," hints at the long trajectory that it took to the curb.

A good starting point in this tomato's story is 1994, when the United States, Canada, and Mexico implemented the North American Free Trade Agreement, or NAFTA. In preparation, Mexico phased out long-standing protections for its agricultural sector. International agribusinesses seized the opportunity presented by lowered tariffs to flood Mexican markets with heavily subsidized U.S. grain, especially corn.[1] Falling grain prices and the withdrawal of state support for small-scale agriculture pushed thousands of peasants off the communal lands they had worked for centuries and defended during the Mexican Revolution.[2] Many trekked north; some made it to the tomato fields of Florida, where a recent investigation found both old and young engaged in backbreaking labor and living conditions akin to "virtual slavery."[3]

This tomato was most likely picked by temporary laborers on a huge tomato plantation in Mexico, working twelve hours to earn a meager ten-dollar daily wage.[4] Industrial farms pick their tomatoes while still green and ripen them through dozens of different chemicals and pesticides. They then send the tomatoes north: in the peak growing season, more than one hundred trucks full of tomatoes cross the border each day.[5] These tomatoes are emblematic of the increasing distance our food travels from farm to fork, as well as the rising carbon emissions that result. Indeed, although we might think of tomatoes as a product of sun, soil, and water, virtually everything used to raise the crop—fertilizers, pesticides, plastic bins, fuels for trucks and tractors—is petroleum based.

The average tomato today contains 62 percent less calcium, 19 percent less niacin, and 30 percent less Vitamin C than just a few decades ago.[6] The products of industrial tomato farms are uniform, tasteless, and nutritionally devoid—because they were bred to be that way. Although tomato seeds originated in Mexico, the hybridized and genetically engineered varieties planted there today, and the chemicals used to grow them, are increasingly the property of multinational corporations like Cargill or Monsanto. These companies loom ever larger over our food system: in the United States, ten agribusiness conglomerates account for half of all food sales.[7]

It took many hands to pick, process, pack, unpack, and put this tomato on display. Nearly one in six employed Americans works in the production, marketing, distribution, and preparation of food. Like many jobs in the burgeoning service economy, food service jobs are poorly paid, unreliable, and offer few opportunities for advancement. In one survey, only 13 percent of employees in the food sector reported earning a living wage.[8] Compared with those in other occupations, these workers were more likely to be employed part-time, lack health insurance, and need welfare benefits.[9] Walmart reaps 18 percent of the $76 billion a year paid out for food stamps, a portion of which comes from workers it pays so little that they qualify for the program.[10] Cruelly, food service employees are still substantially more likely than the general population to be unable to afford enough to eat.[11]

Embedded within this tomato, and every other item on the supermarket shelves, is a history of human exploitation and ecological harm. Yet the average consumer won't see the uprooted laborer in Mexico, the greenhouse-gas-emitting truck that brought the tomato to New York, or even the underpaid worker in the D'Agostino back room. Instead, he or she sees only the products themselves: the forty thousand different items on offer in a typical supermarket.[12] These goods are symbols of America's historically unprecedented superabundance of cheap food (the average family in 2012 spent only 10 percent of disposable income on food, nearly the lowest figure ever recorded) and the high social and environmental cost at which that abundance comes.[13]

In recent years, activists, journalists, and scholars have begun to expose the hidden underside of our food system. Best-selling books like Michael Pollan's *Omnivore's Dilemma* or Eric Schlosser's *Fast Food Nation* chronicled the problematic paths that our food takes to our plates. A wide range of social movements, too, have made increasingly audible calls for reform in the food system, demanding that all consumers—not just wealthy ones a short Prius drive from the local farmer's market—have access to food that is organic, fair-trade, and free from genetically modified organisms.[14]

For all this growing interest in where our food *comes from,* though, there has been comparatively little attention to where it actually *goes.*[15] Then again, the denouement of the tomato's story appears obvious: someone eats it. For most of us, the notion that food should feed people, not go to waste, is a powerful moral imperative. In a country with 17.6 million food-insecure households, it seems instinctual that any excess food surely must be donated to the needy.[16] But as this tomato sitting outside D'Agostino shows, the end point of our food's long journey from the farm is more complicated—and more disturbing.

Perhaps an employee spotted a blemish on the tomato while putting it on the shelf. Maybe she put it on the bottom of the display, where shoppers didn't see it. The store could have received a new shipment earlier than planned. Or it is possible that, out of fear of ever showing an empty display, the store deliberately stocked more tomatoes than it anticipated that people would buy. City Harvest, the largest organization recovering and distributing surplus food in New York City, describes D'Agostino as a "great partner" that donates significant quantities of food.[17] Yet whatever the reason, this tomato was not bought, not donated, and not composted. It was wasted: put in a garbage bag and placed on the curb.

This tomato's sad fate is no aberration. Forty percent of the United States' food supply is never consumed.[18] From virtually any angle, the scale of food waste is astonishing. According to conservative estimates, 160 billion pounds per year are jettisoned during harvest, processing, distribution, and consumption.[19] In 2008 Americans wasted $4.1 billion worth of tomatoes alone—and with them, the approximately 8.9 million hours of labor and 15 billion gallons of water that went into producing them.[20] While the market value of America's food waste ($197.7 billion) is shocking,[21] its potential "value" to meet human needs is even more striking. By one calculation, Americans dispose of enough calories of edible food each year to bring the diets of every undernourished person in the world up to an appropriate level.[22] Yet estimates suggest that less than 10 percent of grocery stores' edible excess gets donated.[23] Still smaller quantities are donated at other points in the food chain.[24] Almost all the rest makes its way to landfills, where it spews methane, a potent greenhouse gas that accelerates climate change.[25]

Examining the trajectory of this tomato, then, reveals a different set of truths about our food system. It is not just that the food we buy has a sordid history of exploitation behind it. It is also that the food that actually gets sold is shadowed by an enormous number of products that, like this tomato, are *never* sold, *never* consumed, but simply wasted. Yet while the average consumer in D'Agostino might spend a long time perusing the store's shelves, he likely won't think for a second about the lumpy black trash bags outside. Even if that shopper opened one, he would probably assume that the food in it was dirty or rotten—even though much of it is just as fresh and nutritious as the food he bought inside. Accustomed to thinking that anything in the garbage must be polluted and valueless, few of us see the massive wealth of one-time commodities that, in modern capitalism, ends up wasted.

The Anticapitalist

Shortly before the garbage truck arrives to begin the tomato's long journey to a landfill in one of the twelve different states to which New York City sends its trash, someone unties the black plastic bag. A hand reaches in, brushing aside some sodden cardboard packaging and a few scattered leaves of lettuce. It reaches the tomato, feeling it to see if it is still firm.

That hand is attached to a thirty-year-old white man named Adam. Adam has shoulder-length, shaggy hair and an unkempt beard; he is wearing a pair of loose, torn jeans and a stained, oversized hoodie. Even before pulling out the tomato, he is already laden with bags of food: slightly soft zucchini from outside another grocery store a few blocks away, an assortment of day-old bagels rescued from a nearby bakery, and some still-warm Indian food recovered from a neighborhood restaurant. In a city where at least some of its forty-one thousand homeless rely on discarded food to survive, the scene seems like an ordinary one.[26]

Many aspects of Adam's lifestyle put him on the extreme edges of society. Adam claims not to have bought food in thirteen years. Actually, by his own account, Adam doesn't buy much of anything, aside from the occasional subway pass, phone card, or box of baking soda for toothpaste. All told, he says that he survives on less than $1,000 a year. When I asked him about taxes, he quipped back, "No income, no taxes." Even if he did have an income, he would be hard for the Internal Revenue Service to find: he lives without a cell phone or government-issued ID. For most of 2008, Adam slept rent-free on a mat in a windowless and poorly ventilated basement underneath an old industrial warehouse in Brooklyn. Aside from a short stint as a security guard, Adam avows that he hasn't worked for pay since he graduated from high school.

Adam insists that he didn't arrive at this lifestyle by choice, but he wasn't driven to it by poverty and deprivation either. As he explained to me during an interview, "I've always thought that spending money unnecessarily, when vital needs are unmet for the world's less fortunate, seemed frivolous and irresponsible," adding that, "for as long as I can remember, I've felt like I had to reduce my impact and live as nonviolently as possible. I've basically always been an anarchist, I just didn't know the word."

Adam grew up in a conservative household in a New Jersey suburb, the son of a pediatrician and a schoolteacher for gifted-and-talented youth. I asked him where his radical views came from, as his parents apparently did not impart them. He responded with a well-rehearsed litany of factors, a sign that he had been asked this question countless times: "I'm a direct descendant of Holocaust victims. Growing up, my moral role models were comic-book superheroes and Gandhi. I've always had a contempt for formal schooling and the inane garbage that's taught through it. And my closest relationships as a kid were with non-human animals."

That last point helps explain why Adam went vegetarian at age eight and vegan at twelve, although he insists that he would have done so earlier "if it weren't for parental arm-twisting." This intense compassion is still evident today. One afternoon, I helped Adam clean out his cluttered living space. As I moved to take a bag of trash outside to the dumpster, he grabbed my arm and exclaimed, "Holy shit, there are flies in there!" He then spent fifteen minutes meticulously removing from the trash the insects that were still alive.

His concern for animals deepened, he said, when he began

conducting personal research into agriculture, thinking, for a time, that he would move to a farm. But, he explained, "I realized that even plant farming, even *organic* plant farming, even *local organic* plant farming, involves a ton of animal exploitation. It hit me that buying *any* food was morally unacceptable. Dumpster diving just came to me naturally after that." Since then, Adam has been living off the detritus of an economic system he despises.

Adam got his start in political outreach by campaigning door-to-door in his neighborhood against the use of backyard "bug zappers." After high school, he eschewed college to become a full-time environmental crusader. From one perspective, Adam's entire life can be read as an ongoing struggle against animal abuse, environmental degradation, and the exploitation of humans. At the same time, his life is also a rejection of the most common ways that activists, social movements, and politicians have responded to these abuses. In a society where claims about the importance of protecting the environment are "ambient—as pervasive . . . as the air we breathe,"[27] Adam is a disenchanted prophet on the margins, relentlessly insisting to anyone who will listen that "green capitalism" or "ethical consumerism" cannot save us from catastrophe.[28]

For example, despite still adhering to its dietary strictures, Adam is scathing in his critique of veganism. Speaking about the proliferation of high-end vegan restaurants and specialty clothing stores in hipster-saturated Brooklyn, Adam pronounced, "Veganism is a bourgeois ideology that worships consumption." Most animal rights activists, he explained, have an unfounded faith in the capacity of individuals to change the world by buying one product over another. The same could be said for purchasers of environmentally friendly detergents or organic-cotton T-shirts. Consumer activism, in Adam's eyes, does not grapple with the ecologically destructive logic of endless growth lying at the heart of capitalism. This logic, he notes, is made visible by our economic system's never-ending generation of waste.

Dumpster diving, for Adam, isn't about perfecting the ethics of his own personal lifestyle. Instead, Adam views it as an instrument that allows him to meet his needs without spending his days working for pay, which in turn frees up his time for political activism. For the last decade, Adam has been the main force behind the Wetlands Activism Collective, an offshoot of the Wetlands Preserve nightclub, a combination music venue and activist center that closed in 2001. Other activists I spoke to recalled that when the bar was still open, Adam would stay in the back office during concerts, working late into the night organizing boycotts of companies that abused animals or violated indigenous peoples' rights. As part of his work with Global Justice for Animals and Environment and Trade Justice New York—two groups he founded and runs largely single-handedly—Adam was arrested outside then senator Hillary Clinton's office building, chaining himself to the door to protest the Free Trade Area of the Americas. Despite working on legislative issues, though, Adam maintains his distance: "When I'm involved in campaigns relating to elections, it's important for me not to vote on election day. It reminds me, 'Hey, I'm an anarchist!' I've never felt like voting could actually change anything."

Change, he said, is more likely to come from the exhaustion of natural resources or global climate change. "Capitalism is going down," he told me confidently. "The question is whether it's going to take us with it, and whether it's going to take the biosphere with it." Sitting inside New York's Grand Central Station, surrounded by an incongruous opulence of shops selling luxury goods to commuters returning home from working in the financial capital of the world, he elaborated on his political vision: "People need to be growing food, setting up housing through expropriation, creating health care collectives, bike repair workshops. We need things that bring the essentials of living to a community level. I don't think we need that complex of a society. We need to move beyond the culture of production." He closed with a comment that seemed particularly fitting, given his ascetic lifestyle: "We just don't need stuff."

Freegans and the Politics of Waste

On this December expedition, Adam is not just looking for things to eat. Instead of stashing the tomato in his bag, he raises it up in the air and launches into a lengthy speech. He denounces the labor exploitation, free trade agreements, and multinational agribusinesses that brought the tomato here. He then lifts a shrink-wrapped package of chicken legs and announces his opposition to factory farming, railing against birds packed by the thousands into cages and fattened on genetically engineered diets for mechanized slaughter. Finally, he grabs a banana, emblazoned with a sticker proudly proclaiming that it is "fair-trade." Adam is unconvinced: he holds it above his head, points it, and defies those who think that products labeled "organic" or "fair-trade" are any more ethically defensible than the tomato or the chicken. To drive the conflation home, he points out that, whether "ethically" produced or not, all these edible products wound up in the garbage anyway. He is, in his words, "waving the banana at capitalism," holding up a mirror to consumer society that exposes *both* where goods come from *and* where they go.

Adam's views on society, his political commitments, and his personal practices are undoubtedly extreme. He's the first to admit that, throughout his life, many of his appeals have fallen on deaf ears. After all, Adam talks incessantly about "capitalism" in an era where the word has virtually disappeared from our popular and political lexicon. More than that: he calls for alternatives to capitalism at a time when most elites and policymakers—and much of the general public—would nod in agreement with the economist Hernando de Soto, who pronounced that "capitalism stands alone as the only feasible way to rationally organize a modern economy."[29]

Yet, on this night in December, despite a temperature with windchill well below twenty degrees Fahrenheit, a gathered crowd of twenty-five gives Adam's tirade their rapt attention. The assembled individuals are difficult to characterize. While a few display tattoos, piercings, and tight black clothing—the unofficial uniform of twenty-first-century urban youth counterculture—the rest are more eclectic. Among them are cab drivers, teachers, doctors, secretaries, artists, and computer programmers; they range in age from high school students to retirees. Most are white, well educated, and from affluent backgrounds. Two-thirds of them are women. A television crew from MTV, a photojournalist from Norway, and a freelance writer from Argentina join them. They have come to participate in one of the collective dumpster dives called "trash tours" that Adam routinely led through New York City from 2003 to 2009.

A report on garbage from the *Economist* magazine claims that "there are really only three things you can do with waste: burn it, bury it, or recycle it."[30] If we follow this tomato for a little longer, though, we see that the afterlives of waste can be more complex. Carried by subway, bicycle, or on foot, this tomato might make its way to a communal apartment, where it will help feed a handful of unemployed left-wing activists. Or, quite possibly, it will find itself at a Brooklyn anarchist community center, cooked and served as

A freegan rescues an ex-commodified tomato, setting it back on a path to someone's stomach rather than a landfill. Photograph by Courtny Hopen.

part of a free meal, composed entirely of scavenged food, for the surrounding low-income community. Others take food from this night's dumpster-diving expedition onto the subway and distribute it to anyone willing to take it. Far from disappearing, then, this tomato provides a window into an incipient but poorly understood social phenomenon: freeganism.

Dictionaries began including the word *freegan* in 2004, although my own investigations suggest that it was coined in the 1990s.[31] Its etymology provides some hint as to its meaning. *Freegan* is a combination of the words *free* and *vegan,* and the logic of freeganism is parallel to that of veganism. Vegans oppose animal exploitation by avoiding purchasing animal products, as both a symbolic act of protest and a direct attempt to bankrupt animal agriculture. At least in theory, freegans expand the theory of change behind veganism to the entire capitalist system, protesting overconsumption, environmental degradation, and human mistreatment by refusing to purchase anything at all.

There are innumerable ways to go about this withdrawal: a document Adam circulated on the e-mail list for the New York–based group freegan.info described no less than thirty-nine different practices that fall under the freegan banner. A partial inventory includes "guerrilla gardening" in fenced-off city lots, wild food foraging in urban parks, free exchange of unneeded goods through a "gift economy" of "free stores" and "really really free markets," squatting in abandoned buildings, repairing clothing and furniture rather than purchasing new ones, bicycling and hitchhiking, developing independent noncorporate media, voluntary unemployment, "couch surfing" to get free housing while traveling, and composting. What freegans are best known for, though, is dumpster diving. Also known—depending on the country—as "scavenging," "bin raiding," "trash trolling," "skipping," "curb crawling," "urban foraging," "trash picking," "doing the duck," or "dumpstering," dumpster diving entails recovering, redistributing, and reusing discarded food and other abandoned goods.[32]

Taken on their own, none of these practices is particularly novel. Freegans do voluntarily what, for many people around the world, is a necessity for survival. Nor is an ideology that celebrates nonparticipation in capitalism anything new. Freegans' actions and beliefs have clear precursors within utopian back-to-the-land communities, the "New Left" of the 1960s, and the radical wings of the environmental movement. The freegan.info website defines freeganism in what could charitably be described as amorphous terms:

> Freegans are people who employ alternative strategies for living based on limited participation in the conventional economy and minimal consumption of resources. Freegans embrace community, generosity, social concern, freedom, cooperation, and sharing in opposition to a society based on materialism, moral apathy, competition, conformity, and greed.

The website's vagueness reflects the unwillingness of individual freegan.info participants to rigidly circumscribe the boundaries of their movement. Explained Cindy, a self-described freegan who has been involved for a decade, "You're either vegetarian or you're not. But you're freegan if you decide you're freegan. It's not a set of rules." Freeganism, others told me, is "contested terrain," a nebulous "moving target." In popular discourse and the media, I've heard "freegans" reduced to "dumpster divers," "people who eat for free," or "cheapskates."

During my time spent with participants in freegan.info, though, our conversations kept circling back to one central theme: the challenge of living ethically in a capitalist system while trying to make that system itself more ethical. Freegans, one told me, are "practicing anticapitalists." Another described freeganism as a form of "conscientious objection to capitalism," based on "nonparticipation in the economic joke that is the capitalist world."

In truth, no freegan.info participant lives entirely "outside" capitalism—and doing so isn't really the point. Instead, by emphasizing the need to boycott the entire economic system, rather than just particular companies or products, freegans assert the futility of small-scale environmental reform or minor changes in consumer practices. As Cindy summarized it, freeganism is at its core "an attack on the mainstream environmental movement for thinking that we can solve environmental problems without attacking capitalism." Instead, freegans see lifestyle changes as a stepping-stone to more radical, transformative, and collective action. As Madeline, one freegan.info activist, put it, "The point isn't my lifestyle and how pure or impure it is. It's not about [taking] shorter showers. It's about making a political point and changing hearts and minds and getting people to take first actions for themselves."

In public, freegans can be reticent to evoke "capitalism" directly and talk instead about "the system" or "consumer society." But regardless of the language they use, freegans reject some of the most basic requirements of a functioning capitalist system: endless economic growth, the valuing of goods by price, and the distribution of necessities based on ability to pay. For freegans, "waste" is proof par excellence that these central imperatives make capitalism profoundly dysfunctional. As the freegan.info website avers:

> *In the globalized system dominated by a relative handful of corporations, vital resources like food and housing are wasted while the needs of hundreds of millions go unmet. All manner of consumer commodities are produced cheaply, offered for sale at high prices, and often discarded unsold by corporations that dismiss the waste as a cost of doing business. These corporations promote disposable goods over reusable ones, design rapidly obsolete products, and ensure that repair is more expensive than replacement. Enormous volumes of still-usable goods go to landfills that poison the exurban*

communities pressed into hosting them, with a disproportionate impact on the poor and disenfranchised.[33]

More than just denouncing what is wrong with capitalism and absolving themselves of responsibility for it by consuming less, freegans see their movement itself as an ongoing experiment with alternative ways to organize society. As Adam explained during his speech:

> *The freegan model for revolution is not just that we can preach this and suddenly people will take to the streets with torches and tear everything down. We realize that many people see the system as their very means of survival. So we believe that the only alternative is to build this new society within the shell of the old.*

Yet herein lies the great paradox of freeganism: it is largely through the collective repurposing of capitalism's waste that freegans are able to put their anticapitalist values—"community, generosity, social concern, freedom, cooperation, and sharing"—into practice.

Freegans' anticapitalist politics and fixation on waste seem like a recipe for obscurity. Yet since the group's founding in 2003, freegan .info has attracted thousands of people from New York and elsewhere to "trash tours" through the city, exposing them to waste and teaching them to recover food and other discarded items. The group has connected with hundreds of others through its bike workshop, wild food foraging expeditions in city parks, really really free markets to distribute surplus goods, sewing skill-shares, films and forums, and dumpster-dived catering at activist events. By 2009, according to its own count, freegan.info had been featured in six hundred media stories, from blog posts written by high school students to Madeline's extended appearance on Oprah in early 2008. Outside New York, there are or have been self-identified freegan groups in the United Kingdom, Sweden, Norway, Austria, France, Canada, Greece, Poland, Spain, Switzerland, South Korea, Japan, and Brazil, as well as a half-dozen U.S. cities from Sioux Falls, South Dakota, to Decatur, Georgia.

Freegans' message about the ecological limits of capitalism, the urgent need to create a more sustainable economic and social system, and the insufficiency of personal consumptive choices to achieve that change have all found a surprisingly broad audience. By examining freegan.info in depth, this book explores one of the most visible and vocal manifestations of a phenomenon that has received growing academic attention and inspired significant popular interest.[34] In my own quest to understand freeganism, though, I've had to go beyond freeganism itself to examine changes in contemporary activism, consumer culture, and—above all—the production, representation, and politics of waste in the United States.[35] In the rest of this introduction I elaborate two concepts, the ex-commodity and fetish of waste, that help illuminate freegans' politics and what they reveal about the underbelly of capitalism itself.[36]

The Birth of the Ex-Commodity

When freegans talk about "waste," what do they actually mean? At freegan.info events documented throughout this book, freegans evoke "waste" to describe all sorts of things. Adam raged against the "wasteful" rapid obsolescence of the salvaged computers he uses. Madeline deployed the same label for excess packaging, and Evie for the "wasteful" wars in Iraq and Afghanistan. Academics claiming to study "waste" have been even looser with the term, lumping concepts and objects including reality television, out-of-place objects, family heirlooms and secondhand furniture, corporate expense accounts, and fecal matter together under the same label.[37]

To understand what is distinctive about freeganism, we need to be more specific. Freegans stand in a privileged position relative to most scavengers. They are not rooting through residential garbage cans looking for plate scrapings or sifting through landfills for consumers' refuse. Nor are they, like the *zabaleen* in Cairo or *cartoneros* in Buenos Aires, searching for unused raw materials or packaging to recycle or resell. Instead, most of the time, freegans dumpster dive outside commercial establishments. What they find are, by and large, perfectly usable consumer goods. If waste is defined as "the rejected and worthless stuff that needs to be distanced from the societies that produced it,"[38] then what freegans are finding doesn't look much like waste. Instead, aside from the occasional blemish on a tomato or tear in a piece of clothing, freegans' finds are indistinguishable from the objects on sale inside a store—commodities. But they are no longer commodities, because they have been expelled from the shelves into the trash can. We might say, then, that what freegans find are ex-commodities.[39]

The challenge, then, is to understand why some products wind up as commodities in shopping bags and others as ex-commodities in trash bags. The social scientific field of "discard studies" provides hints, but, as one critic observes, these studies rarely present a clear linkage between the specific form of the material stuff being called waste and the particular economic and political conditions that produce it.[40] Freegans have their own theories as to why useful goods wind up in the trash, which I report and evaluate throughout this book. First, though, I want to offer my own conceptualization, by drawing on two theorists of commodities and capitalism: Karl Marx and Karl Polanyi.

In the opening line of his magnum opus, *Capital,* Marx observes, "The wealth of those societies in which the capitalist mode of production prevails presents itself as an immense accumulation of 'commodities.'" In simplest terms, Marx characterizes commodities as objects that embody two different kinds of value: "exchange value" and "use value." In our everyday lives most of us see commodities in terms of their use value, or their capacity to "satisf[y] human needs of whatever kind." Yet for Marx, the "capitalist" is interested only in exchange value, or the money that can be earned from selling a good.[41]

This division, often evoked by freegans in their public events, provides a starting point for understanding where ex-commodities come from. As Marx points out, someone interested in the use value of commodities can trade one good for another—books for iPods, chocolates for coffee—and feel satisfied so long as they get a qualitatively different use value out of the deal. For someone fixated on exchange value, this is no longer true. There's no reason to invest $100 in producing, distributing, and selling something if you wind up with $100 at the end of the process: you need to have *more* exchange value than when you started. This basic observation explains why, as the conservative economist Joseph Schumpeter insists, a capitalist economy "is not and cannot be stationary."[42] Indeed, under capitalism, an absence of sustained economic growth—the norm for most of human history—creates crises that threaten the system's very core.[43]

What does this have to do with waste, though? When it came to workers, Marx feels that capitalists would have no qualms about "wasting" their employees' lives and bodies on mindless, physically grueling, or downright dangerous tasks.[44] At the same time, however, in their insatiable pursuit of profit, individual capitalists would obsessively root out "wasted" time or raw material in their factories to maximize production.[45] The result of this combination, as Marx begrudgingly admits, was that capitalism would offer up a "progressively rising mass of use values and satisfactions" in the form of consumer goods.[46] But he never got around to explaining where the demand for this (by necessity) ever-increasing supply of commodities would come from. Instead, he assumes that, except in moments of acute economic downturns, virtually everything capitalism produced would get purchased and used by someone.[47]

Marx does observe that a wise capitalist understood that, for a commodity to have exchange value on the market, it must have use value, too—otherwise no one would want to buy it. What Marx missed, however, was the other side of the coin: that, in a capitalist system, if something lacks exchange value, its use value doesn't matter, at least as far as the capitalist is concerned. When a capitalist produces more than she can profitably sell, she generally doesn't give the unsold excess away for free: instead, she ex-commodifies it! Marx's categories allow us to specify the "ex-commodity" more precisely, as a good produced for the market that has use value but which the capitalist gets more exchange value by *not* selling and instead throwing away. In a sad sense, ex-commodity waste is thus not an "externality" or "failure" of the market but a source of value and driver of production in a capitalist system.[48]

In his later work, unpublished at the time of his death, Marx goes farther. He speculates that capitalism's impetus to endless growth would lead to overproduction and, ultimately, a "major wastage of productive forces" through economic crises that create idle factories or unemployed workers. The solution, he says, is for production to follow a "social plan."[49] Marx's diagnosis proved prescient, even if his prescription missed the mark. The "social planning" of state socialism in Eastern Europe and the USSR systematically "produced" chronic shortages and bare shelves.[50] But, despite mainstream economists' obsession with "scarcity" and the necessity of economic growth, the central problem of modern capitalist economies has—just as Marx predicts—turned out to be exactly the opposite: excess.[51]

What Marx doesn't tell us, though, is where this excess of commodities, produced by capitalism's own astonishing dynamism and innovation, winds up. For that, we need to step outside the factory and into the market, where Polanyi picks up the story. Polanyi recognizes that capitalism does not just produce commodities but also attempts to commodify things that already exist outside the market.[52] Indeed, this process of commodification is central to the origins of capitalism. During the eighteenth-century "enclosure movement" in England, which preceded and enabled the industrial revolution, the bourgeoisie turned the land on which peasantry had survived for centuries into a tradable commodity. Pushed off land they could not afford to rent or buy, the peasantry had no choice but to "commodify" the one thing they did have: their labor. Only by selling their time to factory owners could they buy commodities, like food, which they had previously produced for themselves. Economists usually present the unprecedented expansion of the market into new realms of society during the last three centuries as an inevitable outgrowth of humanity's natural tendency to "truck, barter, and exchange."[53] But this process was anything but automatic. In truth, land, labor, and food were commodified, according to Polanyi, only through the "conscious and often violent intervention" of capitalist landowners and their allies in the state.[54]

Although Polanyi is not alive to say it, he would undoubtedly see the decades since the 1970s as another powerful wave of commodification. The moniker *neoliberalism* aptly captures how today's free marketeers have resurrected the fantastical nineteenth-century vision of an entirely commodified society dominated by the dual logics of market exchange and endless growth.[55] But how could this new wave of commodification lead to ex-commodification? According to Polanyi, capitalism's drive to reduce everything to commodities could, ironically, undermine the very basis of capitalism itself. For example, "in disposing of man's labor power" like any other commodity, capitalist employers increasingly "dispose[d] of the physical, psychological entity 'man' attached to the tag."[56] In short, by subjecting humans and human societies to the whims of the market, capitalism risks annihilating the fabric of nonmarket relationships and institutions on which it feeds. But, Polanyi thought, society would never let capitalism follow its self-destructive logic to its conclusion, but would instead rise up to rein in the market before it imploded.

Polanyi's prognostications about the destructive consequences of unchecked commoditization resonate powerfully in the neoliberal era. Today, the slums of the developing world, swollen with would-be laborers unable to find productive employment, testify that rural peasants are being dispossessed of communal lands faster than new jobs are created for them in factories and sweatshops.[57] In the West, long-term, structural unemployment virtually disappeared in the prosperous post–World War II decades of vibrant unions and burgeoning welfare states. Its recent return bears witness to the disparity between the speed at which "globalization" and "austerity" are closing factories and slashing government payrolls and the rate they create new jobs in the service or information sector.[58] The result is what some theorists have called "wasted lives."[59] More precise would be to call them "ex-commodified workers": people who need to commodify their labor to survive but who can find no buyer for it and are thus unwillingly expelled from the labor market.

This book exposes how neoliberal capitalism is ex-commodifying material goods in much the same way it ex-commodifies workers. As Marx postulates, capitalism is producing commodities faster and more efficiently than ever.[60] But the drive to commodification—made concrete through cuts to government welfare programs, privatization of public services, elimination of economic regulations, and the gutting of labor unions—has undermined the very institutions that, for decades, propped up demand and kept capitalism's tendency to overproduce in check. Debt has bridged part of this rift by allowing people to keep consuming despite stagnant wages. But the fundamental problem remains: markets thrive on the high prices that come from scarcity, but modern capitalist production creates an unparalleled abundance of commodities without paying its workers enough to buy them. Under these conditions, ex-commodification becomes a "rational" strategy for firms to maintain exchange value through the destruction of use value.[61] While ex-commodified workers help hold down wages, ex-commodified goods hold up price. Both work to the advantage of individual capitalist firms but to the detriment of society—and, arguably, the capitalist economy—as a whole.

Housing presents a depressingly illustrative example of how contemporary capitalism depends on ex-commodification. During much of the 2000s, a run-up in lending fueled a construction boom that drove economic expansion. Less noted is that the construction of new houses was accompanied by a veritable "demolition derby" of old ones, peaking at the destruction of 360,000 houses a year in the mid-2000s.[62] Destroying homes in a nation blighted by homelessness, foreclosure, and eviction unveils the perverse rationality of ex-commodification.

If you are a landlord who owns only one house or one apartment, it makes no sense to leave it vacant or have it demolished. But if you're one of the large property owners who increasingly dominates the U.S. economy, it is sickly self-serving to ex-commodify otherwise useful structures in order to raise prices for those left on the market.[63] Banks virtually fessed up to this strategy when, at the height of the foreclosure crisis, they began bulldozing repossessed homes.[64]

Both Karls' analyses, then, are illuminating but incomplete. The wealth of capitalist societies is not just, as Marx declares, an "immense accumulation" of commodities. It is also an "immense accumulation of unused, abandoned, and recycled" ex-commodities.[65] And while Polanyi was right to see capitalism's drive to reduce workers to commodities as inherently destructive, he was overly optimistic to predict that society would never let the market succumb to its own nihilistic impulses.[66] He thus missed how unchecked commodification could lead to waste that reached from human lives to the most mundane of commodities. Indeed, while this book focuses on the ex-commodification of food, I at least hint at how scarcity is being artificially manufactured for a gamut of consumer goods. Today, capitalism obeys its imperative to endless growth and expanding markets by discarding the people and products it itself produced and commoditized.

Fetishes of Commodities, Fetishes of Waste

To hear freegans talk about it, ex-commodities call into question some of the canonical tenets of mainstream economics. Free markets frequently *do not* efficiently distribute goods. Supply often *does not* equal demand. And modern capitalist economies are as much about creating scarcity out of excess as they are mechanisms for providing abundance.

Beyond that, though, freegans believe that ex-commodities offer new strategic possibilities for anti-capitalists. As Adam postulated:

> If consumers became aware of this massive waste, this could pose a serious problem for retailers operating under this model. Some [consumers] might choose to recover discarded goods rather than purchasing the very same goods in the store. On a large enough scale, this could substantially cut into profits.[67]

Beyond hurting wasteful firms, Adam told me that recovering ex-commodities could serve as the resource base for a "global counter-economy to capitalism," which would eventually grow to the point where it could produce its own goods. At this point, there would be no need for capitalism—or its waste.

Yet despite the media attention and increased visibility freegan-ism has garnered in recent years, it is obvious that most people don't make any attempt to recover capitalism's "massive waste." The reason why seems immediately intuitive: it is *waste*, after all, so why would anyone want anything to do with it? Then again, when we consider that ex-commodities are, at least in terms of their usefulness, essen-tially identical to commodities, and that we live in an era where many people are struggling to buy what they need to survive, it becomes less straightforward. In good social scientific fashion, scholars have repeatedly shown that, far from being an immutable characteristic of a material object, the label "waste" is a "social construct," a desig-nation that is, ultimately, reversible.[68] Worldwide, entire economies are built on the "revaluation" of wasted goods and materials.[69] Yet despite the possibility that wasted objects like ex-commodities can be recovered and reused, most aren't. Why don't more people make use of ex-commodities?

This is, of course, tied to a much bigger question: why don't peo-ple see what is really going on under capitalism? Marx argues that, to understand our blind spots, we must return to the commodities themselves. In Marx's framework, the worker's labor is the source of all value and unpaid labor the source of all profits. But when work-ers confront their products in the marketplace, they don't see their own sweat and toil: they see only material goods that are useful and alluring. Marx calls this the "fetishism of commodities," whereby the "social relation[s] between men themselves" that go into production are mistaken for "the fantastic form of a relation between things."[70] This fetishism helps make capitalism seem "natural," both in the sense that the things humans need to survive are "naturally" com-modities and that capitalism is the "natural" way to organize society.

While Marx is interested primarily in the exploitation of labor, others have taken this idea of a "commodity fetish" and extended it in two ways. First, they show how our fixation on commodities and their physical characteristics blinds us to a much wider range of destructive social and ecological processes that go into commodity production than those identified by Marx.[71] The history of the tomato recounted above includes more than labor exploitation, but all these factors are hidden from the consumer in the store. Second, as Marx suggests, capitalist societies imbue mundane commodities with magical, quasi-religious power.[72] Polanyi, too, observes how nineteenth-century proponents of marketizing labor and land fervently promised that "all human problems"—from poverty to war to loneliness—"could be resolved given an unlimited amount of material commodities."[73]

During their public events, freegans, like so many other anticapitalists past and present, attempt to dispel this commodity fetishism. As Adam announced before one rapt group of trash-tour attendees, "We view the commodities being marketed to us and see them for what they are—misery and suffering with a clean coat of paint." His tirade not only exposed the hidden aspects of commodity production but also challenged the transcendent powers contemporary consumer activists grant them. Freegans incisively critique those who endow compact-fluorescent light bulbs with the capacity to halt global warming, organic detergent with the power to protect us from environmental toxins, or fair-trade coffee with the ability to rectify poverty in the developing world.

But freeganism also reveals that, to understand modern capitalism, the notion of fetishism needs to be expanded further. We must recognize that, when we fixate on the material properties and price of commodities in the store, we miss not only the processes that go into their production but also the way they are distributed, consumed, and wasted.[74] This is not a coincidence. As ex-commodification has become more crucial to the capitalist economy, capitalist firms and their allies in the state have devised ever more sophisticated ways to keep ex-commodification hidden. In this, they have followed a more general pattern: whenever society has raised concerns about waste, the capitalist's first instinct has always been to build a taller smokestack, extend the sewage pipe deeper into the harbor, or locate the landfill farther out of town.[75]

When faced with more overt challenges to their wasteful practices, industry grows more overtly pusillanimous. During World War II, U.S. beer manufacturers introduced the first one-way cans, which proved cheaper to produce than reusable bottles but had the predictable result of leaving roadsides teeming with discarded metal. Under pressure from the nascent environmental movement, nearly every state in the United States considered legislation to require deposits on beverage containers or ban flip-top cans.[76] Those "bottle bills" that did pass were largely effective, but most didn't, because the container industry poured money into defeating them.[77] More recently, the plastic bag and bottled water industries responded with a similar barrage of litigation and backroom lobbying to defeat attempts to ban or tax their products.[78]

Thus, under neoliberal capitalism, ex-commodities—like commodities themselves—become fetishized.[79] This "fetish of waste" stems not just from the way waste is physically hidden but also from how its origins are systematically misrepresented. In the wake of the first-ever Earth Day in 1970, the same beverage companies fending off antiwaste legislation financed campaigns like "Keep America Beautiful," famous for the image of a Native American crying over the carelessness of indifferent citizens. These campaigns pinned blame for solid waste on individual consumers rather than wasteful business practices.[80] In 2009 in California, the Plastic Bag Association pushed a bill to ban municipal prohibitions on plastic bags, which it coupled with a commitment to a token fund to finance "litter abatement" and "consumer education."[81] Companies thus glossed over the immense amount of marketing and "consumer education" that went into convincing people they needed to buy products like bottled water, despite their dubious health benefits, ecological (and financial) costs, and resultant waste.[82] In directing our ire toward the individual consumer who puts the plastic bottle in the trash rather than the recycling bin, though, we miss how the overarching logic of a capitalist system makes such wastage necessary.

Finally, this fetish of waste also endows ex-commodities with pseudomagical properties. If commodities have a divine power to save us, ex-commodities are given an equally otherworldly capacity to poison and debase us. The hysterical responses most people have to the idea of eating ex-commodified food—fears that are quite removed from the real risks involved—illustrate how, under advanced capitalism, we have come to equate all "waste" with "pollution."[83] Certainly, there's some truth to this belief: advanced capitalism produces toxic outputs like plastics, spent nuclear fuel, or e-waste in abundance. Yet this endlessly repeated conflation is misleading, blinding us to the fact that some of what gets labeled "waste" is still useful and some of what gets sold as "commodities" is patently harmful and dangerous.

Although never articulated as such, freegan events and statements relentlessly assail this fetish of waste alongside the original fetish of commodities. As Adam reflected in one essay:

> We are led to believe that the goods presented to us in stores are safe, effective, desirable, and worth the money we are spending on them. We have spent lifetimes hearing adages such as "There's no such thing as a free lunch," designed to convince us that only hard work at joyless jobs can guarantee our survival. We are left with the impression that anything we aren't required to pay for can't possibly be worth having. We therefore assume that discarded goods must be unsafe, ineffective, unusable, or otherwise undesirable. Stripping away the marketing attached to goods, it becomes apparent that neither assumption is true: the goods sold to us aren't necessarily good for us, and the ones discarded aren't necessarily bad.[84]

As Adam realized, a combination of marketing, media discourse, and government campaigns narrow and divert our gaze when it comes to ex-commodities. Much of the time, we simply don't see them. When we do, we blame anything and everything *but* capitalism for putting them in the garbage. And we are further confounded by culturally ubiquitous assumptions about the value of newness and fashion, the importance of hygiene, and the dangerousness of anything to which the label "waste" is attached.

These two concepts, ex-commodity and the fetish of waste, drive this book's analysis. As I show, freegans' encounters with ex-commodities revealed to them the limits of contemporary consumer activism, which frequently centers on buying one commodity and boycotting another. These same ex-commodities formed the basis of the underground anarchist societies out of which freeganism emerged and, eventually, became the focal point of freegan .info's public protests. Freegans use ex-commodified food, in particular, to reveal the absurdity of neoliberal capitalism: the production and subsequent destruction of goods that—despite fetishistic concerns about health or safety—are (or at least, were) perfectly usable. In so doing, they undermine the moral justifications that underpin a capitalist economy. Instead of placing their faith in the market, through recovering ex-commodities, freegans took tentative steps into experimenting with a new system outside it. They thus weakened the fetish of waste itself by showing that the real wealth of capitalism is not just on its shelves but in its dumpsters.

Yet, as I reveal later in this book, capitalism—in all its diverse guises—eventually reclaimed its ex-commodities and reimposed the fetish of waste. Perhaps, in so doing, it has consigned freeganism to the proverbial dustbins of history. As I suggest in the Conclusion, though, the lessons freeganism teaches about the nature of capitalism and limits of consumer-oriented reform are not so easily discarded.

Capitalism's Cast-offs

I interviewed Wendy in February 2009, after her Wednesday-night shift as a mechanic in the freegan bike workshop. The workshop was in the basement of the 123 Community Center, an anarchist infoshop in Bedford-Stuyvesant, Brooklyn, that freegan.info shared with the In Our Hearts Collective and Anarchist Black Cross. Upstairs, crammed into a single long room festooned with flyers for past protests, 123 hosted a press for silk-screening T-shirts, a library of anarchist literature, and a kitchen where freegans often cooked meals from dumpster-dived food. Downstairs was the freegan bike workshop, stuffed to the gills with half-completed bike frames and scattered surplus parts in various states of rust and degradation. That night, Wendy, her shoulder-length, salt-and-pepper hair flowing freely and her glasses half-falling off her nose, was moving frantically in the cramped space, helping a mix of hip-looking white activists from Williamsburg and African American teens from the surrounding community with bike repairs. During the two nights a week it opened, the bike workshop was an ongoing platform for "prefigurative politics": attempts to directly, in the here and now, build a *new* society in the heart of the *old* one.

Wendy's activist history is closely bound with the founding of freegan.info. It also provides a window into how anticapitalist activists came to see recovering food waste as a potent political act. Wendy grew up in a middle-class, suburban area of South Jersey and described her parents as "bargain shoppers" who taught her the art of acquiring stuff as cheaply as possible. When Wendy was twelve, she abruptly decided to go vegetarian after a sharp, emotionally charged realization that pork came from pigs that were little different from her family dog. She insisted on an "animal rights" theme for her bat mitzvah and, in seventh grade, tried—unsuccessfully—to start an animal rights club at school. She tried her hand again in college, this time more successfully. At the freshman activities fair, she ran into the table for the campus animal rights group: "I thought to myself, 'You are the people I've been waiting for all these years.'" As she recalled, "I missed, maybe, three meetings in the course of four-and-a-half years with them."

Over time, though, Wendy began to question whether tactics like waving signs or signing petitions were effective vehicles for change. Reflecting on protests outside Kentucky Fried Chicken, she admitted, "We stood by a highway and chanted to people driving by in cars. That's what we did. That was it." It was her encounter with ex-commodities on her first-ever dumpster dive, though, that cemented for her the conviction that animal abuse could not be ended without tackling something bigger: capitalism. The realization that many animals were not just commodified and eaten but actually *ex*-commodified and discarded was overwhelming. As she avowed, "No one deserves to have their life wasted, because that's the biggest disgrace of all: to have a whole life wasted, crushed in a garbage truck. I won't stand for it any more than I would sit and watch my friends die."

For Wendy, waste was more than just an outrage. As she explained it, the superabundance of ex-commodities proved that any political strategy focused on getting people to buy different commodities, without challenging the economic structure as a whole, was bound to fail:

> *Veganism equates your decisions with a direct market decision. Your financial contribution directly effects this change in the market. You use your buying power or whatever. And that's [a] totally perverted version of what the actual picture is.... Your little decision is such a small factor in the greater economic decision of what's produced and marketed.*

The entire notion that individual consumers could be effective activists, she pointed out, rests on confidence in the elasticity and efficiency of markets: that is, that if one person stops buying animal-based food, then the production of animal-based foods will go down. Yet, as she was viscerally reminded on every dumpster dive, food markets are only imperfectly responsive to consumer demand. "I hate that button that says 'Veganism is direct action.' Not even close," she told me. "All the animal rights campaigns that I've seen can't even begin to touch the issues brought up by the industrial world's waste."

After college, Wendy moved to New York City, convinced that "all the activists, all the culture was there—not in the suburbs." New York offered a plethora of different models for political engagement. First, she volunteered with the League of Humane Voters, which attempted to advance animal rights through electoral means. At the same time, she began working with the Wetlands Activism Collective and Food Not Bombs, two anticapitalist groups claiming to practice "direct action" that ignored politicians and sought to change the world through interventions that immediately implemented aspects of the world that activists sought to create.[1]

Over time, Wendy moved toward the latter approach, which emphasized building alternatives to the capitalist system rather than reforming it. Her lifestyle changed accordingly. To devote more of her energy to activism, she eschewed long-term, stable employment, looking for "short-term gigs and only short-term gigs." As she acknowledged, the result was that she was "only barely getting by," but for her, to give up her activism and focus on paid work was something she "couldn't afford, in my own way." She supplemented her small earnings by dumpster diving as much of her food, clothing, and other goods as possible.

Wendy picked up a copy of the pamphlet "Why Freegan?" at an animal rights conference in 2000, around the same time that some people she met started to tell her she sounded like she was living as a "freegan." She met Adam through her involvement in Wetlands. Both of them were using waste recovery to support themselves and wanted to share the strategy with others. Freegan.info was born of the sense that "it's really hard to even find examples of how not to be in capitalism. It's everywhere around us."

The freegan project was an attempt to provide just such an example, and it drew a surprising amount of attention. Over time, freegan.info and its collective dumpster dives went from being a way to support activists engaging in *other* kinds of political action to a form of political action in itself. It is this emergence of freeganism as a form of prefigurative politics using capitalism's waste, particularly ex-commodified food, that this chapter recounts.

Anarchists and Their Garbage

Where did freeganism come from? Social movements are never "immaculate conceptions."[2] They build on the tactics, messages, and ideologies of movements before them. Both in direct links and indirect affinities, Food Not Bombs (FNB) has the strongest claim to being the forerunner of freeganism.[3] That movement's story begins with the Clamshell Alliance, which used nonviolent civil disobedience to protest the Seabrook nuclear power plant near Boston during the 1980s.[4] I spoke with one of FNB's founders, Keith McHenry, an affable lifelong activist with a Santa Claus beard who has spent his life atoning for the actions of the U.S. military generals in his family and who now lives in a yurt in New Mexico. As he explained it, the name "Food Not Bombs" stemmed from a sad juxtaposition: hungry people living in poverty, their condition exacerbated by cutbacks to social services imposed by the Reagan administration, which claimed that there weren't enough funds to go around, and the huge amounts of money somehow available for the military–industrial complex.

He and a few others organized FNB's first protest to dramatize investments that the Bank of Boston was making in nuclear energy that "sounded a lot like the kind of stuff bankers were doing that led to the Great Depression." To drive home the point, they decided to dress up as hoboes and create an impromptu soup kitchen, and invited residents of the local homeless shelter along. The ingredients for the meal, Keith said, were surplus that he took from the grocery store where he was working. As McHenry reflected, serving free food in the commercial heart of Boston provoked people to think critically about the capitalist system:

> The whole idea that food was free really blew people's minds: the message that you could have as much as you want, because it was rescued, and that we didn't anticipate or expect or even need money, and that—on top of that—it was great food which was well-presented. That had a profound impact on people, and that's why we adopted that model permanently for FNB.... It got people to think outside the box about all kinds of social and cultural issues. They started asking: "Why is food withheld from people who need it? Why is food so expensive? And why is food a commodity when everyone needs it?"

By McHenry's own account, the combination of symbolic protest and direct action was markedly successful, and, while cleaning up with his friends, McHenry proposed, "'Let's just quit our jobs and do nothing but this!' And so I put in my two weeks' notice."

In the late 1980s McHenry moved to San Francisco and started another chapter. The San Francisco FNB was openly anarchist and frustrated even the city's liberal mayor with its unwillingness to apply for permits or participate in the "negotiated management" that had been used to police protests since the 1960s.[5] On August 15, 1988, forty-five officers in full riot gear arrested nine FNB activists who were serving a meal without a permit at the entrance to Golden Gate Park. As the police spokesperson explained, "This [the meal] appears to be more of a political statement than a program to feed the hungry."[6] In subsequent years, the struggle escalated, to the point where the *San Francisco Chronicle* asked every mayoral candidate in 1995 what he or she would do about Food Not Bombs. By that time, more than one thousand activists had been arrested, the group had become the fourth-largest food service organization in San Francisco, and an offshoot, Homes Not Jails, had opened up hundreds of squats and was housing up to five hundred homeless people a night.[7]

FNB now claims affiliates in hundreds of cities worldwide, but over time the group has largely moved underground.[8] Indeed, instead of directly challenging the authorities, most FNB chapters believe they are creating the rudiments of a postcapitalist food system by rescuing ex-commodified food and distributing it for free. Of course, the act of serving free food is not itself particularly "political." In many places soup kitchens and food pantries actually legitimate cutbacks to government services by providing a private band-aid that mitigates neoliberalism's worst effects.[9] Keith, and the FNB activists who came after him, see themselves as different, not so much because of what they do but because of how they do it. FNB's chapters are run through consensus decision making and prepare only vegetarian meals, and those who eat are encouraged to share in the meal's preparation (and vice versa). In short, FNB claims that the movement itself is a model for society and that it is thus engaged in "prefigurative politics."

We can partly distinguish prefigurative movements by contrasting them to more conventional ones. The most iconic political actions of the 1960s, such as the civil rights movement's march on Washington, mass demonstrations against the Vietnam War, or even civil disobedience to desegregate lunch counters or bus stations, all shared a common underlying understanding of how to change society. For them, "politics" was all about pressuring external groups, whether voters or policymakers, to address social problems through state action.[10] Other subcurrents of the New Left of the 1960s, however, became disillusioned with the formal democratic process. Offshoots of the civil rights, antiwar, and student movements began eschewing the *indirect* influence of marches, demonstrations, and petitions in favor of *directly* building an alternative society from the ground up.[11] Variations of this approach could be seen in rural communes, the experiments in participatory democracy of the civil rights movement, or the Black Panther Party's "free breakfast" program in impoverished neighborhoods.[12] Although many of these experiments collapsed under the weight of state repression and internal dysfunction, the approach to bringing about social change lived on through the 1970s and 1980s among radical feminists, participants in the "do-it-yourself" punk scene, and antinuclear activists—like those who founded FNB.[13]

There is some evidence to suggest, however, that prefigurative politics have been growing in prominence in the last two decades.[14] The explanation rests in the particular challenges facing any contemporary radical movement. In the 1960s an anticapitalist could buttress the assertion that it was possible to transform the United States into a noncapitalist society by noting that alternatives—however flawed—already existed in the Soviet Union and its satellites. Today, though, a central tenet of politics is, as Margaret Thatcher put it, that "there is no alternative" to neoliberalism.[15] Adam himself articulated the stark challenge facing contemporary anticapitalists:

> *People see the global capitalist economy as intrinsic to their society…[so] bringing that down seems nihilistic and insane. It's like telling someone you can breathe without oxygen. It's just instantly dismissed—that's the response we get when we tell people they can live without capitalism.*

Today's anticapitalist activists must do much more than just demand an end to capitalism; they must show people that there is a viable alternative to it. And, as FNB activists realized when they faced stark repression by the nominally liberal municipal government of San Francisco, they must do so on their own, without expecting the state to rein in the market for them. Incorporating some element of prefigurative politics is thus now a virtual necessity for anticapitalist movements.[16]

One group of anticapitalists has eagerly seized the opportunity to mount a prefigurative challenge to capitalism: anarchists. Although the label "anarchism" evokes connotations of violence or chaos, most contemporary anarchists understand themselves as seeking revolutionary social change through building a "new society within the shell of the old," rather than the more traditional strategy of seizing state power.[17] These anarchists burst dramatically into view during protests at the summits of international organizations, such as the World Trade Organization, G-8, and International Monetary Fund, that swept the globe in the late 1990s and early 2000s.[18]

Those protests are best remembered for their carnival-like character, such as the "medieval bloc" in Quebec hurling stuffed animals at riot police, or for the property destruction instigated by the "Black Bloc" in Seattle, in 1999. Movement participants, however, believed that the way they organized the protests—"horizontal coordination among autonomous groups, grassroots participation, consensus decision-making, and the free and open exchange of information"[19]— was as important as the message of the protests themselves. The chant "This is what democracy looks like!" was more than just rhetoric. Many antiglobalization movement (AGM) activists believed that the movement was developing a genuine alternative to a formal democratic system that they perceived as powerless, corporate-controlled, and unresponsive.[20] In its place, they called for a world organized around "autonomy, voluntary association, self-organization, mutual aid, [and] direct democracy," values they argued their movement itself was already putting into practice.[21]

I dwell on FNB and the AGM for two reasons. First, it helps us embed freegans' politics in a broader field of movements and political ideologies, within which freegans came to understand activities like sewing one's own clothes or operating meetings through consensus as potentially revolutionary. Explained one freegan, "There is this notion that we need an alternative way of life, and it's very strong right now. As a result, even riding a bicycle or going to the farmer's market has become a kind of radical statement."

Second, these movements help explain where freegans' fixation on recovering waste comes from. Unlike the "back-to-the-landers" of the 1960s, today's anarchists are much less interested in developing farms or communities in remote places. Instead, their political strategy centers on an "engaged withdrawal," in which anticapitalists construct a utopian society in sight of capitalist dystopia.[22] Yet how can individuals have time to engage in time-consuming prefigurative politics if they have to work constantly to feed, clothe, and house themselves? And how can social movements without ready access to cash get resources with which to build alternative institutions, given that nearly everything they need is commodified?

At least in some cases, "waste"—and particularly, ex-commodities—has answered both these questions. Keith told me that the original idea of using food surplus for FNB made sense within the budding ecological consciousness of Boston anarchists in the early 1980s:

> There was an entire culture around recovering things. At the same time, we were starting the punk movement, and I would write articles in local punk zines about all of this. So there was starting to be an ideology around recovering garbage and using it. It wasn't about making money from it, but to use it as artwork and as props, as food, everything.

A few decades later in California, the Berkeley-based FNB chapter I worked with continued to put this ideology into practice. The group's operations depended almost entirely on waste in various guises: participants cooked with ex-commodities that were rescued either shortly before or after they made their way to a dumpster, recovered and resold discarded furniture during move-out days at the local university to buy rice and beans, and brought a "free box" filled with scavenged items like T-shirts and eight-tracks to most meals.

Far from being an isolated case, FNB is characteristic of an explosion in waste recovery throughout the anarchist community. The actual form that "waste" takes varies. Some anarchists travel by hitchhiking or train hopping, using "wasted" or "excess" seats to get around. Others take discarded cooking oil, a seemingly valueless restaurant by-product, and turn it into fuel.[23] "Guerrilla gardeners" seize abandoned, unused urban lots and transform them into oases of sustainable food production.[24] At other moments, anarchists focus more directly on ex-commodities. Anarchist "infoshops" are community centers in which people can learn about radical ideas, plan political actions, and share practical skills.[25] Infoshops, which usually operate on a shoestring budget, often outfit their spaces with dumpster-dived goods and serve as hubs for the exchange of ex-commodities among activists.[26]

Sometimes the spaces themselves are ex-commodities. Although the United States never had anything close to the tens of thousands of "squatted" homes and community centers in Western Europe in the 1980s,[27] recovering wasted space remains an anarchist ideal, one I heard frequently discussed within freegan.info. I first met Sasha, a white male freegan in his late twenties with shaggy light-brown hair and a broad smile, in the summer of 2008, after he had returned from a four-month "squat tour" of occupied houses and community spaces in Spain and Latin America. Sasha shared some of the experiences from what he jokingly called "anarcho-tourism" at two open forums organized by freegan.info and held in an art gallery in Manhattan and a community center in Brooklyn.

Sasha debated with more skeptical members of the crowd over whether squatting was "political" or simply not-so-petty theft. In response to one challenge, he countered:

> Squatting...is about moving into houses that already exist, moving into spaces that have been abandoned and have been wasted. It's anti-capitalist in a big sense. Whereas capitalism represents a kind of underlying money exchange, where everything has its value that represents it in a global market, squatting basically says, "Okay, because I can't have this, I'm going to take it anyway."

As his answer evinced, anarchists view squatting as "political" because it denies the right of the owners of needed commodities to ex-commodify "their" private property. Moreover, squatting allows activists to house themselves without relying on the money economy or housing markets. Waste enables squatting in other ways, too: unable to access municipal services, the squatters Sasha met recycled water from the kitchen sink to flush toilets and scavenged materials left at construction sites to make repairs.

The forum also pointed to some of the limitations and contradictions of an anarchist prefigurative politics dependent on waste. As Esther, Sasha's traveling companion, acknowledged, despite squatters' anticapitalist ideals, "One of the big realities is money. In all urban squats that I experienced, you could not completely drop out of the system. There were things that you could not get in other ways. So they were selling things or performing on the street." She summarized the relationships between squats and outside society in terms of an ongoing tension between "dropping out" and remaining relevant and engaged: "The ideal is to be self-sustaining while against the system, and within the system, and almost falling out of the system." Her quote captures tensions that run through this book: the way freegans use ex-commodities to live within, against, and outside capitalism, all at once.

Ex-Commodification from Farm to Fork

Given the amount of time they spend rummaging through dumpsters, it's little surprise that today's anarchists have also developed their own theories of how those dumpsters came to be so full. After his talk on squats, Sasha squatted a bit himself, living with Adam in the basement storage space that housed the freegan.info office. There, lounging between rolls of old carpets, piles of defaced posters from mainstream animal rights groups, and mounds of salvaged bike parts, Sasha offered his own interpretation of Marx:

> Marx develops this idea of overproduction, and the unsustainable quality of capitalism. It occurs because people are being paid too little to buy what they produce. So what happens? Well, the price of the commodity goes down, or the business becomes bankrupt because it can't continue to produce at that price.

But, of course, the final collapse that this overproduction was supposed to precipitate never happened. As Sasha noted, some of Marx's followers have claimed that this "surplus" overproduction would not be consumed by workers but invested in war or imperialism.[28] Today, though, "the surplus is the garbage":

> There's enough to go around for the entire world, but because people aren't able to afford to buy it, it is more profitable for the capitalist to throw things away than to give them out.... The money that was made is harnessed by the capitalists, but the surplus itself...is largely decadent, it's just thrown away.

As anarchists like Sasha see it, ex-commodification is not just an unintended externality of neoliberal capitalism. It is a direct result of long-running tendencies of overproduction and the contemporary wave of commodification. This latter point is crucial: it's not just that anarchists are discovering ex-commodities now—it's that ex-commodification is actually increasing.

A comprehensive history of waste under capitalism is beyond the scope of this book.[29] Nonetheless, we can put Sasha's supposition to a preliminary test by considering one particular case of ex-commodification: food. Capitalist agriculture is inherently problematic, and the reason is simple.[30] In contrast to cars, houses, or clothes, there is a biological limit to how much food people can consume (obesity epidemic notwithstanding). If demand for their products has an upper limit, how can companies engaged in producing, distributing, and selling food achieve the never-ending growth required by shareholders?

There may have once been a time when American farmers did not grow enough to feed the entire country and free markets served to distribute scarce food resources. But by the start of the twentieth century, the problem was the inverse: yields were swelling thanks to advances in plant breeding, fertilizers, and harvesting technologies, and farmers, driven by an increasingly competitive market, were already producing more than consumers would buy.[31] The self-destructive tendency of free markets noted by Polanyi reared its head, as processors and distributors began to destroy part of production to maintain prices:

> In 1920, thousands of gallons of milk were poured into rivers and creeks of southern Illinois. In the fall of the same year, the Potomac River below Washington was afloat with watermelons—a trainload having been dumped from the wharves to avoid breaking the city price.[32]

With the arrival of the Great Depression, agricultural prices nose-dived. It took forces outside the market to save capitalist agriculture. During President Franklin D. Roosevelt's "New Deal," the federal government inaugurated a long period in which the state limited production and found outlets for farmers' excesses.[33] Under the Agricultural Adjustment Act of 1933, the federal government mandated that farmers leave a portion of acreage for certain products unplanted, and purchased surplus food to raise prices. Perversely, much of this stockpiled surplus was left to rot.[34] Public outrage led to the first federal food-aid program: a portion of surplus agricultural production was decommodified—that is, taken off the market and given to those in need.[35]

By the end of World War II, though, silos were once again bursting with excess grain. This time, corporations and their allies in government looked abroad for an outlet. Over one-quarter of aid given under the famous Marshall Plan, through which the United States supported rebuilding war-torn Europe, consisted of surplus agricultural inputs and outputs.[36] By 1956 nearly half of U.S. foreign aid came in the form of dumping agricultural excesses on developing countries.[37] Agricultural policy at home followed a similar trajectory. The government institutionalized food stamps and the Federal School Lunch program in the 1960s to create consumers for the food accumulated through agricultural programs.[38] Although these initiatives served many ends, including controlling urban unrest and undercutting radical movements like the Black Panthers, one of them was to allow capitalist agriculture to fulfill its primary imperative: continued growth. They did so, however, by subjecting the market to social and state regulation, interfering with free competition, and actually removing some of the fruits of overproduction from the world of commodity exchange.

Under the neoliberal push to subject all of society to the market, these policies are being reversed as the exchange- and profit-driven logic of capitalism penetrates deeper into our food system than ever before.[39] Of course, the U.S. government continues to spend astonishing amounts on farm subsidies: $256 billion since 1995.[40] But they go to a steadily dwindling number of small family farms and an ever-more-consolidated cadre of agribusinesses.[41] Moreover, the form of these subsidies has changed. The 1996 Freedom to Farm Act replaced limits to production imposed in the 1930s with direct payments to farmers, regardless of how much they produced.[42] The expansion of federal crop-insurance programs means that farmers can now confidently plant crops no one needs on marginal land with nearly zero risk of financial loss.[43] These changes are obviously not reflections of a free market: instead, they are the fruits of economic actors who have taken state policy and warped it to their own ends.

Another sign of the growing commodification of food under neoliberalism can be seen from the financial industry's burgeoning interest. In 1991 Goldman Sachs took advantage of loosening government regulations to bundle contracts to purchase eighteen agricultural products into a "Commodity Index."[44] From 2003 to 2008, investment ballooned from $13 billion to $317 billion. By the financial industry's reckoning, food was a commodity like any other. As one grain exchange manager put it, "I view what we're working with [food] as widgets.... I think being an employee at an exchange is different from adding value to the food system."[45] Yet food is not a "widget," although treating it as such has very real effects. In 2008 speculators bought an unprecedented amount of futures contracts—agreements to purchase a portion of the harvest—for wheat. Even though the year saw record harvests, food prices spiked, causing hunger and food riots worldwide.[46]

The hand of neoliberalism can also be seen at the other end of the food chain. Food banks and emergency food pantries are now such a normalized part of the landscape that few remember that, in postwar America, they virtually disappeared. Groups like City Harvest in New York emerged only in response to cutbacks in social services imposed under the Reagan administration.[47] Social programs have fared little better under Democratic presidents: welfare reform passed under Bill Clinton in 1996 triggered a $37 per month decrease in food stamps' purchasing power, which is no small figure for a program that provides about $1 per person per meal.[48] Although much has been made of the increase in the number of Americans on food stamps during the Obama administration, their buying power continues to fall.[49]

Slashing food stamps, rearranging agricultural subsidies, and turning food into a financial toy might seem disconnected, but they obey a common principle. Each treats food as a commodity that goes to whoever will pay the highest price. Yet the ongoing commodification actually *reduces* outlets for surplus food, despite continued increases in production. The predictable result? Nearly 10 percent of crops in the United States are never harvested, because it is more profitable to plough some crops under than to feed them to people.[50] Twisted as it might seem, the wanton destruction of food is occasionally openly coordinated: in 2009 California dairy farms called for the dumping of milk from two million cows to raise the price.[51]

Nonetheless, even after (often deliberate) losses in processing, transport, and distribution, and taking into account imports and exports, U.S. farmers provide 3,796 kilocalories per person per day.[52] To put it in less abstract terms, according to the U.S. Department of Agriculture, in 2011 "each American had available to consume, on average, 54 pounds more commercially grown vegetables than in 1970; 17 pounds more fruit; 11 pounds more caloric sweeteners; 37 pounds more poultry; 3 pounds more fish and shellfish (boneless, trimmed equivalent); 22 pounds more cheese; and 35 pounds more grain products."[53] Together, all this food provides vastly more than the 1,900 kcal/day necessary to feed the average person, taking into account children and the elderly. It is far beyond the 2,600 kcal/day scientists claim is an adequate buffer against weather, accidents, or other crises.[54] It is little surprise, then, that since the 1970s, the proportion of the U.S. food supply going to waste has increased 50 percent.[55]

Advanced capitalist countries do not have a monopoly on wasting food. Food waste probably started at the same time as agriculture itself, as farmers planted more than they actually needed to hedge against drought or pests.[56] Even in countries like India with widespread malnutrition, a significant amount of food rots because of underdeveloped infrastructure and poor storage (as well as the dumping of excess food from the West).[57] What makes food waste in the United States, Western Europe, and other developed capitalist economies distinctive is that it happens despite the technical capacity to avoid much of it. The economic logic of neoliberal capitalism makes it inevitable, regardless of the efficiency or thriftiness of individual firms and farms—just as Marx, and Sasha, predicted.

The First Freegans

Recovering all this ex-commodified food eventually had a name attached to it. In 1994, shortly after being released on bail before his trial for serving food in San Francisco without a permit, Keith McHenry—the FNB founder—went on a "Rent Is Theft" speaking tour throughout the United States and Canada. After a presentation in Edmonton, Alberta, he went with a group of local FNB "kids" who were in a punk band to a local health goods store. As he tells it:

At first, we went in, and they had samples everywhere, so we thought we could get breakfast by eating the samples. And we were all vegan, so we were just eating the vegan samples. But eventually, the workers said, "You're just eating samples, you're not even buying anything. You have to leave."

McHenry, confident that any health food store was bound to have a plethora of ex-commodities on hand, suggested that the group go out back:

There were these four massive dumpsters. There were a lot of us, maybe eight or nine people, and I was in a dumpster and discovered this huge wheel of imported cheese from France, priced at like $250. It was covered in wax, and it hadn't even been cracked, and it was so huge that I couldn't even lift it up to the rim of the dumpster.

McHenry, like most people at FNB with whom I interacted, was vegan, but the top-notch cheese was too good to pass up: "I called out to everyone, 'I can't believe I just found this cheese. To heck with being vegan, let's be 'freegan'!' So that was it, where the word came from."

McHenry ultimately left the wheel of cheese in the dumpster, but he carried the tale of the legendary find with him. In Gainesville, Florida, he told the "wheel of cheese" story at the Civic Media Center, an alternative community space. At that particular moment in the anarchist scene, he explained, "the whole energy that was going on made sense [with freeganism]," as more and more people were embracing waste recovery as one way to transform their lives and minimize their responsibility for capitalist exploitation. One attendee—purportedly Warren Oakes, the one-time drummer for the punk band Against Me!—liked the word *freegan* enough to write a short manifesto titled "Why Freegan?" While McHenry originally used *freegan* to refer only to food, the tract offered a much broader vision:

There are two options for existence: (1) waste your life working to get money to buy things that you don't need and help destroy the environment or (2) live a full satisfying life, occasionally scavenging or working your self-sufficiency skills to get the food and stuff you need to be content, while treading lightly on the earth, eliminating waste, and boycotting everything. Go!

Freegans, the author unsurprisingly declared, were those who choose the latter. Freeganism was the "ultimate boycott" directed against "EVERYTHING—All the corporations, all the stores, all the pesticides, all the land and resources wasted, the capitalist system, the all-oppressive dollar, the wage slavery, the whole burrito!" The pamphlet enumerated an array of strategies for "withdrawing from it [capitalism] and never using money," from dumpster diving to politically inspired handkerchief use and skateboarding.

Clearly, the idea of voluntarily "withdrawing from" or "dropping out" of capitalism by appropriating its waste was nothing new, even if McHenry and the pamphlet he inspired gave it a catchy name. While many of the FNB volunteers in the Bay Area whom I talked to were already engaged in freegan practices, only once did someone identify himself to me as "freegan." One day, I was chopping vegetables next to Jeff, a white male in his midtwenties with nose and lip piercings, massive black plugs gauging out his ears, and a black tattoo sleeve up his right arm. He had moved to Oakland from Denver to study urban agriculture and matter-of-factly stated that since he'd arrived, he'd lived on "no money," adding, "I mean, I do work [referring to his activism with FNB and Occupy Oakland], I just don't work for wages." He said that he got almost all his food from the dumpster and proudly added, "My backpack, all my pens, my notebooks—I dumpstered all of them." Squatting was another expression of his resource-recovery practices: "It's all about taking something that's being wasted and turning it into something useful. That's what it's all about. It's like dumpstering a house." When Jeff called himself "freegan," Darrin— another FNB activist in his early forties, who has been homeless for most of his adult life because of his commitment to full-time, anarchist activism—asked, "What's that?" When Jeff explained that "freeganism" meant trying to "drop out" of capitalism, Darrin nodded excitedly, and exclaimed, "That's what I've been trying to do my whole life!" Darrin was, in effect, a longtime freegan without knowing it.

The few available published studies of individuals outside New York who identify themselves as freegan also describe freeganism as a diffuse subculture of youth from relatively privileged backgrounds committed to "dropping out" of capitalism. After interviewing a handful of freegans living in rural Oregon, one anthropologist concludes that freegans are people who "prefer to opt out of the economic system entirely, living in the 'cracks of society' as they say, consuming only what society throws away."[58] Her respondents were completely disconnected from mainstream society, "not permanent residents" anywhere and "not integrated into the community."[59] Another pair of researchers characterize a group of freegans and FNB participants in Australia as nearly entirely white, male, in their midtwenties, and well educated.[60] This juxtaposition between advantaged upbringings and present-day scrounging for survival is not coincidental. As an ethnographer writes of dumpster divers in Seattle, "For those punks who were raised white or middle class, dumpsters and dumped food dirty their bodies and tarnish their affiliation with a white, bourgeois power structure. In this sense, the downward descent into a dumpster is literally an act of downward mobility."[61] Freeganism, for these practitioners, was a kind of politicized poverty—albeit a form of deprivation that was temporary and reversible.

Beyond a basic agreement that freegan practices center on reducing one's participation in the capitalist economy through waste recovery, though, both published and unpublished accounts of freeganism outside freegan.info offer little sense of what the aim of freegans' "politics" actually is. On the one hand, some freegans argue that dumpster diving is itself a form of transformative "direct action" to undermine the capitalist system:

> If shoppers all stopped buying stuff they don't need, and we started rummaging for our necessities through the stuff supermarkets throw away, the supermarkets themselves would soon stop over-ordering and stop budgeting in the immense waste that is a regular part of their economics.[62]

Another laudatory account of freeganism argues that "the dumpster divers are the most logical subset of the anti-globalization activists because they live in a way that does not create any demand for goods and therefore their lives do nothing to propagate the very system they are protesting."[63]

For other freegans, however, living off ex-commodities is not an end in itself but a way to survive and build community while engaging in more overtly political projects, such as protesting against the WTO or setting up squatter settlements with the homeless. As Christian, a tall, handsome investment-banker-turned-sex-worker who was active with the group until 2008, explained to me at one of my first trash tours, "We're activists. We're working to save the rainforest. We're fighting for human rights. This [dumpster diving] allows us to work less so that we have more time for activism." One "how-to" zine for dumpster divers cautions against viewing dumpster diving as a political "tactic" in any meaningful sense: "Dumpstering is a way of reducing your impact on the environment, but it is not a practice that works to directly engender a sustainable world. THAT is a topic for another zine."[64]

In short, freeganism started as just a word, to which a range of people and groups subsequently ascribed their own meanings. Freeganism as a whole is not really a "movement," at least not in the sociological sense of "collective action by people with common purposes and solidarity."[65] As Keith recalled, seventeen years after he coined the term:

> It started as a joke, really. I had just been thinking: isn't it amazing that there's this $250 wheel of cheese here? We were vegan and we found a lifetime supply of cheese. At that point, it had nothing to do with a movement or anything like that, just a really funny thing that happened. It was the young man that wrote the flyer [Why Freegan?] who made it into a theory. But my sense from that flyer is that it was also supposed to be more humorous and playful. He hit upon something that was already happening for many years. It was just that one guy writing about it, not a deliberate attempt to make a movement or to have it be worldwide.

During my time with East Bay FNB, I encountered several activists who could be described as freegans, insofar as they were meeting most of their needs through recovering waste rather than engaging in wage labor to purchase commodities. To them, salvaging ex-commodities was an obvious strategy for reducing their participation in the capitalist economy. But when I mentioned my time spent with an organized group of freegans in New York at one meal in Berkeley to one such activist, he replied incredulously, "Wait, it's like a *movement* there?"

Freegan.info's Wetland Birth

The story of how a diffuse set of anticapitalist practices congealed into a social movement starts with Wetlands Preserve nightclub, lovingly remembered as a "hippie dive bar" that opened in a postindustrial district of Tribeca, Manhattan, in 1989. Patrons described it as "a beautiful flower growing in a crack in the concrete" or "a secret society, a temporary autonomous zone, a late-night slacker's sanctuary, a tripper's refuge, an all-ages hardcore haven"—terms that evoked the prefigurative radical communities to which the club was connected.[66] Its owners billed it as an "environmental nightclub," offering paper straws with drinks and matchbooks made from recycled materials. What's more, the club channeled its patrons toward activism through benefit concerts and weekly "Eco-Saloons." It even included in its operating budget up to $100,000 a year for an environmental and social justice center.

The club itself closed in October 2001, replaced with loft apartments as part of the ongoing gentrification of lower Manhattan, but the Wetlands Activism Collective (WAC) continued. According to its website, the WAC is a "volunteer-run grassroots organization" "focused on resisting global capitalism and its devastating effect on the environment and the lives of human and nonhuman animals."[67] The collective's stated commitment to "draw[ing] connections between animal rights, human rights, and environmental concerns" and opposition to "the commodification of life on all fronts" is similar to the anticapitalist critiques on freegan.info's website. This is hardly a coincidence, given that Adam was the primary author of both. Adam first went to Wetlands in the mid-1990s for a talk on the damage that oil exploitation was causing to the environment and indigenous peoples in Ecuador, and eventually became the collective's activism director.

In the 1990s Wetlands was at the vanguard of New York's direct action scene. As Cindy, a freegan.info activist who had been involved with Wetlands, explained:

> We were doing environmental stuff when really very few grassroots groups in the city were. When I was first involved in '95 and '96, I didn't see lots of other [direct action] activism going on in the city, maybe some community gardening and that was it. So we were active kind of before it was mainstream or in the news.

WAC organized events on behalf of Earth First! and the Rainforest Action Network, two environmentally focused anarchist groups that used direct actions such as "spiking" trees to make them dangerous to cut or blockading logging trucks to protect old-growth forests in the Latin American tropics or northwestern United States.[68] For its part, Wetlands mixed direct action with more classic political tactics, from street theater to civil disobedience to lobbying. Its website lists a huge number of campaigns—and victories—that pressured corporations over animal abuse, workers' rights, and environmentally unsustainable products.[69]

Adam told me that, at an animal rights conference in Seattle in 1995, he described his lifestyle to another activist, who replied that he sounded like a "freegan." At the time, though, Adam was taken aback: "I saw a freegan as someone who's usually vegan, but then someone gives her half a ham sandwich, and since she didn't pay for it, says it's 'freegan' and eats it." As the definition of freeganism circulating within the anarchist scene broadened into the "total boycott" described by the *Why Freegan?* pamphlet, though, the term gained in allure. People like Wendy, Cindy, and Adam were becoming frustrated with trying to protest exploitative companies individually through WAC. The official freegan.info founding story encapsulates this realization:

> After years of trying to boycott products from unethical corporations responsible for human rights violations, environmental destruction, and animal abuse, many of us found that no matter what we bought we ended up supporting something deplorable. We came to realize that the problem isn't just a few bad corporations but the entire system itself.[70]

This sense of the need for a wholesale challenge to capitalism drew them to freeganism, which seemed like a necessary step to get beyond the limits of Wetlands' previous campaigns.

According to Cindy, at one point while the club was still open, Wetlands screened a documentary about waste. Afterward, some of the WAC activists who were already dumpster diving to feed themselves led a group dive. She herself remembers being surprised to learn "that you could get good, healthy stuff from the garbage, not just cake." The surprising number of attendees "planted a seed that this [recovering ex-commodities] was something that people were interested in." Wendy and Adam worked together to create the freegan.info website as a side project of Wetlands in 2003, and Wendy formed a group on the social network "meet-up" around the same time. In 2005 the group began offering a monthly calendar of events, including skill-shares, films and forums, and, of course, collective dumpster dives, or "trash tours."

Why did freeganism take such a particular form in New York? If freegans are right that capitalism as a whole is wasting huge numbers of ex-commodities, the logical corollary is that acquiring food by dumpster diving should be possible just about anywhere there is advanced neoliberal capitalism. And, at least for the United States, this is what some have found: as the author of a famous anarchist travelogue, *Evasion*, recounts, "There was always the consistent and confounding thread running through each town and region in America: edible trash."[71] Adam himself insisted that it's possible to dumpster dive "everywhere"—at least within the range of his travels (not surprisingly, he avoids flying)—although it's a bit more "hit or miss" in the suburbs. Scholars have confirmed the apparent universality of available wasted food with accounts of self-identified freegans and dumpster divers in urban, suburban, and rural contexts.[72]

But while the existence of ex-commodities might be a universal fact of modern capitalism, the municipal governance systems that manage waste vary from country to country and city to city.[73] The dumpster-diving expeditions I have taken outside New York hardly allow for systematic comparison, but they do hint at the variation in what "dumpster diving" actually means. I took one foraging trip in Phoenix, Arizona, with a middle-aged, otherwise inconspicuous woman who claimed that she had recovered and redistributed tens of thousands of dollars of food in the previous few years under the nom de guerre "Ginger Freebird." The take was abundant, but the logistics complicated: in a city built for automobiles, a car was a necessity. Under the blazing desert sun, food spoiled rapidly and dumpster rims were scalding.

I tried my hand dumpster diving in Europe, following the city-by-city guide posted on the open-source encyclopedia, trashwiki. org. In Montpellier and Paris, France, there were fewer doughnuts and more cheese and yogurt than in the United States. Many French grocery stores had compactors, so in the few places where the food was accessible it was gone in a few minutes, harvested more often than not by elderly women continuing the long French tradition of "gleaning" excess food.[74] In Vienna, Austria, food waste was sequestered in

A diver in Phoenix, Arizona, faces one-hundred-degree heat and scalding hot dumpsters, conditions rare in New York City. Photograph by the author.

indoor "trash rooms" with a nausea-inducing smell of rot that made any trip there a short one. The local anarchist community had stolen a master key from the city's sanitation service and distributed copies, but, when I visited, they were concerned that the municipality was in the process of changing the locks. Freegans may be correct when they point out that wherever there are supermarkets, there is wasted food. But accessing that food presents unique challenges depending on the location.

For its part, New York has always been "too large and too densely populated to be typical" in its municipal waste system.[75] The city's Commissioners' Plan of 1811, which laid down its iconic numbered grid, left no space for alleyways.[76] As such, "dumpster diving" in New York involves no dumpsters: bagged-up garbage sits directly on the street. New York's (non)dumpster divers thus do their foraging on well-lit thoroughfares, where they can easily access and examine garbage for useful items, rather than in dark back alleys. Comparing dumpster diving in New York with her native France, one diver explained, "There [in France], I need help just to pass the bags over the rim [of the dumpster]. You need more planning, more organization. Here, if I want to get a doughnut, I can just go out at any time and I know it'll be here. The garbage here is very reliable." The city's density means that there are an exceptional number of establishments, including 24,000 restaurants, 5,445 supermarkets and grocers, 1,700 wholesalers, and 1,000 food manufacturers, producing ex-commodities in proximity.[77]

Although "theft of garbage" and "interfering with sanitation operations" are crimes in New York,[78] two scholars who studied scavengers in the city could not find a single example of someone being ticketed for gathering food or other items from the trash.[79] Adam had interacted with the police only once during his thirteen years of dumpster diving in the city, and in that case, the officer simply stopped to ask, "Finding anything good?" Once again, the contrast with dumpster divers outside New York—who often faced locked gates barring them from dumpsters and feared being caught trespassing on store property—was stark.[80] One frustrated Danish diver shared her own travails over the freegan-world e-mail list: "I am very proud to be a forager but we have problems here in Scandinavia. We must constantly watch for the police because if we are seen to be foraging in a dumpster, the fine is 500 kroner [$85]. Sometimes 'good citizens' use their cell phones to phone the police." In New Zealand, "doing the duck"— the kiwi term for dumpster diving—is flatly illegal.[81]

The comparatively easy, abundant, and legal dumpster diving in New York has earned it a reputation as a forager's mecca. One day, while I was preparing a meal with Food Not Bombs in Berkeley, I spoke about my experiences in New York. Anka, a German émigré with long dreadlocks, chimed in: "Yeah, I couldn't believe how much food there was everywhere I looked in New York!" When I mentioned that freegan.info held public dives in the city, she responded, "I guess you could try to do a public thing here [in San Francisco]. But most of the grocery stores here are already donating their food. So there's not that many places to go here, and they're pretty spread out."

Academics are always tempted to offer convoluted explanations for what is easily accounted for. It may be that freegan.info emerged in New York because that's where its founders happened to be. To be sure, the existence of anticapitalist communities was an essential precondition for the emergence of a strong freegan organization, but this does not explain why it happened in New York City as opposed to other major urban centers. Particular features of the way garbage flows through America's largest metropolis, however, made it a particularly hospitable home for freeganism. Little surprise that the "garbage capital of the world"[82]—a city literally built on top of waterways filled in with garbage and legendary for its waste output—would play host to the most visible freegan group critiquing and recovering that waste.

Prefiguration in Its DNA

The essays on the freegan.info website are the closest thing the group has to any formal statement of mission or strategy, and provide a glimpse into the group's founding political rationality. At least at its inception, the group's strategy was a prefigurative one:

> *Freegans envision a future based on self-sufficient, sustainable communities, where we obtain vital resources in ways that don't exploit people, animals, or the earth, and share them freely to ensure that everyone's needs are met. We believe the best way to shape this future is to put these values into practice today to the greatest extent possible.*[83]

Of course, if this doesn't sound like a realistic model for a complex, high-speed global economy, that was probably the point. In contrast to Marxist–Leninist communists who promised a hyperproductive postcapitalist techno-utopia,[84] freegan.info believed it was "prefiguring" a simpler and slower world. In this respect, freegan.info was drawing from a general sense among contemporary anticapitalists that modern production and consumption are not just exploitative and dehumanizing but also rather pointless. As David Graeber, one of the most prominent theorists of present-day anarchism, argues, neoliberal capitalism is

> *built around the spectacular destruction of consumer goods. They are societies that imagine themselves as built on something they call "the economy" which, in turn, is imagined as a nexus between "production" and "consumption," endlessly spitting out products and then destroying them again.*[85]

In its place, freegan.info's website proposed: "To live in harmony with other beings and our planet . . . we must decrease personal and societal consumption, shrinking our personal and societal economic needs."[86]

In stark contrast to the version of freeganism articulated in *Why Freegan?* and described in studies of freegans elsewhere, freegan .info envisioned freeganism as more than just a dropout subculture or radically autonomous lifestyle. In fact, the website was disdainful of a single-minded focus on achieving personal ecological and ethical perfection:

> *Freeganism is NOT a form of asceticism or purism. Freegans recognize that the society we live in makes us all complicit in social and environmental atrocities—a simple act like flipping on the lights means contributing to global warming and habitat destruction through strip mining of coal. Our goal is to present PRACTICAL alternatives that massive numbers of people can use to make their lives easier and better while limiting their economic support for oppressive corporate practices. Freegans believe that our economic system and social structure as a whole needs to change—not just individual practices—and believe that by creating more humane and sustainable living strategies and building institutions to facilitate them, we can make corporate dominated global capitalism obsolete.*[87]

Even as the website fingers ordinary consumers alongside corporate executives as responsible for "social and environmental atrocities," it insists that any strategy to address those atrocities must be collective.

Freegan.info's ancestry was visible in the group's structure, which closely mirrored that of other anarchist groups but strayed far from what most people would see as "organization."[88] During my involvement, the group had no formal membership requirements, no officers or titles, and only a handful of collectively articulated policies. A rotating facilitator led meetings, and the group made decisions by consensus. Anyone who had attended two meetings and done "some work"—the precise meaning of this requirement was unclear, although it was certainly not stringent—could block any proposal for any reason (although a single block could eventually be overruled). Most projects were carried out by semiautonomous, voluntary "working groups,"[89] which, like the umbrella group, had no defined or fixed structure.

Some individuals who came to freegan.info meetings unfamiliar with this anarchist version of direct democracy and nonhierarchical organization told me that they appreciated how open the group was to newcomers. Others, confronting the Byzantine complexity of getting

A freegan "sewing skill-share" in a community center "prefigures" an economic system where people make and repair (not buy and replace) their clothes. Photograph by the author.

anything done, described freegan.info as "bureaucratic." Either way, freegan.info was copying organizational forms that were widely diffused by the direct action movements of the 1980s and 1990s. Many of the hand signals I saw used in freegan.info meetings, like "twinkle" fingers to show approval or crossed arms for a "block," were taken from the AGM and later became icons of the General Assemblies of the Occupy Wall Street movement.

While the freegans certainly sought to expand participation in their movement—"I want someone in every city saying they're a freegan, saying 'fuck capitalism,'" as Madeline put it—freegan.info's participants had a particular idea of what "growing the movement" meant. When I first attended a freegan trash tour and indicated that I was from New Jersey, Janet suggested to me that I stop coming to New York and bring the freegan movement to my hometown. When interest in freegan.info peaked in 2008, the group floated the idea of "chapters" in other cities. The "guidelines" proposed would allow nearly any group that claimed to be prosustainability and anticonsumption to have access to the group's website, e-mail lists, press contacts, and printed materials. Jason explained the impetus for chapters in these terms:

> Trying to traverse great distances to bring our mission to everyone will just wear us out. We should give our ideas and our structure to other localities, and let them apply them to make their own groups. I can even envision a point where there are self-contained freegan groups in every borough of New York. How cool would that be? ... You don't spread ideas over a massive population by growing your organization to a massive size, you spread them by birthing offshoots.

The e-mail that announced the new guidelines for chapters stated, "We claim no ownership of freeganism, but hope to build the resources and mission of freegan.info as part of a global collective effort." Although the group did at one time have "chapters" in Washington, D.C., and Boston, there was almost no coordination or communication between them.

If its organizational structure and prefigurative focus were what freegan.info shared with other millennial anarchist movements, its emphasis on waste distinguished it. Although the freegan.info home page lists strategies like urban gardening, wild food foraging, and voluntary unemployment as freegan practices, "waste reclamation" comes before all of them. The first image that confronts a visitor to the site is a picture of a woman leaning out of a dumpster, holding a bag of presumably just-rescued potatoes. While FNB and the other anarchist groups considered waste one possible resource for prefigurative practice, freegan.info made it central:

> Through dumpster diving, squatting, guerilla gardening and other strategies, freegans transform waste into resources to meet real

needs, allowing us to live our values of ecological sustainability, cooperation, and sharing while reducing our contribution to capitalism's abuse of humans, animals and the earth.[90]

Dumpster diving, as the website's opening essay states, is a way to "*politically* challenge the injustice of allowing vital resources to be wasted," not just a way to reduce one's individual ecological footprint. Although Adam invariably talked about dumpster diving in deprecating terms, diminishing it to "being a bottom feeder off of capitalism," it is hard not to get the impression from the website he largely wrote that collective dumpster diving is *the* defining tactic in freegan.info's strategic arsenal.

Strident rhetoric about freegan.info as a "revolutionary movement" building a "global counter-economy to capitalism" aside, both Wendy and Adam concur that the group's first organized "trash tour" did not go well. Adam bickered with another WAC activist over whether the tour was about the "politics of dumpster diving" or simply a social event for people who usually dived individually. The grocery stores they visited hadn't put out food that night, contributing to the fracas. Wendy and Adam also agree that the handful of attendees at that event were already at the radical fringes, well-versed in prefigurative politics. To their surprise, though, freegan.info's next few dives began to attract people from outside New York's relatively narrow direct action scene, revealing that freeganism had appeal beyond its anarchist roots.

Diving In, Opting Out

ike most freegans I interviewed, Madeline described herself as coming from a "safe, happy, and decidedly normal" suburban, middle-class household. She nonetheless insisted that inspirations for her later political behavior were presented to her early: her parents were "depression babies" who "grew up with frugality." Madeline recalled that her grandparents cultivated a vegetable garden, preserved food, knit and sewed their own clothes, and repaired broken household items rather than buy new ones—all activities that she now sees as having deeply political significance. She remembered an ethic of nonwasting that pervaded her household and, reflecting on her own vision for a utopian future, told me, "I look at my grandmother's generation, and I think 'not so bad.' They were reusing, they were repairing, they were composting, and they weren't consuming as a form of entertainment."

Madeline's introduction to more overt radicalism came in the late 1970s at State University of New York, Stony Brook, where she studied theater. College for her was a time of emergent awareness: her neighbors across the hall in her dorm were anarchists, and, as she became cognizant of her own bisexuality, she exposed herself to gay-rights activism. She dropped out of college after a year and a half, intent on pursuing an acting career on her own. When she found few opportunities awaiting her, though, she moved to the countryside and started learning about "survival living," cutting her own firewood, trapping animals for meat, and canning food from her garden. She proudly told me that by this point she had almost completely withdrawn from the monetary economy: "freegan," perhaps, without having ever heard the word.

While she found the ethical purity of her rural lifestyle appealing, though, a year of isolation left her longing for more engagement. She took a tour of back-to-the-land communities scattered across the United States and eventually settled in Bellingham, Washington. There, Madeline told me, she worked at a vegetarian restaurant, operated an alternative printing press, and helped found a shelter for victims of domestic violence. Her interest in art and activism converged when she discovered situationism, a philosophy from 1960s France whose practitioners subverted capitalism in everyday life.[1] Situationism led her to challenge the dominant norms of society in unconventional ways, like street theater and graffiti.

Her participation in the cultural politics of post-1960s America, though, eventually brought her into conflict with the state. Police held her and her partner for two weeks after an antinuclear protest, but eventually released her. Later, they caught her spray painting, and the prosecutor charged her with a felony. She recalls the moment as a major turning point:

> While I was in jail, my situationist friends started organizing on my behalf. They wanted to turn me into a poster girl for "the cause," making my story into a parable for free speech versus police repression. But I didn't feel comfortable with being reduced to a set of characteristics designed to fit the typecast profile of a political prisoner.

Madeline, then nearly thirty years old, pled guilty to a misdemeanor and, in her words, simply "backed off." She returned to school at Western Washington University and finished her degree in theater. Shortly thereafter, though, she abandoned the stage. "I just got too tired of being poor," she explained. For the first time in years, she took a full-time job.

As she put it, the next two decades of her life were a "slippery slope" that carried her farther and farther away from her previous commitments. She returned to New York, covered up the gaps in her résumé, and entered finance. To her surprise, she ascended the ranks quickly. Even without previous experience in business, "I just proved to be good at climbing the corporate ladder. I played it like a video game." When she moved to the communications department at Barnes and Noble a few years later, her salary topped six figures, paying for what she dubbed a "dream life." Looking back, she conceded, "I had been bought off. I had been co-opted. And it felt good." Madeline went to anti–Gulf War protests in 1991, but for a decade thereafter, she was by her own admission "no longer politically involved." When the second Bush administration invaded Iraq, she said she was disturbed, but remained inactive.

Things changed only when she read about Reverend Billy and the Church of Life After Shopping, a street theater troupe based in New York dedicated to convincing people to limit their consumption. When I spoke to Reverend Billy, he described the tactics of his combination ministry-theater troupe—performing exorcisms on banks and beatifying antiwaste activists—as "trying to turn society upside down. Change the signals. Drive people out of their old understandings." This blend of politics and performance, social change and everyday life, resonated with Madeline and her situationist past. Later that year, she risked arrest at a civil disobedience action on "Buy Nothing Day" 2004. Her sudden reintegration into activism was, to her, "like living under water for ten years and then sticking my head up and breathing."

By Madeline's account, she then embarked on an intense period of personal change and self-exploration. Surfing the Web and following links from one activist website to another, she encountered freegan.info. The group caught her attention as a more radical version of the Church of Life After Shopping. Out of curiosity, she attended a meeting. The experience was, she laughed, "horrendous": the group appeared to lack any organization or direction, and the meeting consisted of little more than an ideological shouting match between Adam and Wendy.

Something about the trash tour afterward, however, "clicked." When I pressed her to explain why, she replied, "There was just something about the hidden part of waste. Seeing all that food—it was like a microcosm of what is wrong with capitalism." In a sense, the collective dumpster dive appealed because it dispelled fetishistic beliefs about commodities and waste. It exposed the sad truth that much of what gets produced is wasted, that this waste stems not from negligent consumers but the capitalist system as a whole, and that much of that waste, far from being polluted and valueless, is still useful. And, Madeline quickly realized, the experience was not just powerful for her: "I like watching other people have their 'Aha' moments— realizing that there's all this waste out there, and connecting it to capitalism." As she mused, "There's this whole opportunity for more activities than you could ever do in New York City. So I guess it's significant that I stayed with the freegans."

Within the space of a year, Madeline had quit her job, left her Manhattan apartment in a doorman building in favor of a small but tidy flat she and her partner purchased in Flatbush, Brooklyn, and dedicated herself to political work. She became one of freegan.info's chief spokespeople, putting her skills in corporate communication to work honing an anticapitalist message centered on waste. When I spoke again with Madeline in 2012, she told me about her recent work to save a community garden and her deepening involvement in projects to protect food crops' genetic diversity from control by international agribusiness. She also recounted her recent arrest at an Occupy Wall Street protest for raucously banging a pot and pan in a police officer's face. This time, though, she was not backing off but instead suing the NYPD for wrongful arrest.

While Madeline's switch from corporate success-story to full-time activist makes for a dramatic narrative—it even earned her a chapter in a book about life "U-turns"[2]—it is more intelligible within her own history. Madeline got her activist start in the culture- and identity-focused movements of post-1960s America, but eventually came to doubt their efficacy. When she returned to activism, she found a movement that built on the brand of theatrical protests with an emphasis on personal consumption and everyday life that she knew, but which tied these tactics to a direct, prefigurative attack on capitalism.

Freegan from Birth?

Twenty out of twenty-two freegan.info participants I interviewed reported that they came from "middle class," "upper-middle class," or "privileged" backgrounds, a finding consistent with numerous studies on post-1960s far-left movements.[3] Most freegans are childless, college-educated, and unmarried, features of what the sociologist Doug McAdam calls "biographical availability" for activism.[4] Freegans themselves, though, viewed their backgrounds as more than a set of demographic prerequisites. In fact, nearly every freegan I interviewed tied his or her present activism to experiences, emotions, and aspirations from childhood.

Radicalization: Models from Parents and Grandparents

Three of my interviewees insisted that their parents imparted their anticapitalist politics to them. Evie explained that her family life inculcated in her a "daily consciousness about how my actions affected other elements of the world." As such, there was no moment when she decided to become an activist. Instead, she had always operated on the assumption that she would be engaged. The only question was which cause would occupy her time: in her youth, she bounced between work on behalf of Palestinians, political prisoners, and third-world victims of corporate globalization. Her commitments were tied to a strong sense of moral obligation, rather than any reassuring sense that social transformation was imminent. "My grandfather used to talk about the Spanish Revolution," she said, "and he always told me, 'You don't fight fascism because you think you can win. You fight it because it's *fascism*.'"

I met Lola, a tattooed young woman with a septum piercing and a short Mohawk, during the summer of 2008. She paused in New York to spend time with freegan.info while she was traveling across the country by bicycle, train hopping, and hitchhiking. Her parents were academics, and she grew up listening to conversations about the unjust treatment of Native Americans and other minorities at the hands of the U.S. government. More than just hearing about these wrongs, though, she was actively exposed to them: she recalled being just a few years old and going with her parents to rallies on behalf of migrant farmworkers striking for higher wages.

Disillusioned with the public school system, her parents pulled her out in fifth grade: "They basically thought that the child has the best idea of what to learn. So I just would go to the library every day and find topics that were interesting to me." When she returned to public school in tenth grade, she was already heavily involved in movement organizing. She protested against labor practices in Taco Bell and sweatshop conditions in Nike factories—trying, with no avail, to get her peers at school to join her in sit-ins and confrontational protests. "It's hard to get high school students interested in direct action," she bemoaned.

Leia, a Latina in her midtwenties and one of the few participants in freegan.info with a child—a toddler named Uma—also attributed her politics to early experiences. Her father and grandfather, she explained, were "anti-Christian" and had "communistic leanings." Leia's family moved from city to city when she was young, at one point bringing her to a particularly conservative region of Georgia. She obtained a copy of the "Satanic Bible" and tried reading it in class, but her teacher took it away. She also clashed with her teachers over dress. When the school directed students to "Dress for Success," she snidely told administrators her torn jeans and T-shirts reflected her desire to "succeed" as a "dirty-ass punk rock star."

In high school, Leia joined the Spartacist League, a Trotskyist socialist party. Through her involvement in the group, she had her first opportunity to participate in collective, contentious politics, attending protests against the KKK and police brutality. Looking back, she was uncertain about the rigid communist ideology and hierarchical structure of the Sparticists, which were a far cry from the loose, consensus-based organizing into which she ultimately put her energy. Nevertheless, she appreciated the introduction the communists gave her: "I joined them without knowing what I was joining. But they taught me a lot about politics."

As with the other two interviewees, Leia could not offer a precise moment where she became "politicized" or "radicalized." Instead, all three emphasized that they were invariably political. Years later, they were often some of the most forceful voices calling for freegan.info to take part in overt and confrontational anticapitalist actions—of precisely the sort that these women had been engaging in for as long as they could remember.

Rebellion: Against Parents, Schools, and Society

Thirteen freegans offered a divergent narrative, centered on childhood "rebellion" against parents, schools, and society as a whole. Rather than being channeled into leftist movements by their families, these future freegans found themselves resisting parental dictates and formal schooling on their own. Jonathan was a twenty-five-year-old freegan whose shaved head, dark goatee, and thick-rimmed glasses gave him the bearing of an early-twentieth-century Russian revolutionary. In addition to being a freegan, Jonathan was involved with anticircumcision and pro-Palestinian organizing. This was a rather stark rejection of his Orthodox Jewish upbringing:

In my family, the only politics that mattered was whether the Pres-
ident was pro-Israel or not. That's the extent of how political my
parents were. My parents didn't vote, but they did read the Jew-
ish Press. *Nobody in my family is remotely political in any sense.*
They keep to themselves, they work, they support their families, and
that's it. The outside world is just something to fear and hate. They
interact with it as little as possible.

Jonathan claimed that he chafed under the conventions of society
from an early age: "Because I was sort of really good at school work
and stuff, I felt like sitting in class was just punishment, like jail. I did
really well, all the time, yet I still had to sit. I always rebelled against
teachers, rabbis, whatever." When he was eight, he asked to be trans-
ferred to a nonreligious school, a request his father denied. At fifteen,
he declared to his parents' horror that he did not believe in God.

Making sense of Jonathan's early rebellion is challenging. His
political proclivities certainly did not come from his immediate social
milieu: Jonathan insisted that he had little exposure to nonconserva-
tive, non-Orthodox ideas as a youth, and none of his siblings shared
his iconoclastic views. Like many freegans, Jonathan felt that the
seeds of his political beliefs were "just there" for as long as he could
remember.

Other elements of Jonathan's early experiences do, however,
map onto the present. As he explained, his family was affluent until
his uncle got in trouble with the tax authorities, at which point their
fortunes soured. Jonathan was one of the few freegans (alongside
Leia) who described material deprivation in his childhood:

We were pretty poor; I couldn't get proper dental care when I needed
it. My parents live in a small, three-bedroom apartment in Brook-
lyn. They've lived there since I was one. And we were a family of
seven in a tiny three-bedroom. So why did we have to live in such
cramped quarters? It just kind of sucked not having the same privi-
leges as other people.

Rather than crave the perquisites of those around him, though, the
experience left Jonathan disavowing them entirely: "I noticed that
people who did have those privileges, well, I really didn't like them.
People who have lots of money, they go shopping a lot, and buy things

from fancy clothing stores. I was never really into that. I always thought it was a waste of money."

Tall and muscular, Jason had a strikingly different bearing from Jonathan but shared in his adolescent rebellion. He, too, described a youthful obstreperousness that escapes quick sociological accounting. Despite growing up in a middle-class family, he avowed, "by seventh grade, I was basically an anarchist, even though I didn't run into cool adults who could nurture that." He characterized himself as one of "the kids with long black hair and trench coats and Nine-Inch Nails [an alternative metal band] T-shirts." As a result of his and his friends' unconventional aesthetic, which during the 1990s became associated with social outcasts and the perpetrators of school shootings, when his high school received bomb threats, "Everyone always suspected us." Once, the police interrogated one of his friends, and Jason recalled feeling like he was the only person who thought that there was something wrong with this intrusion. These experiences were disillusioning, but disconnected from any political ideology: "I remember thinking, 'Man, cops suck, this system sucks, it all sucks.'"

Although it's difficult to be sure whether these words reflected Jason's feelings at the time or his perception looking back on the past, he clearly saw his background as crucial to his involvement in freeganism. As he reiterated, "I was always radical. Sometimes it was latent, sometimes it wasn't encouraged, sometimes it was covered up by other things. But I was always radical." What Jason lacked, however, was a cause into which he could channel his frustration.

Recycling, Reuse, and Reduction

Finally, there were six interviewees who described little in the way of early radicalization or youthful rebellion. In their own way, though, they claimed to have deep roots out of which their freeganism eventually grew. These freegans linked their pasts and presents by highlighting a continuity of personal practices around waste and consumption.

Janet, a high school Spanish teacher in her midfifties, assured me that she grew up feeling "appreciated, loved, and comfortable." Yet she was always "intrinsically nonwasting," despite the material abundance of her family life and an inability to recall external influences that might make her that way. She recollected that, even when she was a teenager surrounded by shopping-obsessed peers, she never wanted new clothes: "If someone gave me a sweater, I would leave it hanging in my closet for a year before wearing it. I preferred hand-me-downs." Even when she did engage in more mainstream adolescent pursuits, like listening to music, she did so with a frugal twist: rather than buy records, she waited for a favorite song to come on the radio and tape-recorded it.

Lucie, a French student who became involved in freegan.info in early 2012, offered a similar story. She, however, had a clearer explanation of where her obsession with reducing consumption came from:

> My parents are kind of crazy for not wasting. My father, when he needs hot water, and it comes out cold from the tap, he puts a bowl under to take the water and not to waste it. My mother, she would repair any object. I've seen her taking things like toothpaste from a tube with a syringe not to waste the insides. They don't waste food at all: we always eat the yogurts two months after the expiration date.

Despite growing up in affluence, Lucie thoroughly internalized her parents' nonwasting ethic:

> I grew up in a wealthy environment, I never lacked anything, so I had all that I wanted when I was young. And as far as I can remember, I've always wanted nothing, and I'd say, "I don't want this, I don't want this." I never wanted anything, no material things, no toys or clothes.

I asked Lucie if there was any ideological or political dimension to her early nonwasting practices. She laughed, "No. Now I see it, but of course it didn't, because it started when I was four years old: 'What do you want for Christmas?' 'Oh, I want nothing.' It wasn't political."

Lanky with a goatee and scraggly hair, Gio gave another version of the "recycling, reuse, and reduction" narrative. Gio's parents, he confessed, were "pretty conservative," having fled to the United States from Cuba during 1959 revolution. Nevertheless, in high school, he developed "a reputation as a moocher" because, at lunch time:

> I would see my friends with a half-eaten slice of pizza, and I would say, "No, no, no I'll eat that." I would basically clean up after everyone

else, eating other people's leftovers, what other people at the table considered garbage that they were going to throw away, and I thought, "That's still edible, that's still food, don't throw that away."

A turning point came when one of his friends pulled an uneaten slice of pizza out of the garbage and ate it: "Everyone thought it was totally gross. But I was like, inspired. I thought 'Wow, he's taking it to another level. I've never thought to eat out of the garbage.'"

As with Janet, his aversion to waste could not be traced to any easily identified influence: it was simply there. In a way, these freegans were never captured by the "fetish of waste." Gio told me, "I've never had that stigma, I could always see beyond the idea that 'If it's in the garbage can, it's garbage.'" Still, he did not adopt thrift and nonwasting with any broader objective. Instead, he had a reflexive sense that "waste" was simply stupid.

As all three different narratives highlight, while freegans' transitions to becoming freegan were full of moments where freegans chose a more radical path where others did not, they nonetheless explained those choices as attempts to be true to their own inherent activist core.[5] Analytically, the divergent narratives of "radicalization," "rebellion," and "recycling, reuse, and reduction" also hint at the divergent meanings that they attached to freeganism itself, presaging some of the movement's later fissures.

Frustrated Lifestyles and Vegan Disillusionment

How did these diverse childhood experiences converge on freeganism? Unsurprisingly, many freegans with narratives of "reduction" or "rebellion" had their first exposure to overt and collective political action during college (all but Leia and Adam had a college degree when I interviewed them). Sowmya, a student of environmental technology in New York but originally from Bangalore, India, told me that she had always believed that "without activism, life is useless." She then rattled off a list of organizations she was involved with when she was in college: the World Wildlife Fund, Greenpeace, and People for the Ethical Treatment of Animals (PETA). As Sowmya explained, "I began with animal rights, and I still see myself as an animal rights activist." When Sowmya first moved to New York to continue her education, she attended, by her own report, almost every antifur protest she could find. Yet these experiences led to disillusionment: looking back on hundreds of hours of sign waving, chanting, and leafleting, she said, "I'm not sure what any of that accomplished."

Her story was not exceptional. Even in the face of divergent experiences in youth, sixteen of twenty-two freegan.info participants said that they were vegetarians or vegans prior to becoming freegans (by comparison, the figure for the U.S. population writ-large is 5 percent vegetarian, 2 percent vegan, with some overlap between the two).[6] The origins of freeganism as a movement may lie in the anarchist community, but as individuals, freegan.info participants almost always began with animal rights.[7] As such, except for "radicals," freegans' political socialization initiated in movements deploying a standard mix of symbolic protests and lobbying for legislative reform.

The intensity of freegans' commitment to veganism and animal rights was evident during our interviews. David, a graduate student involved in both freegan.info and FNB, who invariably wore T-shirts advertising animal rights, avowed to me, "I do not believe it is okay to kill animals for anything no matter what" and that "I would never promote the consumption or use of any animal product." Similarly, Cindy once told me that she would not approve of keeping a beehive for honey, even if not a single bee was harmed: "I don't believe in humans having dominion over animals and I don't believe in non-human animals belonging to humans." Often, more casual attendees of freegan events arrived by way of the animal rights community. As one participant in a wild food foraging tour whispered, "*freeganism* shares the same root as *vegan*, so it must be good."

This fervent concern for animals was not just held by freegans individually but also espoused by freegan.info as a collective. Statistics about the harmful impacts of animal agriculture were among the first mentioned on freegan pamphlets or in "waving the banana" speeches.[8] On an ethical level, most freegans thought that there was no problem with eating meat from a dumpster, because doing so did not funnel money to animal exploitation. Yet, in contrast to other studies, which find that many freegans practice "meaganism" (eating animal products if they come from the trash),[9] only three of my interviewees ate dumpstered meat. When freegans cater for other activist events or hold freegan feasts, the food they prepare is almost strictly vegan. During trash tours, specialty vegan items like soy ice cream or seitan are quickly snatched up while choice cuts of beef or salmon go unclaimed. When

Sasha said he dumpster dived behind McDonald's during one speaking tour through Middle America, his admission drew judging glances from those around him. He was almost compelled to add, "Well, it's really not convenient to be starving all the time."

To some extent, freegans stay vegan out of force of habit; others, because they think animal products from the dumpster are unsafe. More importantly, though, many freegans saw being vegan as not just one part of their moral identities but central to it. "I like staying vegan while being freegan," Zaac explained. "It reminds me that I'm doing all this for the animals." At the same time, though, freegans almost all talked about becoming freegan as a way to move *beyond* veganism. Given that many freegans' first activist experiences were with vegetarian, vegan, or animal rights organizations, then, it is worth taking a step back to consider what kind of movement the modern animal rights movement (ARM) actually *is*.[10]

The first organizations created to promote vegetarianism in the West emerged in Britain in the nineteenth century. Vegetarianism was one cause amid a general ferment of interest in social change among the growing middle class, with vegetarians involved not only in advocacy for animals but also pacifism, abolition, women's rights, and prison reform.[11] As such, both its practitioners and the general public saw vegetarianism as a challenge to anyone who would "dominate, subordinate, exploit, and oppress one who is 'inferior,'"[12] whatever their species. Well into the early twentieth century, vegetarians were lumped in the popular imagination alongside "communists, anarchists... and other non-conformists."[13] Even today, the ARM retains some of this past association with demands for systemic change. For many contemporary anarchists, for example, a vegan diet is part of "prefiguring" a future nonviolent society, which is why vegetarianism is one of FNB's core principles.

Nonetheless, the mainstream ARM as represented by groups like PETA and the Humane Society of the United States shares little with its nineteenth-century predecessor. Veganism is "super-trendy" and animal rights a "hip cause,"[14] but growing acceptance and popularity have, in the eyes of freegans, come at a price. While they themselves were deeply concerned for other species, many freegans nonetheless questioned the ARM's single-minded focus on animals. Cindy told me, for example, that Wetlands used to collaborate with animal rights' organizations in antifur protests, but when she and others pushed for these events to address human labor conditions and sweatshops, "we got slammed" by those who wanted to focus on any animal except *Homo sapiens*. As David lamented, "You [don't] have to be progressive or radical or critical of the oppressive institutions around us to be vegan. And a lot of people who are extremely oppressive and extremely fucked up and involved in these institutions are still vegan." Research confirms that many contemporary animal rights groups are focused on a "narrowly defined set of issues … with little regard to their implications for other ideological questions."[15]

Freegans tied the ARM's failure to address the interconnections between human and animal oppression to the movement's narrow demographic profile.[16] Survey data suggest that participants in the ARM are overwhelmingly white, educated, and wealthy.[17] One ethnographer found that fewer than 5 percent of participants in vegetarian groups were people of color.[18] Freegans like Lola saw this, too: "Veganism has really exploded in the hipster community. Everyone is riding their fixed gear [bike] and eating the weirdest food they can find. In one sense, it's exciting because people are looking at the world in a new way." Her tone then shifted, "But a lot of the vegans I know are yuppies and very classist. They eat at overpriced restaurants in gentrifying neighborhoods. They don't think about the social impacts and exclusivity of their dietary practices." A lot of vegans she knew, she added, eat "crappily." The epithet had a double meaning: "There is this laziness to a lot of vegans that you can just eat Oreos and drink orange juice. And then there are the people who buy only processed soy products. So they're supporting a corporation that is destroying fields and taking over family farms. Then there's all the plastic!" She went silent for a few seconds before adding, "I guess in college I realized just how abusive it still is to be vegetarian."

As Lola attested, over time many freegans became skeptical of the ethics and effectiveness of the ARM's signature tactic, purchasing animal-free products. They came to this conclusion through different paths. For Sowmya, disillusionment came from the realization that an isolated vegan's actions were just a drop in the bucket: "People think 'Oh, I'm vegan or I'm vegetarian and I'm going to save the world' and now they have a halo. But it's way beyond that. It does make a difference, but it's negligible." Future freegans also began to question the ethics behind vegan commodities themselves. Adam, for example, told me of his shock when he realized that "vegan" food production destroys wildlife habitat and that the machines used to harvest "vegan" crops kill millions of small rodents.[19]

Others focused on the nonanimal abuses behind vegan products. When one trash-tour attendee asked me if I *really* thought that harm to bees meant that vegans should eschew honey, Zaac interjected, "You don't even need to think about the bees! Think about the working conditions for the honey collectors. Think about all the chemicals they use." As Zaac later elaborated, "A lot of vegans are locked into a constant competition to prove, 'I'm more vegan than you,' so they fret about a trivial amount of cow bones in refined sugar but ignore the petroleum products in a vegan item's packaging."

Freegans gradually linked problems with vegan products themselves to concerns about the corporate entities selling them. When small-scale farms and grocery cooperatives first marketed organic and vegetarian products in the 1960s, big agribusinesses perceived them as a threat.[20] Now, though, food providers, from large distributors to fast-food chains, have recognized vegetarians as an affluent niche who provide a "new marketing and profit-generating opportunity."[21] Organic sales have grown at an extraordinary 20 percent per year clip since 1990, but their sellers have steadily eroded the standards behind them.[22] More and more product lines marked as "organic," "vegan," or "fair-trade" are owned by large corporations that—aside from using organic inputs—rely on "conventional" agricultural practices in the worst sense of the term.[23] Money that goes to purchase these products thus supports the bottom line of companies that also market foods that are anything but organic, vegan, and fair trade.

Marketing researchers have long recognized that many consumers use the organic shelf at a supermarket as a cue that anything placed there is "ethical."[24] But, as freegans realized, just reading the label to see if a food contained animal products or was fair-trade was no guide to whether a foodstuff was truly produced or distributed in a just manner.[25] Money is too fungible, and globalized capitalist economies too interconnected, for it to be so easy. Noted Wendy, "You can buy only the vegan stuff at the buffet bar at a place like Whole Foods, but you're funding everything at that bar if you buy from it." Even the epicenter of ethical purchasing for many in the contemporary food movement, farmer's markets where consumers can buy organic food directly from local producers, often sell crops picked by drastically underpaid migrant laborers.[26]

The haul from one freegan's first expedition in New York City. Many items are "organic," "vegan," or otherwise marketed as "ethical." Photograph by Marie Mourad.

Some of the earliest freegans connected all this to the ARM's unwillingness to challenge capitalism. *Why Freegan?* explains:

> *The vegan theory is essentially a boycott of any products that injure animals in their production. The vegan consumers are flexing their monetary muscle and "voting with their dollars" for the products that don't injure animals. These dollars are voting for Coca-Cola, big corporate grocery stores, greasy-fast food (we all know Taco Bell vegans), and worse. Shouldn't truly conscientious folks seek something more? I don't vote because no matter who I vote for, the government always wins and when you "vote with your dollars," consumerism always wins, capitalism always wins.*

And, as the author adds for good measure, "The packaging from vegan food doesn't take up less space in the landfill or consume less resources just because the food is vegan."

Adam summarized the same point in more succinct terms: "For all of the ridicule that vegans face from the mainstream public, ultimately they are still playing within the rules. Whether a consumer responds to one marketing pitch or another, they are still buying in, still acting as a cog in the capitalist machine." As far as he was concerned, under neoliberal capitalism, even the morals of animal rights activists had been commoditized and sold back to them in the form of high-end veggie burgers and cruelty-free cosmetics. The profits eventually cycled back into the same agricultural system vegans thought that they were escaping.

The Limits of Pocketbook Politics

This brief history of the animal rights movement might seem like a detour, but it illustrates a much larger story. The rise of prefigurative politics charted in the previous chapter is, in truth, a sideshow on the radical fringes compared with the broader transformation of more mainstream American activism since the 1960s. In response to the demands for authenticity, uniqueness, and self-actualization from the "New Left" or hippie movements of that decade, clever executives and marketers took concerns about individual identity and expression and packaged them into commodities.[27] Since then, calls for collective liberation coming from the gay rights, women's, or environmental movements have all been channeled into niche markets and specialty products.[28] The growing difficulty of getting the state to legislate for social change through collective action, too, has pushed more activists to adopt individualized "lifestyle" or "identity" politics in the neoliberal era.[29]

If many people choose to express their concerns about the environment, animals, or workers through buying things, they can be forgiven for it. After all, we are accustomed to addressing problems in our personal lives through consumption, so why not address collective problems the same way? Still, there is something incongruous about making the purchase of commodities the central means of political action. As one sociologist wryly observes, "The planet is warming, biodiversity loss is rampant, freshwater sources are dwindling and tainted, and public health is at risk due to environmental pollutants. One of the latest efforts to stop the looming socio-ecological catastrophe(s) is shopping."[30] Consumer activism accepts the fundamentally neoliberal notion that we are primarily citizens not of nations, communities, religions, or ethnicities but of the market.[31] The ARM is thus just one example of how movements once committed to changing capitalism now place enormous faith in the power of capitalism to effect change.

But, as freegans realized in their forays into veganism, the idea that consumer activism is a useful strategy for fighting injustice depends on a certain view of how capitalism works. Vegans believe, in effect, that the free market will carry the preference for more kale and less bacon that they express in dollars at the cash register all the way to the factory farm, which will raise fewer pigs as a result. This is the "story the environmental [and other consumer movements] tells itself"[32]: that individual consumer demand exerts a powerful influence over the shape of the economy as a whole. It is a modern manifestation of the commodity fetish, by which the things we buy are "granted mystical powers to create significant progressive changes," even though changes in markets or corporate practices have virtually *never* come in response to individual consumer decisions.[33] What's important to realize here is that this story rests on the idea that markets are efficient. Consumer activism wouldn't work if the things that consumer activists are boycotting still get produced yet wind up ex-commodified in the trash.

This portrayal of how capitalism works isn't just a tale circulated among activists. It's also the story that the boosters of free markets have told us for a long, long time. Early advocates (like Adam Smith) for "economic liberalism"—the kind of liberalism that calls for free trade and private property—viewed themselves as "waging a relentless battle against 'inefficiencies,' or wastes, of all sorts."[34] During the British enclosure movement of the eighteenth century, English politicians and intellectuals claimed that the unoccupied "common wastes" that peasants used for grazing, firewood, and hunting were actually underutilized "wasted commons."[35] Zaac, from freegan.info, talked about how colonists used the same claims about "waste" in the Americas:

> The central mythology used to justify manifest destiny was [John] Locke's concept of waste. The idea was that if a rich, elite landowner lets apples rot on the ground, then he doesn't deserve those trees, so we can take them. This was never really used to displace the aristocracy, though, but instead the native peoples who "underused" the land, in the colonists' eyes.[36]

Today, discourses of "waste" and "inefficiency" are central to the neo-liberal project of expanding the role of markets worldwide.[37] Advocates for neoliberal policies from Great Britain to Mexico have argued that, however we feel about the impacts of commodification on labor conditions or income inequality, it "works."[38] One reason neoliberal policies work is that, thanks to the magic of price signals and supply and demand, they reduce waste.

Lest this seem like idle pontification, it's worth noting how much this market mythos is drilled into us. As one introductory economics textbook details, because capitalists are driven by competition and the desire for profit, "Manufacturers are continually seeking ways to produce their products with less input, as well as less wasted output."[39] One study that examined texts used to teach administration, business, and economics found that, within them, "competitive private enterprise is always deemed more effective and efficient than non-profit-making organizations...since they reduce the waste of resources," whether "resources" are defined as money, goods, or time.[40] Even the left-wing magazine *Mother Jones* offers the same claptrap: "to save money, reduce risks, improve quality, and remain competitive, companies in nearly every sector are continually engineering waste, inefficiency, energy intensity, and toxicity out of their manufacturing and distribution."[41] This may be true for the individual firm, but, as Marx suggested, this fixation on the efficient production of individual commodities may blind us to the waste produced by the system as a whole.

This same battery of assertions about "waste" and "efficiency" has provided a powerful vocabulary for deriding any alternatives to capitalism. Newspaper portrayals of the communist countries of Eastern Europe frequently pointed to how "wasteful" they were compared with the "cleanliness, efficiency, and thriftiness of Western capitalism."[42] Closer to home, public statements in defense of neoliberal policies are frequently couched in the notion that we cannot tolerate "wasteful" government programs.[43] Yet only certain types of programs get tarred with the "waste" brush. Noted one public-opinion surveyor:

> *Suburbanites say they oppose government waste, but they clearly do not oppose it across the board. Waste, in their lexicon, is defined as those programs that spend billions upon billions of dollars to help*

cities, minorities, and the poor. Equally expensive programs that pri-
marily benefit the white middle class are not deemed "wasteful."[44]

Under neoliberalism, cutting public transportation or education
based on claims of "wastefulness" is an easy way to spur consumption
by forcing people to turn to the market. These policies depend, however, on the fetish of waste. Economists and policymakers constantly
tell us that governments, nonprofit organizations, or individual consumers produce waste but free markets don't. At the same time, they
buttress the fetish of commodities by suggesting the markets have
an almost supernatural capacity to respond to our wants and desires
that government or nonprofits do not. Often unknowingly, consumer
activists who "vote with their dollars" subscribe to this free-market
mysticism.

For the founders of freegan.info, their first experiences dumpster
diving exposed the disconnection between these representations and
capitalist reality. Wendy recalled the first time she found the waste
outside a supermarket and thought to herself, "What the hell is this?"
Reflecting on her early sorties into salvaging ex-commodities, she
explained:

> *I've seen first-hand that if a bunch more vegans or health-conscious*
> *people move into an area over a period of time, they [grocery stores]*
> *are not going to sell less meat, they're just going to sell more soy*
> *products. They'll add more products to their shelves, but when has*
> *a store ever sold less meat? The place doesn't not have meat soup*
> *because they have vegans; they just have both. And if a package of*
> *meat isn't sold, it's probably just going to get thrown out.*

From this, she concluded that pretty much anything—even lobbying
politicians she despised—would be more effective than buying tofu.
The discovery that over 20 percent of meat and seafood produced in
the United States goes to waste fueled Adam's outrage, as he realized
that "sentient beings lived lives of suffering and died in terror and
agony merely to be discarded as a waste product."[45]

Seeing this did something more, though. It convinced him that
the choices of an individual consumer have no power to change the
course of the capitalist behemoth. As Adam told me:

All the time, I see vegans wearing T-shirts that say, "I saved 84 animals this year." And I always think, "No, you didn't. Eighty-four more animals got thrown in a trash can because you are vegan." There's not some guy at the store saying, 'Bob went vegan this week, let's order one less chicken.' There's nothing that precise going on in terms of how stores are ordering commodities.

As Adam made clear, his rejection of veganism as a form of transformative political action was also a rejection of the dominant narrative of how capitalism works. Ex-commodities were the physical proof that the shibboleths of mainstream economics were patently false.

Searching for an Activist Fit

To some extent, though, our narrative has gotten ahead of itself. At the time that future freegans were becoming disillusioned with veganism and other forms of consumer activism, few of them had discovered the existence of ex-commodities. Nonetheless, each perceived the same basic flaws: staid and ineffective tactics, a failure to draw linkages between different issues, and an obsession *either* with personal consumption choices disconnected from broader, systemic change *or* a naive faith in voting, lobbying, or pressure on elected officials. Lola reflected on public demonstrations at her university, telling me:

People seemed obsessed with fashioning their activism in the image of the civil rights or antiwar movements of the sixties. But when you think about it, things haven't really changed. And if they have changed, they haven't progressed. So why do we keep doing the same things?

Jonathan, who had been working with groups organizing against the Iraq War—many of which were dominated by activists who had gotten their start in the movement against the Vietnam War—offered a similar assessment: "I started to feel disaffected and distant from those previous groups that I had organized with in college. It just didn't feel like we were hitting the nail on the head. I didn't feel like I was really getting to where I wanted to be."

Yet most freegans did not have a readily available alternative into which to channel their energy. Although drastically different models of political action existed in the "prefigurative" experiments and "direct actions" of anarchist movements, few freegans (aside from the "radicals") were aware of their existence. After all, aside from occasional dramatic moments like Occupy or the anti-globalization movement, anarchist movements are largely hidden away in marginal spaces like abandoned-lot gardens, short-term squats, and scattered infoshops. So how did freegan.info participants go from single-issue, consumption-oriented activism to an anticapitalist movement that *rejected* purchasing commodities?

My interviews suggest that, for most freegans, the jump came after an intense period of personal research. As one interviewee in her midfifties described:

> I've always been into figuring things out, looking underneath things, understanding things that don't make sense. And this whole thing [mainstream environmental and animal rights movements], it doesn't make sense. I don't think that thinking about these things is a waste of time. Activism in the wrong direction—that's what the people that are in control of the world want. They want you to take to the streets and scream and yell and have that be worthless.

Such inquiries led many freegans to see capitalism as the key issue their previous activism had left unaddressed and the failure to confront it their greatest flaw. Sasha explained how, when he first came to New York, he was "studying hardcore" and realized that "the stuff that I was reading was presenting itself really heavily in my daily life." His investigation, he said, "dismantled this wall that was guarding me from a life outside of capitalism, outside of the structure of daily life which seems so natural. I guess I just came to the conclusion that Adam was actually making sense and he was actually making more sense than someone I hated on TV that night." He eventually realized that, "if I really believe this stuff, this isn't just philosophy anymore, it's real life." Similarly, Jason's fundamental shift in orientation started, he said, when he began doing research into the roots of environmental destruction, which led him to the self-described "anti-civilization" author Derek Jensen. His readings made him realize, he said, that "my life was about living in this comfortable cushion of exploitation, and I'm not doing anything about it." After a pause, he said, "I just started hating everything." He felt that, at that point, he was "anti-this and anti-that" but hadn't found a way to "put it all together and think about what was a rational way to respond to this aside from being anti- a lot of things."

One study on transitions to veganism found that reading and self-directed research represented ways that future vegans "conspicuously and purposefully" learned more about a given consumptive practice, such as meat eating.[46] The problem for many freegans, however, was that personal research on one issue, such as the harmful ecological impacts of animal agriculture, invariably led to another, such as the destructive impacts of *all* industrial agriculture. In effect, what freegans faced was an out-of-control spiraling of one issue into another, in which any ethical concern eventually led back to the conclusion that only a total overhaul of society could address an individual problem. One of Adam's essays on the freegan.info website highlights the almost paralyzing effect that knowledge of the real origins and end points of commodities could have:

> For argument's sake, let's look at vegan Boca Burgers. Freegans see the card-stock wrapper and think of the serene forest erased from the future. They look at the bleached stock and think of the tons of carcinogenic organo-chlorides invading waterways. They note the inner plastic "freshness seal" and see barrels of petroleum, some as oil spills killing fish and birds, some as climate-changing carbon emissions from the fuel for shipping and factory power, some processed into plastic that will choke our rivers and seas for thousands of years after its one-time use. Freegans remember the deer shot and insects poisoned as "pests," and the worms, voles and other creatures crushed by the enormous machinery used by modern agribusiness. They remember the farm worker, underpaid and overworked, sending funds home to a country impoverished through imperialism by a government serving the interests of the wealthy corporate elite. They realize that most industrially-produced soy is genetically modified, and that the genetic code of those plants is "owned" by a corporation. Finally, Freegans realize Kraft Foods bought Boca because it saw the huge profits it could make off people who are trying to eat more healthily and responsibly.

I saw this dynamic play out not just internally but between freegans over and over again. One attendee at a freegan event would highlight a problem with one consumptive choice and propose an alternative. Someone else would interject and point to how that practice, too, would foster exploitation, waste, or environmental degradation of some kind. The conclusion was always the same: *every* choice a consumer makes within a capitalist society is morally repugnant.

Around this time, many freegans, especially those who weren't already "reducers, recyclers, and reusers," reported a growing awareness of waste. Often, this started as yet another aspect of capitalism to be concerned about. Annabelle said that she had "always been a bleeding heart liberal," but, in her midtwenties, she read Elizabeth Royte's *Garbage Land*, which follows the "secret trail of trash" through New York City.[47] Afterward, she said, "I started wondering why I couldn't compost in my backyard, and I started noticing things about how people were taking care of their municipal waste, and I found it really hard to deal with." Similarly, Anna told me that during a period of personal intellectual ferment she "got really interested in what's going on with waste." Now a teacher in her late forties, she had spent an extended period of her life working with a shoestring theater troupe in Ecuador, which often prepared props and costumes with found or recovered objects. As she observed, "I've collected stuff along the years: old clothing, old jewelry, old stuff, it's always ended up with me. I've either reused that for my plays or for my own stuff, and I kept on thinking, 'Where does all that stuff in the States go?'" That the answers to these questions were hard to come by only fueled suspicions that something deeper was afoot.

A few freegans claim to have come to their own conclusion that recovering waste was a way out of the ethical impasse. Rather than buy "eco-" or "animal-friendly" commodities, some realized that they could simply recover discarded ex-commodities and disavow responsibility for their production. Jordan, a graduate student at NYU, described an illuminating experience with waste at college move-out day:

> There was a relatively empty box set up for students to place their unwanted but still-good food and furniture in, and one hundred yards away, there was a giant dumpster overflowing with things that should have been in that box. Me and a few frustrated friends began sorting through the dumpster.... Where we had expected to find a few dollars' worth of things that had been discarded, we found hundreds of dollars of sealed, nonperishable food, cosmetics,

medical supplies, furniture, and everything else people fit into col-
lege dorms.

Even as soon-to-be freegans were peering past the fetish of the commodity, which masks the exploitation that goes into production, they
were also seeing the simultaneous production of ex-commodities,
usually hidden by the fetish of waste. Before finding freegan.info
itself, though, few viewed these practices of waste recovery as political statements in and of themselves. Instead, they served as ways to
make ends meet and live sustainably during the search for efficacious
activism.

So far, my findings confirm a well-worn sociological conclusion
that participants in radical social movements tend to have deep, preexisting involvements in other activist groups.[48] My findings, however, offer a slightly different answer to the question of *why* these
connections matter. Freegans did not adopt more radical beliefs and
more encompassing forms of action because positive, empowering
political experiences left them wanting more. Nor did connections
they created in movements for animal rights or ethical consumption carry them to freegan.info. Instead, freegans looked back on
their prior activism with frustration and disillusionment. As Jordan
articulated:

> Did any of that [my prior political experience] lead me to be an
> "activist?" What's an activist? Seems to me that many of the people
> I know who call themselves that are deeply satisfied in a way I'm
> not. Not satisfied with society per se, but satisfied with their life and
> situation because they find their work to improve it to be satisfying.

It was not through interchanges with others in the movements in
which they participated but through independent research inspired
by disappointment with those movements that most freegans came
to see capitalism as at the core of the problems they wanted to
address. At the same time, freegans were, to varying degrees, building practices of waste reduction and recovery into their lives. The discovery of freegan.info helped freegans pull these diverse threads of
their lives together into a form of political action that they saw as
efficacious and meaningful.

Taking the Freegan Plunge

At some point during their unsatisfying travails through environmental or animal rights activism, each of the individuals I interviewed encountered the term *freegan*. Many initial impressions were far from positive. Janet remembered that she first heard about freeganism from a former student, who told her that she had a freegan boyfriend who didn't work and expected her to pay his rent. As Janet perceived it, *freegan* meant "freeloader": she admitted, "It seemed sort of negative when I first heard it." Leia's first experience with a freegan was when a friend refused to chip in for the phone service in their shared apartment, citing "freegan" principles that allowed him to use a free phone but not to pay for it.

Something changed, however, when they encountered freegan .info. For over half of the freegans I interviewed, this discovery came through the Internet. Sowmya said that she learned about freegan .info while searching for activist groups on meetup.com. She went to the freegan homepage and, upon seeing the group's simultaneous denunciation of human, environmental, and animal abuse, thought to herself, "These are all the causes I am so passionate about." For her:

> Freeganism answered a lot of questions. I've been involved in a lot of social causes and something was missing in each and every movement. For example, the animal rights movement—PETA, for example—they wouldn't address environmental issues. And the environmental groups I was involved in wouldn't acknowledge animal rights. I felt like this was my chance to be involved with something that I know is going to create a change.

Consistent with other research on the growing importance of the Web in activist recruitment, the Internet furnished a way for freegan activists to become aware of the movement without following preexisting social ties or organizational links.[49] Yet freegan.info's website only piqued activists' interest because its critiques of capitalism and of most activism within capitalist society resonated with ideas they had already been slowly developing.

If the freegan website's grandiose statements about a total boycott of human, animal, and environmental exploitation were the bait, the first collective dumpster dive was the hook. Even with their pre-existing awareness of the flaws of the industrial food system, many freegans found their visceral encounter with New York's vast stream of food waste emotionally wrenching. Indeed, dumpster diving remained a morally charged activity long after the first trash tour, one that brought new people into the group as well as reaffirming the commitments of those already involved.

On one night in January 2012, the group approached a Food Emporium, which was discarding its excess New Year's Eve party supplies. The area was an absolute mess, and the bins overloaded with food. As we walked up, Janet halted and exclaimed, "Oh my god, this is going to be outrageous." And it was: we found immense amounts of meat, produce, flowers, bread, and a wide range of packaged goods. Although the plan for the trash tour was to move quickly between numerous stores, we lingered at the spot long after everyone had taken all that they could possibly carry. When I asked Madeline whether we should move on, she sighed, "It's like an elephant grave-yard. Right now, we're just here mourning the food." We had created piles of food on some barrels outside the trash bins, but ultimately we had to put it back to avoid the ire of the store's employees. As we did so, Janet woefully stated, "My heart is really breaking right now."

In my interviews, I had a chance to probe farther into what, specifically, was so affecting about the trash tour. Most respondents, after all, were already well aware of the injustices of the economic system in which they lived by the time they found freegan.info. Nevertheless, realizing that *useful* waste had been hidden from them amplified their outrage. Lucie explained why, for her, waster food was so poignant:

LUCIE: *It's direct. You value food when you see it. You know it's something that you need, or other people need. For other things, the impact is indirect, if you buy clothes that have been made in another country by children, you know it's bad but you don't realize it. I was really shocked by the quantity of food.*

AB: *But now you're used to it?*

LUCIE: *No, I'm not used to it. Every time I see it. I think when you arrive, when you really see all the wasted food, even if the rest of the time we know it exists, when you see it in the dumpster, you have a*

The reality of ex-commodification: plastic cups thrown out because they were more profitable in the trash than on the shelves, not because they were "useless." Photograph by Hannah Plowright.

> *feeling of being responsible for it. If you're in front of the dumpster, you have a choice, to leave it or to save it, to rescue it, in a way.*

It is important to qualify that the sight of waste alone rarely turns someone into a freegan. Plenty of people have had the fetish of waste dispelled at freegan events and never returned. The appeal of freegan .info to those who became more consistently involved stemmed from the way that seeing waste affirmed long-standing doubts about other forms of political action, even as recovering ex-commodities pointed to a way forward.

Those who had presented a "reducer, recycler, and reuser" narrative of their pasts emphasized how the trash tour made them realize how far they could take waste-recovery practices. In 2005 Janet received an e-mail from the Wetlands Activism Collective, which she had become involved in through animal rights activism, that discussed dumpster diving for food. She was incredulous: "Are they really able to eat that way?" When she attended her first freegan.info trash tour, though, she was "hooked from moment one." As she elaborated:

> *All my life I've been concerned about wasting. What changed and made me more extreme was the discovery that there's all this food. I think that a lot of people will stop and pick up a lamp on the curb- side, with the sign that says "Take me." But it seems like a big step to go to taking food. And I never really believed it was possible to find good things in the garbage on a regular basis.*

For Janet, dumpster diving for food was a signal to herself and those around her that she cared more about reducing waste and challeng- ing environmental degradation than complying with social norms. As she defiantly told one assembled group before a dumpster dive:

> *It is a big step to do something that is repugnant to other people. And this [dumpster diving] certainly is: to open the trash, put your hand in, pull stuff out, and later (or right then) consume it. It is horrifying and disgusting to some people and it will cause them to judge me negatively.*

Dumpster diving food was what switched her from having "freegan tendencies" to being a full-fledged "freegan."

The collective dumpster dive symbolized something different for individuals who had long since been "radicalized" and were already relying on recovering ex-commodities to survive. Lola told me that, for her, finding a group that engaged in dumpster diving en masse and with a political objective validated practices in which she'd long been engaged on her own:

> Before I heard the term [freegan], I thought it was something not acceptable to do, something I'd hide. People asked where I got something, and I'd say "Oh, I bought it." But really, I got it for free. Then I heard about freeganism and I got so excited—it all made sense, it was all the stuff I was already doing. I just learned that there are organizations and groups living this life, rather than just me. Just knowing the term freeganism has allowed me to be more open about it.

For Leia, on the other hand, seeing the ex-commodity abundance going to waste affirmed her belief that wealth could be redistributed on a massive scale. Her communist influences shining through, she told me that "freeganism is the most tangible proof I've ever seen that we have the resources to socialize the economy. There's wealth that we could be distributing to people who need it." The idea that freeganism "made sense" was a recurring one. In these cases, embracing freeganism was less about a radical change in ideology or everyday practice than it was tying preexisting beliefs and activities to a collective project that made ex-commodity waste its centerpiece.

For freegans who had been "rebelling" without a clear sense that doing so was effective, freeganism was compelling because direct waste recovery felt simultaneously tangible and transformative. Jason had heard about freeganism in college, but thought it "sounded really difficult." He tried dumpster diving once, but the haul was limited. Looking back at the first tour that he attended in 2008, Jason told me: "The first time I went dumpster diving [with freegan.info], I brought a laundry sack, and I filled it up, and I couldn't even carry it, I had to drag it on the subway. I wanted to just tell everyone, 'Someone just revealed to me the best thing in the world.'" What made dumpster diving great, he explained, was not just the free food. It was that it showed him that there really was an alternative:

> I realized that, if you go out, and you look, you can find people, you can find things, you can find networks and groups of people that will be there to help you. You can get help from fellow people. It's

not just, "Go to work, go to the bank, go to the store, and go home, and then go to the bar." Every place you go and every interaction you have doesn't have to be based on money. The world is just free. There's stuff out there for free, there are people you don't have to spend money to be with, there's fun out there that you don't have to spend money to have. It just feels really good.

What made this sense of liberation possible, in the end, was uncovering usually disguised ex-commodities: "Trash cans and alleyways, they're mysterious and off limits. But with freeganism, you're opening all these doors, and suddenly, there's all this stuff."

These divergent meanings attached to freeganism never entirely converged. Nonetheless, whether or not they would admit it, dumpster diving for food was the turning point of all my interviewees' transitions to freeganism. It reflected a critical turning point, albeit one that came after a long and gradual process with an economically and socially favored starting point. As Jordan articulated it:

Freeganism never felt like a choice for me. It was the result of many experiences, none of which seemed particularly radical at the time. I think this is how it has to be. The psychological barriers our friends, parents, and marketers erect around trash cans and the halos they put around stores are powerful; they don't dissolve overnight.

For freegans, dumpster diving represented a final rejection of the idea of purchasing "ethical" commodities as a mode of political action, an idea in which they had been losing faith for some time. And through meeting their most basic need for food without spending money, freegans thought that they had found a way to reject the diverse consequences of capitalism that concerned them seemingly at once. By doing so with a group, though, they moved beyond a concern with perfecting their own lifestyles toward a united attempt to challenge capitalism through a constructive, prefigurative experiment in building an alternative. All these realizations flowed from seeing the ex-commodities they were confronted with on the trash tour, which unraveled the fetishism of commodities that told them that consumer activism was effective and the fetishism of waste that instructed them that trash cans were "off limits."

Waving the Banana in the Big Apple

Going by appearances, Cindy seemed to exemplify freegan.info's connection to the "back-to-nature" hippie movements of the 1960s or "deep ecology" direct action movements of the late 1980s and 1990s. Her long blond hair—occasionally dyed blue or green—was generally pulled back in braids or tucked under knit caps, making her appear younger than her thirty-two years. For her, even freegan practices like dumpster diving were a way to get back to nature—in this case, *human* nature:

> *Humans are scavengers, I've always identified as that. We are the ravens and the coyotes of the urban environment, and we have a knack for scavenging, and we have a natural knack for not letting things go to waste. We want to crawl into that abandoned building and make it our little nest, and find the food that's being discarded, find that unused patch of ground and make it grow green things. Being a scavenger is to be human in a good way, as opposed to human in a bad way, as our urban society sadly so often represents.*

Humans may have their own ecological niche, but as she explained it, the key ideological impetus behind her activism was "all about not putting ourselves above other species," adding, "I'm concerned about insects, I'm concerned about plants, I'm concerned about all that."

Cindy began rebelling against environmental destruction at a young age, when developers started clearing the woods behind her house in a suburb outside Milwaukee. She commenced by writing letters to the mayor, but said she received no response. Foreshadowing her later disillusionment with institutional avenues of politics, she shifted tactics, scheming with her brother to pour sand into the gas tanks of the bulldozers. She insisted that she would have gone through with the plan had her mother not found out and put a stop to it.

During college, Cindy went to Wetlands for a social event but wound up becoming involved in the Activism Center. Like many others, she appreciated the way Wetlands linked human, animal, and environmental concerns, but her involvement came with frustrations, too:

> *You boycott this one company on one issue, and you realize you have to boycott it on two other issues as well. And you just realize, it's not boycotting one company or another. It's the system. That was my introduction to realizing that capitalism is the problem.*

When freegan.info spun off into a side project of the WAC, she was one of the first to join. A decade later, when I asked her to encapsulate her critique of capitalism, she returned to the interconnections between environmental and other issues: "Any system that puts profit ahead of anything else is going to be a problem and is inherently oppressive. Any system that's based on limitless growth is not possibly sustainable on a planet with limited resources."

Each year for the past decade, Cindy has left New York in the early spring to participate in the Buffalo Field Campaign, a project that publicly shames hunters who kill bison straying outside Yellowstone National Park. Cindy openly admits that the campaign is "single issue," focusing exclusively on one large, charismatic mammal to the exclusion of the broader social and ecological justice issues that concern her. But, as Cindy explained it, sometimes she simply needed an opportunity to be outside and connect with nature. Given her clear preference for life in Montana over New York, I asked Cindy what brings her back to the city, and she replied, "I don't want to wait around for civilization to collapse. I don't want to drop out. That's what I do in Montana for three months, but then I've got to come back." Like other freegans, Cindy struggled to balance an urban existence with a desire to withdraw from capitalism and live in harmony with the environment.

One factor that kept Cindy coming back was her belief that she had found an effective form of political action that depended on the city itself: freegan.info's bimonthly public "trash tours." By her account, baring "waste" to trash tour attendees provided a succinct and relatable introduction to the moral failings of capitalism:

> *Seeing all the waste exposes very clearly the priorities in our society, that making a profit is more important than feeding people, than preserving the environment, than making use of resources, than honoring people's time, labor, love, and effort. What we see with waste is that once something cannot make money, it is discarded and of no value. It's left to rot in a landfill and create a new ecological nightmare.*

As Cindy saw it, trash tours' capacity to attract media and outsiders, and convey to them an indictment of capitalism through ex-commodities, made them a compelling form of symbolic protest. The obvious disjuncture between a capitalist system that celebrates efficiency and threatens scarcity yet creates and then hides a superabundance of useful waste was part of why, as Cindy said, "You can't go home from a trash tour and say 'Yeah, that's okay.' You have to question." Yet ultimately, for Cindy, trash tours were not just indirect ways to raise awareness but also a form of prefigurative politics. Freegan.info, she told me, was "more successful in attracting and bringing in people than any other group of which I've been a part" because it "spoke to real needs" and addressed those needs by redistributing ex-commodities.

One night in summer 2008, shortly after she had returned from Montana, Cindy pulled Janet aside and told her, "I have to leave. The waste has just gotten to me. I can't take it." She left the tour early, looking overwhelmed by the mountains of wasted food—much of it meat and other animal products—we had found. We all knew, however, that far from dropping out and moving to the countryside, Cindy would be back.

All the Sidewalk a Stage

When speaking with the media or newcomers, participants in freegan.info invariably emphasized that there was much more to freeganism than dumpster diving. As Adam insisted to me over and over, "A freegan getting their food from the trash is like a vegan eating tofu. Lots of vegans eat tofu, but not all of them do." A glimpse at the group's monthly calendar, however, shows that the vast majority of freegan.info events were dumpster dives, and many of those that were not (like freegan feasts or catering for other activist groups) involved consuming scavenged food. Collective waste reclamation was what distinguished freegan.info at its founding, and participation in dumpster dives was the critical juncture in individuals' long transitions to becoming freegan.

Freegan.info's "trash tours" started as a way to bring together anarchists who were already dumpster diving on their own. They were as much social as political events, with little clear organization or messaging. However, the group's early trash tours attracted people who were *not* already dumpster diving on their own, *not* previously integrated into the direct action scene, and who did *not* have the same idea about what a freegan event should actually be. Influenced by newcomers like Janet and Madeline, trash tours began to develop a structure that mixed direct action to recover and redistribute wasted ex-commodities with elements of more classical symbolic protest, intended to grab the attention of the public and mass media. The result was a visible and almost theatrical form of waste recovery. It was, as far as I can tell, unique: as one pamphlet written by freegans from outside New York City noted, "Freegans, in general, tend to be far less public about what we do" than freegan.info.[1]

Freegan.info took advantage of the peculiar way ex-commodities circulate through New York to choose places and times conducive to public presentation. Accounts of freeganism outside New York describe diving in the "dead of night" from "midnight to 2:30 a.m." to avoid being caught trespassing by employees still working the store.[2] By comparison, freegan.info tours generally started between eight and ten p.m. and wrapped up before midnight. These more amenable hours made dives late enough that individuals who had jobs could attend, but not so late as to risk a confrontation with city sanitation employees or leave security-conscious attendees on the city streets past midnight.

There is trash all over New York City, so presumably freegan .info could have held most trash tours in Brooklyn or Queens, where a majority of them lived. Nonetheless, nearly all events were in affluent, busy neighborhoods in Manhattan, such as the outskirts of New

York University. Before inviting newcomers to go dumpster diving in a previously unexplored neighborhood, the group first would hold a "trash trail blaze" to determine which stores threw away the best food. By doing so, they avoided what happened on the first-ever trash tour: finding only sincerely useless garbage. When individuals unfamiliar with freeganism join the group, then, freegan.info can be almost sure that the tour will be able to show them a great deal of ex-commodities, including food, clothing, toiletries, or other house-hold items, in a short period of time. Over half the events I attended in my years with the group followed a carefully rehearsed route along Third Avenue in Murray Hill, Manhattan, that in the space of a few blocks brought attendees to two D'Agostinos, a Gristedes legendary for throwing out packaged food, and a Dunkin' Donuts.

My own informal conversations suggested that many people who came to trash tours saw themselves as "ethical consumers," engaged in precisely the kind of neoliberal activism freegans themselves spurned. The itinerary of trash tours almost guaranteed that these commodity-conscious consumers would receive a jolt. Many of the group's routes stopped at Whole Foods or Trader Joe's. These grocery chains sell organic, vegan, and fair-trade items in abundance in front but expel enormous quantities of ex-commodities out back. Indeed, many freegans speculated that these stores were actually more waste-ful than their mainstream counterparts, because, in their attempts to appeal to high-end shoppers, they offered a wider range of exotic products and held their goods to more stringent standards.[3]

Dives themselves were anything but free-for-alls. Before group leaders released trash tour attendees to begin searching the garbage outside a given store, a representative of freegan.info welcomed the group and enumerated a series of unwritten "rules" of dumpster div-ing. The first instructed that individuals deemed to be diving out of necessity took precedence. If the trash tour encountered other dump-ster divers, they were allowed to finish first. The second rule was that group activities like communal freegan feasts took priority, and indi-viduals could claim goods only afterward. As Cindy admonished one assembly of around twenty newcomers, "Remember, this is trash. It doesn't belong to you, it doesn't belong to me, it doesn't belong to anyone. So we really should share." A final rule declared that trash bags should be opened from the top, rather than ripped apart, and that areas in front of stores should never be left a mess. Once again, this rule had emerged from careful calculation: as Janet explained, "In the long term, they [store owners] may be our enemies, but in the short term, we are considerate, because they can make this much harder for us." Madeline then jumped in to say, "Generally, we leave the area super, super neat—just with the bags a little bit lighter."

Anarchists or not, freegans took these rules seriously and consistently reminded trash tour attendees to abide by them. Several times, I watched freegan.info participants spend up to a half hour cleaning up the mess left on the sidewalk by previous divers. During one dive outside the NYU dorms on move-out weekend—one of the rare times we were actually in a dumpster—a man came out of the building pushing a trolley overflowing with abandoned desk lamps, office supplies, and snack food. He started shaking his head as he approached, and when he was within earshot, said in a thick New York accent: "When the truck comes in five minutes, you guys gotta be outta there—and all of that," he said, waving at the pile of goods we had created on the sidewalk, "needs to be gone."

Janet replied, "We know, that's why we always clean up when we're done."

He responded, "And another thing—if one of you gets hurt in there, who do you think is going to have to pay for it?"

Once again, Janet's response was calm: "Yes, and we're always very careful."

He returned a few minutes later with another cart of trash and walked up to Janet, who was now standing on the sidewalk, and said, "You know, I'm being a nice guy here. I could just call the cops on all of you."

Janet nodded understandingly: "We know, and we appreciate that."

He went on. "I don't want to have to pay some ticket because you all made a total mess. I've been spending all morning putting this stuff in there," he said, making a motion as if he were throwing something into the dumpster, "and I don't want to do it again."

Janet announced shortly thereafter that she had to leave early, but stated, "Alex is going to be in charge, and he's going to make sure that everything gets put up back in there, because they can ruin this for us if they want to."

These rules had an apparent strategic logic. The freegan insistence on sharing, for example, was not only a prefigurative projection of their ideological commitment to nonmarket systems of distribution. It also ensured that newcomers who were tentative about actually reaching into a bag of garbage would be able to take food items home with them and, in turn, share those items and their experiences on the dive with others. By being respectful and clean, freegans tried to ensure that they could return to the same places over and over and be confident of finding food. It was also clever from the viewpoint of presentation, because it allowed freegan.info to center its opposition on impersonal corporations, not more sympathetic small business owners or employees.

When I asked Madeline why the group was so adamant about its rules, she pointed out, "Well, we actually care about public relations," adding, with a sigh, "unlike a lot of anarchists." Indeed, freegans themselves saw their trash tours as structured, almost scripted, performances. Janet was freegan.info's most reliable trash tour leader: in over fifty tours I went on with the group, she attended every single one. Standing in an atrium at the entrance to Columbia University before one tour, she explained the event in pedagogical terms to the assembled group of around thirty-five people:

> When I do this [dumpstering] on my own, no one stops or says anything.... I just felt like, well, there's still more, because my own personal actions were good, but they weren't affecting enough people. But when I joined the freegan group, I realized, well, here we're able to do something that's educational. It does sometimes feel like acting. I know that when I'm doing this alone, it has a different feeling. When we do this together, it feels like a party.

In this theatrical spirit, Christian even occasionally came to dumpster dives in costume, wearing recovered employee uniforms for the stores where the group was dumpster diving or an orange construction vest. In his view:

> We're trying to make freeganism sexy and more appealing ... make people look good. We're dumpster diving, we're dirty, we have clothes that are hand-me-down or trash clothes. But if we put a little more effort into it, care about how we look, we can make it a lot more appealing.

The notion that a social movement would try to make their events "appealing" and "educational" may seem obvious. Nonetheless, as scholars of anarchist movements note, many contemporary anti-capitalists put little stock in appearances, assuming that their movements will spread like a "contagion" without overt recruitment.[4] Freegan.info's approach reflected the cross-fertilization of its anarchist founders with more image-conscious newcomers.

Guerrilla Redistribution and a Bonanza of Bagels

While individuals dumpster diving for food is a common sight in New York City, twenty people doing so simultaneously is not. As such, it was difficult for pedestrians not to take notice of a freegan.info trash tour. Anyone who stopped was likely to be confronted by Adam, who typically came to tours laden with freegan pamphlets (printed on the blank side of paper rescued from recycling bins, of course) and clipboards of sign-up sheets for the group's e-mail lists. One night, when Adam paused his evangelizing to grab some food, he shoved a wad of flyers into my hands and instructed me, "The masses are walking by—educate them."

Part of what made a trash tour different from a more ordinary street protest, though, was that freegans approached bystanders not just with movement literature but also ex-commodities themselves. During one event that Janet dubbed the "freegavaganza," the group split into teams of two, fanned out through the city to dive, and, at a predetermined time, returned to Union Square. As freegans slowly trickled back in, they built a mound of recovered goods: some people found produce and bread, while others brought shoes, makeup, a box of unopened condoms, and a functioning vacuum cleaner. The group then began pushing the items on nearby pedestrians, turning a culture of acquisitiveness on its head by using the allure of free stuff to convince people to stop and talk. Anyone who paused to examine an item subsequently learned that it came from the trash. Passersby were, in effect, forced to confront the fetishism of waste head-on: individuals could either take an item for free, and thus acknowledge that not all waste is polluted and useless, or leave it, and thus ignore the use value that they could hold in their hands and see with their own eyes. Either way, the freegavaganza was both *directly* and *materially* challenging capitalism, by redistributing free goods and reducing people's need for the market, and *symbolically* critiquing it by undermining the fetishism that keeps people buying new things despite the ex-commodified wealth around them.

Usually, freegans' redistributive efforts are more opportunistic and ad hoc. One night, Christian grabbed a loaf of bread and some avocados, planted himself on the sidewalk, and started handing sandwiches to unsuspecting pedestrians. Most were caught too off-guard to do anything but take them. On another night, the group found an extraordinary number of boxes of unexpired Mallomars—disgustingly saccharine marshmallow cookies. Janet started calling out, "Wait, wait, these are for you" and shoving boxes of sweets into pedestrians' hands when they halted in confusion. (Adam was skeptical of this strategy, owing to the cookies' questionable nutritional content. When I pointed out that people seemed quite happy to be getting free junk food, he noted, "We could give out crack vials, too, and that'd make people very happy.")

One particularly memorable evening—January 18, 2008—the group was diving outside Balducci's, a chain so infamous for its high-quality garbage that freegans had dubbed it the "food museum." Suddenly, Cindy cried out "Holy shit," and the attendees rapidly encircled her to view two overflowing bags brimming with packets of organic, fair-trade coffee. At $12.99 a bag, there was nearly $1,000 worth of coffee in front of us—far more than the eight people on this trash trail blaze could hope to consume. "Just take as much as you can carry," Cindy exhorted us. "Give it away. Coffee is something that people buy and it's a horrible, destructive crop."[5] Janet turned to a pair of skeptical-looking newcomers and said, "Go on the subway and tell people 'This store had so much they were throwing it out.' Don't say, 'I got it out of the garbage.' Tell them, 'It's past date, are you afraid?' But no one is afraid of past-date coffee." She then trundled toward the nearest subway station laden with bags of dark roast.

Of course, hundreds of dollars' worth of coffee or fifty boxes of Mallomars were not the usual takes from freegan.info trash tours. Instead, what the group found most consistently was fruit, vegetables, and baked goods.[6] The quantities of this last category were so reliably enormous that there was even an anarchist ditty that celebrated subsisting off them:

They have wasted untold millions and they waste more every day

While the workers keep producing, they keep throwing it away

But the freegans are uniting and we vow to never pay

For the donuts make us strong.

Freegans themselves caution against the long-term health effects of the all-pastry diet. Still, there's no questioning the items' allure. Most bakeries throw out their entire stock at the end of the day, and typically place all their food items together in a single bag. Even reluctant trash tour attendees rarely could resist reaching into a clean trash bag to grab a muffin, bagel, or doughnut—often still warm. I've never been on a trash tour where we couldn't find bagels.

I suggested previously that the combination of overproduction and commodification makes ex-commodification inevitable. But I didn't talk about *where* or *how* it happens. Once again, there is something self-evidently paradoxical about waste on such a fantastic scale. Food retailing is an incredibly competitive business: with more and more stores like Walmart entering the industry, and more people eating out, sales at traditional grocery stores have actually declined in the past decade.[7] This would seem to militate against wasting inventory. Baked goods are a particularly confusing kind of ex-commodity, because there are no long supply chains or complicated logistics involved in getting them to the shelves. Most stores produce their baked goods on-site or nearby, so why not simply produce a little less and not throw out dozens of loaves of bread and racks of cupcakes every night?

Why, to put it another way, does capitalism make so much cake? The freegans developed their own explanation for the inevitable baked-good bonanza. As one e-mail bouncing across the freegan.info Listserv hypothesized:

> *Pizzerias, bakeries, bagel and doughnut shops charge so much more for goods than their cost to make them, so they'd rather have too much food and discard a great deal of it than risk losing sales. While the food is still perfectly edible at the end of the day, they prefer to discard it, write it off on their taxes as spoilage, and make everything again the next day, so they can brag to consumers that they are getting their bread or pizza or doughnuts fresh from the oven.*

The infamous bread bag: "In New York, I can decide what flavor of muffin I want and find it in the trash in five minutes." Photograph by Hannah Plowright.

Consistent with this claim, one bakery chain, Au Bon Pain, actually expects its stores to have $80 worth of inventory at closing time to ensure that their shelves never go bare.[8] As this policy suggests, stores are fearful that any customer leaving unsatisfied will go to their competitors. They hedge against this possibility by keeping their shelves full up until the last minute.

This never-miss-a-sale creed extends beyond just baked goods. Stores try to increase their share of the finite amount that gets spent on food by promising freshness and offering a huge array of choices. In an era where agricultural subsidies and technological advances have made the raw materials of our food system (i.e., the food itself) unprecedentedly cheap, stores can deliberately overstock and make up for ex-commodification with the high-priced commodities they sell. One night, Janet contemplated a box of Nilla Wafers within its sell-by date before announcing to the crowd: "They're overordering so that they can have abundance in their stores so that shoppers will never say, 'Oh, they don't have Cheerios today.' They'll always have Cheerios because they have too much. And they're throwing it away." In interviews, many managers actually admit to excess stocking for precisely this reason.[9]

According to freegans' sidewalk theorizing, though, grocery stores create so many ex-commodities partly because they're selling more than just food. As Janet elaborated:

> It's not just a problem that, "Oops, we have a little extra." That wouldn't be the reason that you're seeing something like this [refer-ring to the box]. It's a deliberate effort to overstock their shelves so there can always be—especially in the beautiful, giant chains—a sense of abundance. The shopper has this feeling of well-being walk-ing through the aisles and seeing abundance wherever they go. And so they want to buy more.

This image, Janet postulated, depended on stores' projecting lim-itless choice, quality, and supply. All these rested, invisibly, on ex-commodification. None other than the president of Trader Joe's affirmed this interpretation when he explained to the *Harvard Business Review*, "The reality ... is, if you see a store that has really low waste ... you are worried. If a store has low waste numbers it can be a sign that they aren't fully in stock and that customer experience is suffering."[10] The lunatic yet inexorable deduction from this statement is that even in a world of perfectly efficient markets and omniscient store man-agers, stores would still prefer not to sell everything on hand, since unsightly empty shelves could disrupt the "customer experience."

The frenetic scramble for increased market share creates ex-commodity waste in other ways as well. Freegans often oscillate between laughter and sadness when they encounter absurd new flavors of Oreos—jettisoned months before their sell-by date and still packaged—in the garbage, mingling with bizarre flavors of coffee creamer and yogurt pots in strange new shapes. Although it's hard to "invent" truly new food, grocery stores and distributors nonetheless introduce nearly nineteen thousand new products a year, a rate far higher than that for nonfood goods.[11] But by the U.S. Department of Agriculture's classification, 95 percent of these products are "not innovative" and "offer a fresh image rather than truly novel benefits." Not coincidentally, 90 percent of them "fail" to sell well enough to be profitable. As freegans discover, this often means that they wind up in the trash.

To be fair, sometimes the ex-commodities that freegans find on a trash tour appear to have made their way to the garbage out of sheer negligence or by accident. Boxes containing eleven sticky bottles of olive oil are an infrequent but celebrated discovery. Gio proffered his explanation for this specific yet recurring find: "A store orders a box of twelve bottles of X. One is broken. The store is paying for twelve, they're not going to take eleven, so it just gets thrown out. We see that with eggs all the time: one is broken, and they throw out the dozen." As Janet pointed out before handing off her box of Nilla Wafers, though, most of the waste freegans encounter seems too systematic and too reliable to be a mishap: "It's not just this store. It's not just this chain. It's not just this neighborhood. It's not just this night. It could be on any night if you check it out on your own and see for yourself."[12]

Stores, of course, invariably reply that they offer unlimited abundance and choice and fresh-baked goods and a "fresh image" for their products because that's what consumers want. The failure of so many "innovations," however, suggests, as two researchers conclude, that "the food industry is not responding to consumer demand, but rather blindly offering consumers sets of repackaged, reformulated, and reengineered products in hopes that a few of these products will turn out to boost corporate profits."[13] Even if we do believe that stores are meeting demand, there's no question of who pays for a business model that takes cheap ingredients and transmutes them into high-priced commodities: consumers. A source no less radical than the U.S. Comptroller General determined that "consumers ultimately bear the cost of losses in the form of higher prices."[14] The freegan.info website presents a more thorough analysis:

> *Consumers subsidize this waste not only through the stores' escaping their tax burden using waste as a write-off, but also by high retail prices. As waste is factored as a cost of doing business, the expense is being passed on to the consumer in the retail price of everything we buy. The fact that stores consider such massive waste economically justifiable ... is suggestive of the massive gap between actual cost of the goods we buy and the profit margin added to their retail prices.*[15]

Most people don't realize that the commodities they see on supermarket shelves or in the bakery display case are mirrored by nearly identical ex-commodities outside in garbage bags. Yet, as freegan trash tours expose, the two are inextricably linked. The constant introduction of new products, overproduction to never miss a sale, and insistence on projecting an illusion of abundance are ways that stores add exchange value to inexpensive foodstuffs.[16] And, in so doing, they destroy use value through ex-commodification.

Putting Trash on Camera

Passersby are not the only witnesses to freegan.info trash tours: reporters were also a nearly ubiquitous presence. At least since the 1960s, the mass media have played a fundamental role in certifying social movements as legitimate (or illegitimate) political actors, conveying (or silencing) movement claims, and helping (or hindering) the search for new activists or resources.[17] Many radicals are unhappy about the power the media have acquired over them: David Graeber, for example, reports that anarchists "tend to abhor the corporate media" and rarely attempt to frame their events to garner television or print coverage.[18] One reporter found that many dumpster divers refused to speak to her because of her corporate affiliations.[19]

At the same time, some of these same anarchist groups have sought to "be the media" themselves, turning movement messaging via the Internet, social media, or pirated radio stations into the embryo of a postcapitalist news system.[20] At least in principle, freegan.info celebrates do-it-yourself, not-for-profit media outlets like Indymedia, which grew out of the antiglobalization protests of the 1990s and early 2000s. Yet there's no denying that freegan.info's most significant exposure to the general public has come through mainstream outlets. As Janet told one group of trash tour attendees during her welcome speech in 2007:

> *Apparently we're fascinating to the media, probably you've seen us on something. We've been on radio, television, newspapers, magazines and next up, Oprah. We've been amazingly popular. We don't solicit. They just come and they keep checking us out and following us.*

At every single event I observed that the group had dubbed "open to media," journalists of one kind or another—from college students writing final papers to professional filmmakers—were present. The freegans' own media database listed several hundred stories published in dozens of countries, giving some truth to the freegan joke that they had been covered by "just about every country rich enough to send a film crew."

The mainstream media were present at freegan.info's inception, and the development and expansion of the group has been indelibly linked to this ongoing coverage. Wendy recalled a PBS crew asking Wetlands activists where they did their dumpster diving. At the time, "taking cameras with us was a big deal, because before that, dumpster diving had been a big secret." She said that the media attention exploded in 2004, when a student who had attended one of the first trash tours sold his story to *Newsday*. As Adam observed, "It was obvious from the beginning that the media was going to be all over us." He was right. By 2006 the group was fielding more than a dozen media requests a week, and the freegans implemented strict rules about where and when the media could film or interview them.[21]

Adam was always derisory of the coverage, sure that the reporters were interested only in portraying freegans as "weirdoes with garbage." No doubt the breaking of a social taboo around contact with waste was a bigger draw for the media than freegans' anticapitalist message. Notwithstanding much of the coverage's weak content, though, freegan.info's capacity to effortlessly garner media attention proved irresistible. As Cindy explained:

> *In the days of direct action campaigning [with Wetlands], we were locking ourselves to doors and dropping banners off of skyscrapers to get the* Daily News *to cover a story about the environment. And*

Jason talks to a puppet, the host of a Japanese TV show, not aware if or how the freegan "message" will be translated and transmitted. Photograph by the author.

> *here, all of [a] sudden, a national news outlet came to us [freegan .info], and said, "Hey we're interested in what you're doing!" and that was a shock to us.*

Ultimately, even Adam could not say no, admitting, "I'm not as worried about them portraying us as crazy as I am worried about them just ignoring us."

In my time with the group, freegan.info never actively solicited the media by sending out a press release for an event. Still, freegans often went out of their way to accommodate journalists. A Japanese media crew asked for a group representative to be interviewed by a puppet, a request that seemed bizarre but to which Jason reluctantly agreed. For her part, Janet once took a media crew behind a Laundromat in the dead of winter, combining barely liquid detergent from discarded bottles while shivering uncontrollably. She did it, she said, because she wanted the media to see that freegans could get more than food from the trash.

As Janet's story suggests, freegan.info participants aggressively worked to shape media representations of their movement. Before events, the group designated one person the "media wrangler," whose main job was to prevent the media from interviewing anyone who hadn't been schooled in the group's main talking points. Quinn recalled:

> *They [freegan.info] had a line. They had scripted interactions, and they had media trainings for members. At other places, I've seen an aversion to working with the media. But they took that head-on. There was also a centrality to it. It's an anarchist idea that everyone gets to say what they want, but freegan.info had a united front to the media, which I liked, even if we were taught to personalize it.*

At one media training, Adam proposed preapproving media questions, providing appealing stock footage rather than allowing outlets to shoot their own images, asking to see quotes before they were printed, and turning down media requests from organizations that were likely to provide unfavorable coverage. He added that the group needed to think about framing: replacing the word "disposable," which implied "convenience," with "shoddily made." The discussion of presentation then transitioned to a discussion of positive versus negative language, particularly with respect to "alternatives to capitalism" versus "anticapitalist." As Janet argued, "There are a million different ways to talk about all the issues related to capitalism without ever coming out as explicitly against capitalism, which causes people to just seize up."

Another way that freegan.info controlled media images was through its vigorously enforced rule against eating in front of cameras during trash tours. When outside observers were not present, freegan.info participants ate straight from the trash with relish, often holding long conversations about group strategy while clustered around a grocery-store compost bin. One night, when the sole cameraman present wandered off with Adam, Janet found a watermelon and sliced it, creating an impromptu feast for people already chowing on melted soy ice cream Evie had discovered. When the cameraman started walking back toward us, Janet chided me to stash the ice cream and wipe the residue from my face. If that cameraman or any other media outlet wanted to see freegans eating discarded food—and they probably did—they had to come to a freegan feast, where the food had been carefully cleaned and prepared. Thus the media and its viewers had to confront what freegans saw as the truth about ex-commodities: that, aside from having once been bagged up and put on the curb, they were virtually indistinguishable from commodities purchased at a store.

It is difficult to evaluate what impact this surprising surfeit of media coverage had on public perceptions of freeganism or in diffusing its critique of capitalism. There were moments, however, when both the impacts and challenges of an anticapitalist group engaging with capitalist media became accentuated. In 2008 Oprah Winfrey invited one member of the group to be interviewed for a special talk show on the topic of "how far would you go to live your beliefs?" The organization went through a lengthy and acrimonious debate about whether it was ecologically unprincipled to fly someone to Chicago for an appearance on a television show punctuated with corporate advertisements and product placements. Ultimately, the group opted to send Madeline, because of her work experience in communications. While walking to one trash tour before her appearance, she defended the decision, noting, "It's hard to argue with that level of exposure. And I've been inspired at times by things I saw in the mainstream media. You just have to leave out the language of lefty magazines, like 'anarchism' or 'commodification.'"

While Oprah herself did not attend a freegan.info dive, she sent a proxy. During the trash tour they filmed, Madeline explained, "It's not toxic waste," after which the reporter observed, "The food is still in its original packaging and has been discarded largely for cosmetic reasons, not because of poor quality." The reporter's conclusion was surprisingly incisive:

> *Freegans believe that, in a way, we are slaves to buying. When you think about it, we work so hard, but for what? To buy more. Whether it's a house payment or a car or food, we just want to continue to consume. Freegans have decided to kind of try and turn their back on it completely and stop buying stuff.*

Certainly, "anticapitalism" was slighted in Oprah's coverage, which presented waste as a result of individual actions and a problem that could be solved with personal choices. Nonetheless, by talking about the pointlessness of consumption and how increased economic activity results in little more than waste, it at least nodded to core freegan messages. As far as the group was concerned, to expose the abundance of ex-commodities and challenge the ceaseless drive to consume more was to chip away at the material and cultural foundations of capitalism, even if doing so was far from Oprah's intention.

In terms of tour attendance, the effect was undeniable. Before showing the clip of the "trash tour"—with Madeline sitting by her side, wearing a prim purple suit jacket and pearls—Oprah quipped, "If you're watching, I know you're not going to go on a trash tour after this show."

"You might, you'll be shocked when you see this," the reporter replied.

On this count, Oprah was wrong. Shortly after the story, a stream of middle-aged women with limited prior histories of political engagement started coming to freegan.info events. The story's impact may not have been measurable only in New York: one avid dumpster diver I interviewed in Phoenix told me, "I never would have thought about it [dumpster diving], but I saw the show and thought, 'If Oprah says it's okay, it must be okay.'"

If the story's consequences for awareness were clear, its consequences for fighting capitalism were more disputable. One night in 2008, the group was joined by an older Dutch woman who told me she had seen the freegans on Oprah and had "come all the way from Holland to see us" so she could "get this started in my own country."

I pushed the woman for more detail: "You came all the way here to see freegan.info?"

"Well, and to go shopping on Saks Fifth Avenue," she added.

At the end of the tour, she came up to me and said, "I'm so moved." After a few seconds, she added, "but are freegans still allowed to buy nice things?" The spectacle of dumpster diving and the ideology behind it, clearly, were easily disassociated.

The anticapitalist implications of freeganism were not lost on everyone, though. Another night, I spoke with a middle-aged woman wearing a stained Disney sweatshirt. She said that she had come to New York from South Carolina to visit a sick friend but had remembered the freegans from Oprah and wanted to check freegan .info out. She opened bags with relish and gushed with enthusiasm about the quantities and quality of food. Her gusto for acquiring ex-commodities made me think that her impetus for coming was free stuff. Nonetheless, after the "waving the banana" speech, I overheard her talking to a pedestrian, who had asked her what was going on. "All this waste is due to capitalism," she stated in a matter-of-fact tone.

Engaging with the media is far from the kind of "direct action" or "prefigurative politics" that was originally at the core of freegan.info's politics. It was, however, effective in exposing America's largely hidden waste stream to a wide audience, even if those stories rarely connected the waste back to capitalism. It brought people to the group who might otherwise never have had the networks and contacts that direct action groups often rely on for recruitment. I consider the media coverage's downsides more fully in the final chapter.

Anticapitalism 101

Although the emphasis freegan.info put on "messaging" contrasted with the anarchist norm, the question of whether trash tours should be "educational" was a source of disagreement from the start. Jason explained his own perspective on the topic:

> I don't think it's good for people to hear about dumpster diving without really learning some of the facts about environmental destruction or taking a serious look at sustainability and climate change. I think if you don't, then your efforts aren't really coming from the right place. You're probably not going to be that into it, and later something else will distract you.

Eventually, the group concluded that attendees *did* need to leave with some clear take-away "messages" about freeganism, capitalism, and waste and took the decision to institute "freeganism 101s" prior to trash tours.

The most common questions people asked were revealing. At one event in the indoor seating area of a Whole Foods Market, Madeline opened by stating, "We're here tonight to take a long, hard look at capitalism." Yet the attendees, by and large, were interested in more mundane issues. In fact, at nearly every 101 event I attended, the same three questions arose: "Is there really so much waste?" "Why don't stores donate the food?" "Does anyone ever get sick?" Each question in its own way revealed the powerful hold of the fetishism of waste: the impression that waste is minimal, inevitable, and valueless. In my experience, most people came to trash tours hoping to find good food but still assuming that any food that was still good would be donated and that any food thrown out was in reasonably bad shape.

After a few minutes on the streets, though, these preconceptions were inevitably thrown into doubt. Attendees faced mounds of food indistinguishable from the food on sale a few feet away behind store windows. As one African American teenager commented, "I thought there was nothing in those bags—but Madeline, she schooled me!" Even outside stores that publicly announced that they gave their surplus to charity, waste was abundant. Two hip-looking twenty-somethings wearing tight pants and denim jackets paused next to one trash tour and queried, "Wait, don't stores donate that stuff?" As freegans were quick to point out, stores often defended the decision not to donate by citing liability concerns, even though the Bill Emerson Good Samaritan Act shields them from lawsuits, and no store has ever been sued for giving away its surplus.[22] Such questions offered a quick introduction to a sad reality: stores in a capitalist economy exist to make money, not feed people.

The inescapable observations that there is a lot of waste, that most of it isn't bad, and that very little makes it to the hungry are all basic. Freegans attempted to connect these truths back to capitalism during their "waving the banana" speech, which they delivered near the end of every tour on which there were newcomers. The speech gave freegans an opportunity to talk about freegan practices other than dumpster diving and to invite attendees to subsequent meetings, working groups, and events. More importantly, though, the speech was a platform for elaborating freegans' anticapitalist critique. One night, speaking to a group of twenty-five people, with two camera crews straining to film her at a good angle, Leia announced:

> Here we're seeing all of this waste that is produced by the capitalist system, which is a system that exploits the earth, exploits workers, exploits resources, and all these products get onto the shelf.... It's really sad to see all the stuff going into the trash, thinking about all the workers that are underpaid to make all of this stuff. People don't consider the value behind the labor that goes into producing these things. People don't think of the value in terms of the actual taxation it causes on the earth.

Her opening remarks pointed to the first, classic fetish of the commodity: that the goods we buy are the product of social and ecological exploitation. She quickly moved, however, to the fetish of waste, meditating on the presumption that objects labeled "waste" lack value:

> It's really interesting if you look at the way we relate to the products we get from stores. Even though we just got it out of the trash, it's very useful stuff, it's yummy, it's nutritious, but in this system that we live in, all of this stuff is considered to have no value as soon as it's put in the trash. When you go into the store and you buy it, it's like, we're trained to think that in that moment value is placed in it...and obviously that's not true. It's a really fine line: it's valuable when it's put into a white plastic bag, and not valuable when it's put into a black, big ugly bag on the side of the street.

She transitioned to the prefigurative aspect of dumpster diving, asserting that recovering ex-commodities allowed freegans to live in ethical plenty even while not partaking of capitalist consumerism:

> We're actually living amongst massive amounts of wealth, and until we actually reclaim it and share it with everybody around us, everything is going into the trash. Meanwhile, we have an opportunity to live in abundance. It's all actually there, we're just trained to think that it's only valuable if it came from a store.

Leia closed by evoking a moralistic and quasi-religious condemnation of waste, presenting freeganism as the true way to live up to widely shared values:

> So I say we all take all the stuff that we find and give it out to people, share it, and put the value back into it. It's really there. And also it's paying homage to all those people that work to make all the food, and pay homage to the lives that go into this. To me it's sort of like saying "grace," in a way. It's a spiritual thing for me.

By the time she finished talking, the crowd around her had nearly doubled.

The rhetoric of the "waving the banana" speech was that much more compelling because freegans used ex-commodities as props to drive their points home. Before the speech began, the speaker instructed those who were diving to pile up the goods they found. As Adam jokingly described it, this was done for "propaganda purposes": particularly tasty, rare, or expensive items somehow always found their way to the front of the display, and freegans left the display up for as long as the media were still taking pictures. Adam was particularly adept at taking the ex-commodities we found and connecting them to current events. "If you're wondering why 100,000 people in Southeast Asia died in a tsunami [in 2004]," he stated, holding up a package of shrimp, "it's because mangrove forests are being cut down to create shrimp farms." He gave another speech in 2007, as debates about immigration reform raged in Washington, D.C. He lifted a shrink-wrapped piece of Styrofoam containing two corncobs and said, "If what worries you are 'illegal immigrants,' you might ask why we're subsidizing corn and sending it to Mexico."

Through its engagement with the media, public and performative direct action, and careful use of props, freegan.info billed itself as "the friendly face of anticapitalism" in New York City. As should be clear, this image was something that the group cultivated over time. When the group started, the "waving the banana" speech involved a lot more "waving"; by 2008 it was more of a "holding the banana" speech. Even the most ideologically extreme participants in the group usually tried to make freeganism seem eminently reasonable during a speech. Jason motioned to the display one night and announced:

> We always just stockpile all the food we find and we just look at it. This big cornucopia could sustain all of us for quite a while.... The reason [this food] get[s] to the supermarket is, let's be honest, not to feed any of us. That's not the purpose, otherwise it wouldn't be in the garbage. The purpose of this was to get us to put it into a cart and go up to the register and get us to exchange money so the people that own this grocery store can get a little bit richer.

He then turned to the commonsense notion that quality food should not be wasted:

> Conservative estimates put one-third of our food in this country going to waste, and that is completely insane considering that one in seven children in this city—not just all over other parts of the

Janet gives the "waving the banana" speech at a freegavaganza, showing (not merely claiming) that "capitalism" wastes good food, appliances, and clothes. Photograph by the author.

world, but in this city—goes to bed hungry. What sense does it make that we're finding all this food in the trash? Does that make sense? No, it doesn't.

Jason was right. For most people, the presence of edible, clean food in the trash—rather than a donation bin—*doesn't* make sense.

I don't want to overstate the appeal of freegan.info's events. Despite the hundreds of media stories focused on it, the group never had more than fifteen active members at a time. Some freegans were remarkably cynical about the group's allure: as Wendy told me, "Well, the fact that there are things that you need, and there are things that people are throwing away is alluring. Then there's the taboo, breaking the taboo, people are allured by that kind of thing." Another was even more nonplussed: "I think half of them [newcomers] come because they like to get high and watch people pick stuff out of trash."

Nonetheless, some longtime participants, like Cindy, stayed involved because they were convinced that trash tours had an impact:

> I think that in making changes, for individuals in their everyday lives, freegan.info has been very effective. I hear people talk about how coming to our events really did change how they viewed the world and how they lived their life in a very extreme way.... I really haven't felt that in other types of activism, and I've been involved in a lot of campaigns.

Given the barriers to anticapitalist organizing in a neoliberal era, freegan.info's ability to bring an anticapitalist message to new audiences was, at least, notable—even if, as I show in later chapters, they struggled to turn this attention into sustained social change.

Thrift, Profligacy, and the Spirit of Capitalism

When I asked group members why freegan trash tours seemed to grab attention and, occasionally, spark personal transformations, they almost always brought it back to "waste." Cindy explained that, in her eyes, "Everyone has to acknowledge the problem of waste. Anyone who can make a rational decision is going to realize that this [waste] is a problem." Similarly, Janet told me that freeganism "makes sense . . . because waste is offensive to almost everyone." But this only begs the question of what makes "waste" a compelling topic.

Adam begrudgingly postulated to me that freeganism was more appealing than the other causes he had been involved in because waste reduction was an opportunity to invoke "old people and traditional values." One group member offered a more sanguine appraisal: "We're promoting old-fashioned values of frugality, generosity, wise conservation of resources, community-centered life, and civic responsibility." What both of them hinted at is that the *idea* of waste has been just as closely bound up with the evolution of American capitalism as the *material* stuff of waste itself.[23]

On its own, capitalism's central imperative of "production for production's sake, accumulation for accumulation's sake" is,[24] to quote the sociologist Max Weber, "absolutely irrational."[25] Most people throughout human history have viewed economic production as a means to leisure, status, or sociability, not as an end in itself.[26] Precisely because capitalism's root impetus is so unappealing, capitalism must provide *other* forms of moral justifications that convince people to contribute to a system that may not serve their best interest or collective values.[27] These moral motivations constitute what Weber famously christened the "spirit of capitalism."[28]

This spirit was, and is, in varying ways intertwined with fetishistic ideas about commodities and waste. As Weber explained, for the Puritan colonists, thrift, judicious stewardship of resources, and diligent labor were ways to demonstrate that one was part of God's elect and chosen to go to heaven. With luxury consumption also damned as "waste," the Puritans had no outlet for the fruits of their labors other than to reinvest them in further production. Even as the intensity of their religious fervor wore off, though, they maintained the capitalist mind-set of economic growth as an end in itself.[29] At least during these early days of capitalist production, though, the way that capitalists talked about and represented waste was in line with their practices toward it. Put another way, early American capitalists condemned waste rhetorically and then acted to eliminate it. Entire industries in colonial America were built around reusing scrap metals, rags, or bones.[30] In effect, by transforming waste into commodities, middle-class Puritans could metamorphose themselves from sinners into saints.

Waste and related concepts of efficiency and thrift have remained central to discussions about the ethics of economic life into the twentieth century. Upper-class reformers, for example, often scolded the poor for "wasteful" habits like gambling or drinking and extolled their own "thrifty" practices of saving and reuse.[31] Similarly, in World War I, government agencies admonished people to "use it up, wear it out, make it do, or do without,"[32] and housewives were told to save fatty acids for soap, fruit pits and nut shells for gas masks, and other organic waste for pig feed and fertilizer. On the home front during the next world war, citizens who had just lived through the deprivations of the Great Depression eagerly participated in collections of scrap metal to make munitions. A "Consumer's Pledge Song" harked back to Puritanism, warning, "Do not be extravagant and waste / For wasting is a sin."[33]

Evidently, though, the song's lyrics did not echo for long. Through American history, moral injunctions to thrift and nonwasting have served any number of ends, including achieving spiritual salvation or victory over Germany or Japan. One of them, however, was to further capitalist expansion. In the eighteenth and nineteenth centuries, an era where industry did not necessarily produce enough to meet all of society's need for commodities, eliminating wasted material and reusing scraps in production was crucial for driving the capitalist machine forward.[34]

Over time, though, the key challenge for continued growth has shifted in exactly the way Marx predicted. By the 1950s, economists began to realize that the key threat to capitalism was no longer *not enough* but instead *too much*. And just as a nonwasting spirit of capitalism was drilled into the population when it served capitalism in one period, it was drilled out and replaced with a new ethos when it had outlived its purpose. Keynesian economics, which dominated American economic policy and public discourse after the war, suggested that by spending, not saving, and consuming, rather than reusing, individuals could contribute to the health of the economy. Profligacy was patriotic, while, according to the editor of *Fortune* magazine, "thrift is now un-American."[35]

There was a persistent lag between the introduction of products that made people's lives cleaner and more convenient and people's willingness to adopt them, however.[36] After World War II, corporations found that citizens who had just lived through the Great Depression were not willing to abandon frugality and buy all that companies could produce, even if they were paid enough to do so. The solution was to convince consumers to waste more.

Mostly famously, firms introduced "planned obsolescence," or the "deliberate curtailment of a product's lifespan,"[37] on a large scale. Automakers realized that even without honest improvements in technology, they could use rapid changes in "style"—such as useless accoutrements like tail fins—to "destroy completely the value of possessions even while their utility remains un-impaired."[38] Excessive packaging, too, helped companies squeeze more exchange value from consumers without adding any use value. In the fifteen years after the end of World War II, the volume of packaging in the waste stream increased 50 percent.[39] Still, getting people to buy these products was no easy feat, though, and advertising spending tripled in a decade.[40] The eventual outcome, as the *Time* business section approvingly noted, was that "US consumers no longer hold on to suits, coats, and dresses as if they were heirlooms.... Furniture, refrigerators, rugs— all once bought to last for years or life—are now replaced."[41]

Food is a paradigmatic example of how corporate manipulation and a capitalist-dominated state combined to promote a new spirit of capitalism that encouraged people to waste more. In the postwar decades, agribusiness honed techniques like promotional sales, advertising to children, prominent placement of high-cost foods, and steady expansion of packages, plates, and refrigerators to get people to purchase the heavily subsidized, "edible food-like substances" that American farmers were producing in (over)abundance.[42] The federal government, too, has been a major player in the five-hundred-calorie-a-day increase in food purchases per capita since 1970. U.S. Department of Agriculture nutrition advice, heavily manipulated by the agricultural lobby, has almost invariably told people to eat *more* of "good" things rather than *less* of "bad" ones.[43] The resulting "culture of bulimia" encourages us to oscillate between binging on excess food and then purging ourselves of it through crash diets or cosmetic surgery.[44]

Does this mean that the everyday consumer in Western societies has entirely abandoned the old spirit of capitalism that asserts that creating waste is sinful? Even if at an aggregate level modern capitalism requires that we be magnificently wasteful, as individuals, we've never entirely relinquished practices of thrift. Studies of household economies consistently find that people will go to great lengths to pass on, donate, and reuse even monetarily worthless objects.[45] Recycling attracts an enormous number of people with a range of demographic characteristics and political ideologies.[46] In New York, Mayors Rudy Giuliani and Michael Bloomberg both had to backtrack on attempts to cut or reduce recycling services after public outcry.[47] The persistence of an ordinary, everyday concern for waste that can be seen with glass bottles is perhaps even more evident with respect to food.[48] One survey found that wasting food provoked more "green guilt" than any other behavior associated with damaging the environment.[49]

Of course, people—not just "capitalists" but *people,* likely including many people who encountered or even participated in a trash tour—are incredibly wasteful. The average American produces 4.4 pounds of garbage a day and chucks 25 percent of the food he or she purchases.[50] So is our professed concern with waste a sham? Not entirely. Beliefs and practices can pull people in different directions: we can value thrift and nonwasting and convenience and disposability all at once, even though they are mutually exclusive. And our lives can be structured such that we loathe waste but, in the hustle and bustle of making do and getting by, we produce it anyway.[51]

Perhaps more importantly, waste in contemporary America is hidden. To some extent, it has to be. As I noted in the previous chapter, the neoliberal spirit of capitalism relentlessly celebrates the purported efficiency of markets and the dangers of nonmarket waste, but capitalism itself requires waste on an unprecedented scale. Given this contradiction, it is no surprise that, as researchers found, if people "were confronted with the amount of waste they had individually produced, they would inevitably be shocked."[52] But the point is that, under contemporary capitalism, we almost never *are* confronted with our waste.

For most of human existence, households have lived in proximity to their wastes.[53] Yet innovations like garbage disposals and sealed waste bins have made waste a steadily less perceptible part of social life.[54] My favorite anecdote of the ethereal nature of modern waste comes from the anthropologist Robin Nagle, who found that male New York City sanitation workers could stare blatantly at women without fear of reproach, because, to the city's inhabitants, they were simply *not there.*[55] At the pinnacle of our waste disposal assemblage is the sanitary landfill, a technical apparatus designed to "render waste invisible as rapidly as possible."[56]

At the same time, we have gradually redefined "waste" itself. In the old agrarian economy, "waste" meant something "underused" or "inefficient" but which had the *potential* to be put back into the production cycle, like scrap metal or old rags.[57] For an increasingly urbanized society, though, waste no longer seemed like a potential source of value but like a *negative* value that threatened health and order.

Progressive Era reformers reinforced this sense of waste as something valueless, with frequent conflations of poor sanitation with the "filth" of urban corruption and the moral "pollution" of the working classes.[58] Under the sway of the bourgeoisie, municipal governments shifted from treating waste as a valuable resource to be recovered for production to a "technical problem" that simply "needed to be put in its proper place"[59]—preferably far from upper-class neighborhoods. In short, under neoliberalism, the fetish of waste has grown steadily more blinding, even as waste itself has become more essential to the functioning of capitalism itself.

The Strange Appeal of Eating Trash

In deriding capitalism as "wasteful," freegans are in good company. Given that critiques of capitalism are often sung in the same key as capitalism's praises, it is little surprise that anticapitalists have frequently used waste to refute the moral spirit behind capitalism.[60] Thorstein Veblen gained widespread notoriety in 1899 for his *Theory of the Leisure Class,* which playfully lampooned the "conspicuous waste" of the wealthy in Gilded Age America.[61] In the 1920s American socialists developed a critique of capitalism that hinged on the waste of materials and labor created by unbridled free market competition.[62]

Just as capitalism's moral spirit changed in the twentieth century, so too did the use of waste in anticapitalist critiques. The old socialist claim that capitalism was "wasteful" because it created unemployment and lavished goods on the upper classes, for example, made less sense in a postwar era where employment was widespread and workers found themselves increasingly consuming the fruits of their own production. Instead, books like Vance Packard's *Waste Makers* derided the planned obsolescence, packaging, and advertising that were the new face of capitalist waste.[63] Herbert Marcuse, considered one of the most prominent thinkers of the "New Left" of the latter half of the 1960s, similarly denounced the "socially necessary waste" of capitalism, which consisted not of unused factories or workers but of *over*-used "parasitical and alienated functions" that produced useless, homogeneous goods but no real human value.[64]

In a sense, then, it might seem like freegans aren't doing anything new. Their events invoke well-worn criticisms that capitalism is wasteful and call for restoring age-old values of thrift. What freegans

A mixture of excitement and outrage is expressed as freegans gather unexpired, un-opened chips—and challenge newcomers' preconceptions about why things end up in the trash. Photograph by Hannah Plowright.

add to the debate is not fresh rhetoric but *evidence*. During the hey-days of the Puritan and the postwar spirits of capitalism, represen-tations and realities of waste were aligned. Today, the two are wildly out of sync: neoliberalism produces waste even as it denounces it. Ex-commodities are the incontrovertible proof of this disjuncture.

Freegans don't just say that capitalism is "wasteful": they have the ex-commodities to prove it. When socialists at the start of the twentieth century or New Left thinkers of the 1960s talked about waste, they were speaking in the abstract, comparing the present productivity of capitalism with an imagined socialist future without the waste of unemployment, idle factories, or useless goods. But the waste of neoliberalism is not just an idea but physical ex-commodities that freegans can wave in people's faces and use to challenge the mag-ical dangerousness we attribute to waste head-on.

In attempting to prove, rather than just argue, that capitalism is wasteful, freegans get a boost from the peculiarities of New York City itself. Despite 2,023 sanitation trucks picking up more than eleven thousand tons of trash a day, New York's municipal sanitation system often appears on the verge of bursting at the seams.[65] New York has perpetually struggled to implement a modern waste disposal system and ranks near the bottom of cities for the effectiveness of municipal waste management, recycling a mere 15 percent of its garbage.[66] There is a clear tension in a city that produces waste in exceptional quantities and a waste removal system that is particularly unsuccessful at keeping the ex-commodities in that waste stream hidden.

More so than in other locales, then, trash tours in New York encounter a windfall of ex-commodities that freegans can use to flip the moral spirit of capitalism on its head. As Adam once observed, "One of the buzzwords of capitalism is efficiency. We hear it all the time. But a really efficient economy would be a cooperative economy, a gift economy in which things are shared freely." While few of us would agree with this argument if it were presented to us in a textbook or a classroom, from the sidewalk, his point was hard to deny. The capitalist system really does generate a lot of waste, and through noncapitalist means, freegans are able to turn that waste back into wealth. Freegans do not just answer the questions posed by newcomers in the freeganism 101 sessions but offer supporting evidence when they explain that grocery stores exist to make money, not feed people; that this explains why stores do not donate good food; and that, in a capitalist society, objects without sufficient exchange value are wasted even if they still have use value. Capitalism, as freegans have realized, really does violate most peoples' common sense—it's just that this violation is usually hidden.

Arguments about the "exploitative" or "alienating" nature of capitalism are not likely to win huge numbers of converts anytime soon. Beliefs around food are notoriously sticky.[67] But freegans aren't really asking people to change their minds. As Madeline put it:

> *The chances that someone off the street will espouse human extinction, primitivism, and extreme animal rights are nil. Real anarchism is when you appeal to what people already know. People know these things already. They know the stuff they're buying isn't making them happy. They know that we're hurting the earth. But you have to give them something to practice. Get their hands dirty.*

Trash tours centered on demonstrating an extant but disguised disconnect between how most of us think our economic system *should* work—and how capitalism *claims* it works—and how it actually *does*.

That people "already knew" that "waste" was a bad thing was abundantly evident throughout my research. Even in a city not known for its politeness, most pedestrians wished the freegans "good luck" when told that the event was an attempt to reduce waste. Or, as two elderly women told Janet one night, they condemned food waste as a "sin against God." During tours, waste continued to serve as it had throughout American history: as a flexible metaphor for anything perceived as unfair or inefficient. One night, a cab driver stopped his car to watch us root through the trash outside a supermarket. I was assigned to hand out fliers, so I walked over to his car, gave him a calendar of freegan events, and explained to him why we were dumpster diving. When I started talking about waste and how stores throw out still-edible food, he cut me off and launched into a tirade about the way oil companies were harming cab drivers in the pursuit of "wasteful" profits. Another observer, upon hearing the freegans' justification for dumpster diving, adopted the same terminology to assail the "wasteful" wars in Afghanistan and Iraq. Jason, perhaps exaggerating slightly, once remarked that, "I've never met anyone who disagrees with the basic idea of freeganism."

Of course, few people confronted with ex-commodities for the first time responded by quitting their jobs and renouncing capitalism. A sizable minority stumbling on a trash tour would spend a few minutes looking over the scavenged food items offered to them. A smaller number would leave their e-mail address with a group organizer; a few of this latter group might even come to a freegan.info event. Even those unwilling to "get their hands dirty" in a trash tour could tell an roommate about the good food they found or directly (if infinitesimally) take a bite out of capitalist accumulation by taking free food rather than buying it. Because the trash tour was a *collective* performance that drew on broadly shared values of thrift and non-wasting, the range of ways people could contribute to freegan.info's anticapitalist politics was surprisingly wide and flexible.

A New World Out of Waste

On first blush, Zaac seemed like an unlikely candidate to be a "primitivist"—that is, someone who believes that human beings should return to a preindustrial, preagricultural lifestyle. Born in Greenwich, Connecticut (one of the richest areas in the United States), to a father who ran a corporate headhunting firm, he attended the University of Connecticut to study computer science. At the time of our interview in 2009, he was still a Greenwich resident, with a job he described as "forty hours a week doing stuff that I don't find important." More specifically, Zaac programmed touch screen computers in rich people's houses, work whose social function was, by his admission, "making it easier for them to watch TV." Zaac didn't deny the incongruity between his job and his freegan ideology, but explained the trade-off in terms of his usefulness as an activist: "How effective would I be if I'm worried about a place to sleep? My job allows me to be the change I wish to see."

The first few times I met Zaac, he was wearing the same T-shirt from Farm Sanctuary, an animal liberation organization, that read "Peace Begins on Your Plate." Like many freegans, Zaac's passion for animal rights led him to become a vegan and, when he realized its limitations, a freegan as well. One look at Zaac, though, makes it clear that his interests go far beyond just recovering waste or helping animals. When Zaac showed up at one freegan.info reading group meeting, he showed me a well-worn, spiral-bound notebook. Inside, written in cramped handwriting, were summaries of a vast array of bicycle repair manuals, guides to edible wild plants, recipes for herbal remedies, and radical anticapitalist literature. As he told me, straight-faced, "You never know when you might need a summary of [the prominent early twentieth-century anarchist] Emma Goldman's writings on a note card." More strikingly, Zaac was wearing a backpack that he had built out of bike tubes and was clad in sandals he put together from discarded fire hose. Attached to his backpack was a trowel he used to dig up edible plants he encountered in his travels, as well as a milk jug containing wild greens he had found in the suburbs.

I asked Zaac where his interest in making his own clothes and bags came from, and he told me that he started in high school when he built a tree house out of dumpstered materials. "I've always been a little crafty," he explained, evoking the same intrinsic drive to deviate from social expectations as other freegans. When I queried him about what he saw as the purpose of these skills, he seemed a little unsure: "I don't know where exactly my learning is going towards, so I don't know what I'm aiming for." He went on to add:

> When I buy something, I don't feel like I own it. I'm afraid to sew it, patch it up. This backpack [that I built myself], I can feel it. I know what's wrong with it; I know what's right with it. If something's not working, I can cut it up and make it work for me in a new way.... Once you make something, you can control exactly what it's going to do.

Ultimately, he said, now is the time to gain such knowledge, since to him the environment is nearing collapse and "you don't wait to learn to sail until you're on the sailboat."

Learning how to create physical objects wasn't the only skill Zaac was developing in preparation for the globe's bleak future. Zaac told me that, on weekends, he often looked for wild herbs in the forest or went "mushrooming" with a group in Greenwich. Foraging was part of adopting a new outlook toward the world around him: "When you're my age and you go through the woods, you're supposed to learn how to hike faster. But I'm all about slowing down and becoming more engaged." The contrast between freegan forager and a vegan farmer, to him, was stark: "You could cut it [the forest] down and make a deep ecology farm, or you could just see what's already being offered." Zaac put these skills into practice in 2009, during a months-long bike trip into the remote reaches of Canada, turning back only when he could no longer forage enough plants to survive.

Despite his dire predictions about the biosphere's future, Zaac did not share the hermit-like, isolationist tendencies of "survivalists" or "preppers." When Sowmya arrived at one reading group and reported that Adam couldn't attend, owing to untreated back pain, Zaac rifled through one of his notebooks until he found a medieval herbal pain remedy. Zaac frequently taught "skill-shares" for the freegan group, taking particular pleasure in repurposing cast-off, wasted items and empowering others on how to make them into something useful. Zaac's commitment to making new things out of waste, then, was much more than a strategy for minimizing his carbon footprint: it was a way to embody and enact his vision for the future on a quotidian basis.

As Zaac saw it, "There's just something about this whole withdrawal practice—being a vegan, riding a bicycle instead of a car, foraging instead of buying—that one starts to embody what they're actually talking about. They seem to kind of go with each other internally." Yet clearly not all aspects of Zaac's life "go with each other internally." There was a particularly glaring disjuncture between Zaac's back-to-nature ethos and life in a Connecticut suburb of New York City. Like other freegans, Zaac simultaneously celebrated living more "naturally" even as he consciously continued to spend much of his time in what would seem to be the most unnatural of places—a city.

Although thus far I've looked primarily at how freegans used wasted ex-commodities to criticize capitalism, this was only ever one-half of the group's political equation. Freegans also engaged in myriad activities, from wild food foraging to community bike workshops and sewing skill-shares, outside their trash tours. Their goal in so doing was to plant, in the heart of New York City, the seeds of a postcapitalist world. Through using waste in creative ways, freegans experimented with new modes of valuation, daily rhythms, and ways to relate to the environment that—although far from overthrowing capitalism—were starkly at odds with normative modes of thinking and acting in capitalist society.

Foraging for Flora, Fishing for Garbage

The intensity of freegans' beliefs about the need to get "back to nature" was on display during the group's monthly reading group, where—away from the audience of a trash tour—radical prognostications flowed freely. For most of 2008 we met in the food court of Grand Central Station, feasting on leftovers from harried captains of finance commuting between Manhattan and the suburbs. More than just a glorified book club, the reading group claimed to be the "research wing" of freegan.info, developing both critical analyses of the past and blueprints for the future. One month, our reading came from Jim Mason's *Unnatural Order: Why We Are Destroying the Planet and Each Other*, which argues—in brief—that "our current social and environmental problems...began several millennia ago when our ancestors took up farming and broke the primal bonds with the living world and put human beings above all other life."[1]

Adam seized on the book's "anti-civilization" message to argue that "the foragers were the ones who got it right, everything else is basically fucked up." Despite his indefatigable work to save humanity, there was an air of misanthropy in his views: "Humans should stop living anywhere but the ecosystems we're evolved for.... We need to stop adapting every ecosystem for us, rather than staying where we're adapted to. We're basically an invasive species on the vast majority of the planet. It's time to wipe the slate clean."[2] Evie challenged him, pointing out, "There's six billion of us—we have to figure out a way to get from A to B that isn't cruel." She concurred, however, that "there was a point where human beings stepped out of nature and decided to control nature, and that's where we went wrong."

Discussions like these gave voice to a primitivist current in freegan.info that questioned not just capitalism but industrialism, agriculture, and civilization itself. At the root of this belief system was the idea that these forms of social organization deviated from the "natural" way for humans to live. As Jason framed it:

> My vision is that eventually we live in a world where we don't have any of this modern technology. Live with the land, on the land, and everything we get comes from nature.... I don't like talking about going back to pre-civilization, but going forward to post-civilization. Civilization is fundamentally, inherently crazy and unsustainable. And eventually it exhausts itself. I think we can be mature, responsible beings, but still be wild animals. That's what other animals on the planet do, why should we be any different?

While some in the group were skeptical of these sorts of discussions—"You can't just turn back the clock to a million B.C.," Madeline was fond of pointing out—the group nonetheless created a support-ive community for espousing and developing these views.

On first glance, there was a host of contradictions between these visions of nature and freegans' metropolitan lives. While I discuss these very real incongruities in the next chapter, freegans nonethe-less *did* find ways to put some of these abstract principles into prac-tice. One example was the wild food foraging tours that freegan.info occasionally organized during temperate months. It was during one tour led by Zaac through Inwood Hill Park on the northern edge of Manhattan that the idea that freegans were getting "back to nature" in the cracks and crevices of the urban environment occurred to me. One attendee, a traveling anarchist who made ends meet through dumpster diving and occasional gigs as a Web designer, told me that he often foraged for wild food in city parks in California but wanted to try it in New York. He was surprised to discover that many of the plants in this park were similar to those at home, despite the vastly different climates of the two areas. When he pointed this out, Zaac responded, "There's lots of biodiversity in the rainforest, but there's unique species here [in the city] too." The city, in brief, was an ecosys-tem in its own right.

As a way to provide for freegans' material needs, wild food for-aging is wildly ineffective. Wild mushrooms, the chief object of our search that day, are difficult to find, and only an experienced mush-roomer can identify those that are safe to eat. Even Zaac, who had spent hundreds of hours learning scientific names of mushrooms, techniques for finding them, and tests for determining which were poisonous, readily admitted that he got an infinitesimal proportion of his food from foraging. The most practical advice Zaac could offer a novice like me was that it was possible to eat the dandelions growing in Prospect Park, albeit only if I cooked them properly. And, he added, they would still be wrenchingly bitter. Moreover, in contrast to trash tours, wild food foraging rarely received any media attention or gath-ers a public audience.

Despite all these limitations of wild food foraging as a form of collective action, the freegan group was invariably thrilled whenever Zaac agreed to lead a tour. As I discovered, wild food foraging had sig-nificance that transcended its seeming impracticality. Hunting wild burdock root and edible flowers may not have provided much in the way of sustenance, but it did offer a tangible means through which freegans reconstructed human-made urban parks as "natural" and "wild" spaces. Within the context of a wild food foraging tour, mundane objects like mushrooms became "patches of anarchy... [revealing] nature at work."[3] Simple acts of respect for plants during such a tour, too, were emblematic of a reconfigured mind-set toward nature as a whole. As Zaac cautioned us before our tour, "You see a bunch of ostrich ferns growing in a clump together. If you know to only pick half of them, they'll grow back. But pick all of them, and it dies."

Zaac's admonition reminded us that our relationships to the plants we collected on the tour were a form of prefigurative politics, in which we were enacting new ways to think about and act with respect to nature. As with trash tours, wild food foraging expeditions entailed finding value in unlikely places. During a follow-up interview in 2013, Zaac explained, "Things that seem to be waste aren't waste when you look a little closer. In Hurricane Sandy, a huge number of oak trees fell down, but I helped to organize mushroom cultivation workshops on those trees that had fallen, so they didn't have to go to waste." Although freegan literature often described the group as supportive of urban farming, and some like Madeline or Jonathan were actively involved in community garden projects, others saw wild foraging as better reflecting their environmental ideals. Foraging practices suggested that much human cultivation of food—even sustainable production in an urban garden—was unnecessary, if only we saw the often-overlooked plants already growing around us.

Freegans envisioned themselves as a band of foragers living off the resources of the urban environment in another way: through dumpster diving. Some scholars have described the huge quantities of waste flowing through cities as a kind of "urban metabolism," a "system of flows so fundamental to the city's well-being that its work is a form of breathing, albeit with an exchange of objects instead of air molecules."[4] Rhetoric aside, there is nothing particularly natural about New York's vast waste-disposal apparatus. Indeed, part of the message of public trash tours was that ex-commodity waste is *unnatural*: not an inherent and inevitable part of human society but a historically specific product of capitalism.

At other times, though, freegans talked about ex-commodities as if they were "natural" resources. Zaac often invoked "foraging" in an ambiguous way, suggesting that searching for wild turnips or trash

Finding value in unlikely places: Zaac, Janet, Madeline, and others hunt for wild mushrooms on a downed tree. Photograph by the author.

required the same basic ethic: "The difference between foraging and agriculture is trying to control nature, versus preparing yourself to respond to whatever nature throws at you." Even though freegans knew that waste did not come from "nature," they occasionally spoke and acted as if it were a fixed part of their physical environment. One weekend in 2012 I went to Governor's Island with Jonathan and Lucie for a free art festival. We had been discussing the recent closure of the Occupy Wall Street encampment, and I commented that the island had large tracts of open space that could be expropriated. Jonathan replied, pensively, "Yeah, but what would you eat? You'd have to go into the city to dumpster [dive], and there are only ferries on the weekend."

Lucie laughed, "You remember that food comes from places other than dumpsters, right? You *could* farm it."

"Oh right," Jonathan replied. "I forgot."

Taking advantage of the city's "natural" resources required freegans to develop specialized knowledge of where and when garbage became available. David expressed his pride in this localized expertise, telling me (a bit hyperbolically), "It's gotten to the point where if somebody calls me and says 'It's Thursday at 7:00 p.m. and I want vegan ice cream,' I can say, 'Oh, go to the such and such store on this street and there will be frozen vanilla and chocolate.'" Freegans claimed that, without this practical knowledge, they were faced with scarcity. Leia told me that when she moved to New York, she was "starving" because she couldn't find food. Even though she had lived off waste in Minnesota, she was accustomed to looking in back alleys and dumpsters: she learned how to effectively forage in New York only when she attended a freegan.info event and was taught how. Of course, it's unlikely that Leia would let herself starve—she'd break down and buy food eventually—but the comment nonetheless highlighted the strength of her commitment to living off whatever the urban environment offered.

Gaining skills in dumpster diving provided another way for freegans to see themselves as living naturally, even in a city. Lucie described what she saw as the parallels between being an "urban forager" and a hunter-gatherer:

> When you go dumpster diving...you do things in the natural way. It's like going harvesting or gathering...[or] going in the forest to find food. You need to explore, first, to find good spots. Then you need to really work for your food: it's harder, you need to open bags, to search, to climb into a dumpster...It's always surprising. You don't know what you're going to find. It makes it more natural. It's like going back to the time when people would go into natural spaces to get food.... When you have crops, and you're a farmer, you know

*what you're going to get. The freegan way is more like hunting, or
maybe fishing.*

In contrast to a modern industrial food system built on standard-
ization and predictability, dumpster dives were full of unscripted
moments. As one freegan exclaimed before a trash tour, "It's always
unpredictable; that's part of the adventure of it!" I witnessed first-
hand the excitement that bubbled up whenever there was a particularly rare find, like a box of tempeh or a pomegranate.

Freegan Senses, Freegan Bodies

For freegans, living off dumpster-dived food entailed not just new
attitudes and practices toward urban waste but also toward their own
bodies. Scholars have argued that the design of modern cities directs
our senses toward some aspects of the urban environment—like the
wealth of commodities on sale—and away from others, like pollution
or poverty.[5] As he often did, Sasha reconnected this abstract, academic theme to freeganism, telling me, "our sensitivity is oppressed
by society, and our senses are polluted through industrialism." While
Sasha's commentary might seem cerebral, the way we use our senses
is undeniably implicated in the production of ex-commodities, albeit
in largely hidden ways.

In the Western world, 30 percent of fruits and vegetables that
are harvested are rejected by producers or distributers and diverted
as animal food, compost, or waste.[6] The vast majority of this "trimming" is carried out on the basis of aesthetic—that is to say, visual—
criteria. The Florida Tomato Committee, for example, "decrees the
exact size, color, texture, and shape of exported slicing tomatoes. It
prevents the shipping of tomatoes that are lopsided, kidney-shaped,
elongated, angular, ridged, rough, or otherwise 'deformed.'"[7] None of
these regulations have anything to do with safety, taste, or nutrition.
Yet by all accounts, this summary judgment and execution of food
based on sight has gotten harsher over time. While wholesalers forty
years ago could sell lettuce with a few holes in the outer leaves, today
even bargain supermarkets would reject these products.[8]

Supermarkets invariably repeat that, in offering immaculate produce, they are only responding to consumer demand.[9] Placing blame

on consumers or distributors is, in this case, a chicken-or-the-egg problem that misses how both are bound up in the same system. As Madeline framed it at one freeganism 101 event:

> Our society wants blemish-free food. So when food is not perfect, the stores try to get it out of sight as quickly as possible. It's not individuals, it's the system. The stores are trying to extract surplus value, to borrow a Marxist term. But our system ends up with a huge amount of waste and unrecognized costs.

However we apportion the culpability, the impacts of our collective obsession with appearance are clear. Consumers get perfect (looking) produce, stores increase profits in a competitive market by incorporating the price of fruits and vegetables culled at different points of the supply chain into what they sell, and huge amounts of "waste"— really, completely edible ex-commodities, albeit in nonstandard shapes and sizes—fall out in the shuffle.

Freegan practices of relating to food required the senses to be attuned in a different way. Writing of her own experiences as a sanitation worker in New York, Robin Nagle found that "when garbage is the organizing frame of reference, familiar geographies are radically changed ... instead of upscale residential blocks lined with lovely homes and trees, I saw clots of dark bags, metal cans, plastic bins that went on and on and on."[10] Similarly, for me, becoming a dumpster diver meant turning away from the neon signs, advertisements, and window displays that to me had previously signaled the presence of commodities for purchase. Instead, I had to pay attention to subtle and difficult-to-discern hints that gave away the presence of ex-commodities, such as the faint smell of food, a bag sinking into the curb (suggesting it was particularly heavy), or a store employee walking back inside after depositing trash on the sidewalk.

The senses are necessary not just for finding food but also separating out the ex-commodities from the genuine garbage. Before opening a bag, experienced freegans feel them from the outside: soft, rounded lumps could mean food, while more angular ones suggest packaging. Sight, freegans frequently emphasized, could be misleading. In response to a question about the health of dumpster-dived food during one presentation to a class at New York University, Adam shot back, "We have false ideas about what constitutes fresh food. A lot of food tastes better when it looks worse. But those are not the tactile and aesthetic qualities people look for when they purchase produce." During the trash tour afterward, Adam discovered a bin filled with discarded tofu, chicken, and cheese from one grocery store's hot food salad bar. As a vegan, Adam wanted only the tofu, but in the darkness, the difference was hard to see. Adam fearlessly plunged into the mixture and pulled out a sauce-covered white chunk, explaining how to identify whether it was meat based on its texture and the way it broke when crushed between the thumb and forefinger.

In using their senses to determine what was safe to eat, freegans were bucking the wider trend. Playing up consumers' fears of the toxic products of modern capitalism has, ironically, proved to be a fruitful way for capitalists to sell commodities designed to protect us, from organic food to natural cleaning products to bottled water.[11] These same fears create ex-commodities. In a context where people live farther and farther from food production, and agribusiness jealously guards where and how its commodities are produced, consumers have justifiably become more anxious about the safety of their food.[12] In response, since the 1970s businesses have offered an array of "use-by," "sell-by," and "best-before" dates, slapping them even onto nonperishables like pasta or beer.[13]

Although the U.S. government has concluded that there is "little or no benefit … in terms of improved microbiological safety" for these labels, 91 percent of American consumers report having thrown out an item because it passed its "sell-by" date (which, itself, is supposed to be used only by the store and has *no* connection to food safety).[14] Another study found that consumers evoked labels as the explanation for 30 percent of instances where they discarded food, citing the (incorrect) belief that these labels reflected food safety.[15] As with aesthetic standards, we don't need to believe in secret corporate scheming to recognize who benefits from this situation. Producers, processors, distributors, and retailers all make more money when consumers don't trust their own senses and throw out food that has passed a conservative sell-by date. This probably explains why the National Association of Food Chains has repeatedly and successfully lobbied against federal legislation that would standardize date labeling.[16]

Once again, freegans reframed the practicalities of surviving off dumpstered food into a form of direct action that challenged the power of retailers to determine what was, and was not, good to eat. In response to one of the frequent queries newcomers make about food safety, an experienced freegan quipped, "I never look at the sell-by date, it's irrelevant to me. It's about the condition of the food: you smell it, you taste it, and if it's horrible, don't [eat it]."[17] Eating safely meant cultivating knowledge that freegans claimed had been lost:

> *Not knowing about food, and thinking about safety standards, that comes from living in the city.… If you take a yogurt, and you don't know what it is and you don't know how it's made, and all you know is the expiration date, then after the expiration date you'll throw it away. If you know how a yogurt works, you know it could be good two months after. You just taste it.*

The irony was that freegans actually knew very little about where their food came from. In contrast to organic and local food movements' obsession with intimate consumer knowledge of food's origins, freegans were often unsure of why the food they found was in the dumpster at all. An item might have been thrown out because of the store overordering and minor blemishes and decay, neither of which changed the food's physical properties or capacity to nourish. On the other hand, large quantities of certain types of food waste might be due to a product recalled because it is frankly unsafe. One summer we eagerly collected a surfeit of peanut-butter-based products until Cindy e-mailed us a report announcing that they may have been contaminated with salmonella (some, skeptical of anything coming from the Food and Drug Administration and aware that such recalls tend to be extremely broad, ate from the peanut-butter bounty anyway).

Nonetheless, when reporters asked—and they always did—"Does anyone ever get sick?" freegans relentlessly insisted that no one ever does.[18] In part, they explained, freegans were careful to clean the food they rescue before eating it and were smart enough to recognize when something is truly trash. They also used the question of hygiene to make a political point: as the website's "Health and Safety" page points out, "Dumpster diving plant-based items that have been discarded by stores is probably safer than buying animal products from the shelf and bringing them home."[19] Reports on the declining regulation and monitoring of meat safety in the American agrifood system chain substantiate that this claim is not as outlandish as it may seem.[20] While some other studies claim that illness is a regular corollary to a dumpster diet, on an auto-ethnographic note, over seven years I have never gotten sick from eating dumpstered food.[21]

There's no question, however, that the freegans pushed the boundary between ex-commodity and just plain trash. As Janet confessed, "I mean, we wouldn't do this if it were totally disgusting. But the line between what's edible and what's not edible definitely shifts a little bit." Many freegans put stock in the "hygiene hypothesis," a notion circulating in punk, anarchist, and back-to-the-land communities that modern hygiene has weakened humanity's natural resistance to disease.[22] As Janet elaborated during one freeganism 101 event:

> We're all raised to think garbage is dirty: "Don't touch that. That's been on the floor. That's been in the garbage." Most of us probably have strong immune systems and touch things all over the place that are germy.... The first time I went on a trash tour I didn't take anything like an apple or pear, I only took citrus, like an orange or a banana. Now I'm braver and I just wash them well, and if I'm not sure, I'll peel them. But now I take almost everything.

Leia put it more pithily: "People in this country are a lot more freaked out about dirt than they need to be. We need a little dirt in our lives for our immune systems to be strong."

Eating slightly rotten and over-the-hill foods served as personal affirmations of a commitment to an alternative lifestyle and markers of more natural lives. Playing with hygienic standards, though, was also one of the most attention-grabbing aspects of freegans' symbolic critique of capitalism. As the anthropologist Mary Douglas famously theorized, all societies hold powerful "pollution rules" that separate the clean and dirty, sacred and profane, virtuous and wicked.[23] Some scientific research even suggests that "disgust" is an emotion with a strong evolutionary basis, helping us avoid disease.[24] The modern-day fetish of waste takes the emotion to new heights: we are now frequently disgusted by *anything* labeled "waste," even when it is something our ancestors—or even our grandparents—would eat with relish.

Thus when freegans ate "polluted" food and showed that it was still good, they attempted to flip the object of disgust onto the companies that created ex-commodities in the first place. The perfect example came when an ABC reporter asked, "What do you say to people who say, 'There you are on the street, digging through trash, this is gross, this is disgusting'?"

You could almost hear Madeline's corporate experience when she deftly replied, "I'd say what's gross and disgusting is the fact that this food is being thrown out in the first place."[25]

As Lisa, a middle-aged, well-dressed woman, reflected after one trash tour, "I think it's funny that there's this stigma against eating from the trash, but there's no stigma against putting it in there in the first place. And think about it; that tomato on the shelf, you have no idea where it was fifteen minutes ago. It could have been on the floor!"[26] As freegans showed, the fetishism of waste partly comes through our overreliance on sight and misconceptions about hygiene; by adopting new practices and norms, freegans were prefiguring a "post-fetish" world.

Rhythms of the Urban Forager

Freegans enacted a different, more natural society in another subtle way—through the rhythms of daily life. Rhetorically, freegans celebrated how their lifestyle "liberated" them from a never-ending cycle of work and consumption, allowing them to spend more time engaged in unpaid activities with more flexible schedules. For Janet, "there's a hugely freeing sense to knowing that anytime I'm hungry, I can go a few blocks and find something. It almost feels like this city is more mine than it ever was before." For his part, Zaac felt that his involvement in freeganism had opened his eyes to the flaws of the rigidly segmented, linear conception of time he saw around him, as well as pointing to an alternative:

> People have this notion of going through life as fast as possible. You get a job, and then you go as fast as possible, and retire, get along with life. I feel like foraging as well as a lot of notions pointed out within freegan.info, within a wider context, disprove that theory that this is the way that life is.

Nothing encapsulated freegan beliefs with respect to time better than Zaac's long bike trip to Canada. When he told nonfreegans about his plans, he noted, "They all said 'You're going to die. You're going to get sick. The weather is going to be bad.' But it always works out. You stop and pick things up along the way. It's problematic, sure, but it turns out OK."

Despite claims of personal liberation, though, freegans' deep-seated desire to turn the flow of time into an ongoing series of direct actions created its own constraints. Although food is ex-commodified at reliable places and times, other ex-commodities freegans needed to find in order to avoid spending money, like clothes, toiletries, and appliances, appeared less predictably. One evening, the group was walking from an organizational meeting to the site of the trash tour. On the way, we came upon a dumpster filled with reams of quality printer paper—a rare find that could be used for producing fliers and pamphlets guilt-free. The group spent nearly a half-hour collecting it, even though it made them so late for the subsequent tour that, when they arrived, the attendees had already left. Noncapitalist strategies for getting goods such as waiting for an item to appear on "Freecycle" or for a friend to pass on a used one nearly always worked eventually, but even freegans accepted that this entailed postponing the comforts of immediate consumption.

When I began to dumpster dive necessities myself, traversing the city on foot took much longer than it had previously. I zig-zagged across streets to examine any garbage that looked remotely promising, paying far more attention to the journey itself and what I could find during it than to reaching my destination. I struggled to maintain a barrier between time spent "diving" and time spent "not-diving." For the majority of freegans who continued to live with one foot in capitalist time—holding normal jobs or socializing with nonfreegans—this form of direct action against capitalist time could be frustrating. I myself often missed the last train back to New Jersey owing to the slow, nondeliberate pace with which Adam combed the city at night for useful waste.

Even ex-commodified food carried its own temporal binds. While a grocery store might be open sixteen hours a day, the best window for dumpster diving was a few hours between when stores close and garbage trucks appear. One night, I was working in the freegan office with Adam when he looked at the time on his computer and said, "It's eight-thirty. We can almost get dinner." For Adam, who had no access to a refrigerator or kitchen, eating like a forager meant gathering food at the times it was available and going without otherwise. Marion articulated how dumpster diving required a mix of patience, skill, and self-abnegation:

> I try to project and say, "This is what I have, I probably won't go on this day because of the weather." But I have to plan in advance to make sure I'm prepared. Usually I know when the stores are closed, and that means that, usually, ten to midnight is the good range. It gets laborious, to stay on the street, late late at night, day after day. So I try to limit it to get what I need, at least. It can so easily turn into still [being] on the street at 1:30 in the morning. It's exhausting for me.

Marion elaborated that freegans must save (some might say, "hoard") goods for when they might need them:

> There's no item that I can't find. It takes diligence and you can't really go out and say, "I need an orange right now." Well, with oranges, you almost can, but with some things, you can't. I have the most bizarre collection of stuff, because I do this and think the need for it may come up later, but it's such a bizarre item that I will take it. I've got an industrial-sized bag of arrowroot, and I use about half a teaspoon a year.

Planning and foresight were required to even partly pull back from the money economy. Back-to-school season, for example, was harvest time for office supplies; college move-outs in May presented a rare opportunity to find instant oatmeal, towels, and toiletries in abundance.

Although most freegans continued to have jobs, their urban foraging did reduce their need to commodify and sell their labor by allowing them to get some ex-commodities for free. Yet, as one scholar points out, while freegans substituted "working for food" over "working to pay for food,"[27] they are nonetheless still *working*. But the implications of each sort of labor are distinct. Capitalists, as Marx observed, depend on their control of workers' time in the factory to produce a profit.[28] More than that, though, capitalism requires that individuals create rigid divisions between productive hours spent laboring for the capitalist and time spent *not*-producing, during which the worker can only passively consume whatever commodities the capitalist has on offer.[29]

These temporal imperatives of capitalist society have, predictably, impinged on practices around food. In a neoliberal economy, employed Americans have consistently been pushed to spend more hours working and less in leisure, as well as accept increasingly flexible (that is to say, unpredictable) schedules, all in exchange for stagnant wages.[30] The result has been a constant downward march in time spent on food: the average American spends only forty-two minutes a day eating at home, and even less cooking and washing up.[31] Unsurprisingly, less time cooking means more meals are prepackaged and preprepared. As always, we can argue over whether neoliberal restructuring or consumer laziness is responsible for this shift: as with aesthetic standards, producers claim that they are just giving people what they want.[32] But then again, if consumers naturally wanted bland, unhealthy processed food, companies could have saved the billions they have spent marketing it. Decades of campaigns, for example, pounded in the notion that a "good" mother does not produce food from scratch in the home; instead, she purchases and serves ready-made meals designed by agribusiness employees.[33]

The "deskilling" of the populace from one-time cooks who produced meals to consumers who merely microwave them has clear implications for waste. Processed or cooked offerings from supermarkets, like baby carrots, rotisserie chickens, or hot-salad bars, are wasted at higher rates than their unprocessed counterparts.[34] The materiality of food, after all, is "unforgiving":[35] cutting skins or removing peels drastically diminishes food's shelf life. The best evidence of this comes from the dumpsters themselves: on trash tours, we found far more cut pineapple than whole fruits, more individually packaged pasta salads than dry pasta; more cookies than flour, eggs, or sugar. As with baked goods, stores make up for the prepared food they ex-commodify with the additional markup on the commodities they sell.

By recovering preprepared or packaged food, freegans believed that they were rejecting the principles of the food system that produced them. But they were also cultivating values and practices that could have a more significant, if indirect, impact. Packaging, as some scholars argue, creates a world where people trust labels, not their senses, to tell them what food is good and rely on industrial machines, rather than their own skills, to cook it.[36] The availability of more varied and complex ingredients year-round, juxtaposed against our lessened ability to make use of them, leads inexorably to waste.[37] Freegans saw dumpster diving as a way to retrain themselves to use food in more creative ways. Explained Maximus, one freegan in Boston:

> Most people walk into the kitchen and think, "What do I want?" which quickly transforms into, "What product should I buy?" We think differently. When we walk into the kitchen, we ask, "What do we have? What can we make with it?" We use whatever resources we have available.

Freeganism, as should be clear, takes time. It rejects some of the undeniable conveniences provided for us by our food system (a fact that helps explain why freegans struggle to reach out to harried and overworked middle-class and lower-class people). Yet unlike wage labor in capitalist society, which produces commodities whose origins are fetishized and invisible even to the laborers themselves, freegans understood what their labor was going toward: practices that cherished time spent on food, recovered lost skills, and accepted unpredictability as a necessary part of a sustainable world.

Reworking Waste into Wheels

After one freegan feast in Jason's apartment, eight of us stayed around for a skill-share, which began with Zaac removing a handful of yucca leaves from his backpack and placing them on the floor. He demonstrated how to scrape off the flesh of the leaf, leaving only the internal fibers, which he instructed us to weave into cord. After half an hour, Zaac had created a drawstring for his hat, while the rest of us had a few sloppy, short strands of what could only optimistically be described as "rope." No one seemed dispirited. Instead, the group was so enthralled by the event that, immediately after, participants animatedly discussed plans for similar trainings in canning and preserving fruit, sewing clothes, and making wine.

As with wild food foraging, these do-it-yourself skill-shares were impractical ways to meet material needs. In the city, even a modestly experienced dumpster diver could easily find discarded rope without the exertion required to weave it himself or herself. By taking yucca leaves from outside a gas station and reworking them, though, freegans showed how objects connected to what they saw as the worst aspects of capitalism—cars and fossil fuels—could be imbued with radically different moral meaning.

The power of manual skills in enabling these transformations was, according to many, a core element of freegan practice. During one event where Janet, Adam, and Wendy were speaking to a class at NYU, Adam lectured the group about the uselessness of their formal educations: "We live in a profoundly deskilled society. We've been infantilized, and very few of us know how to do anything outside of our little narrow box of employment." Activities like "mending brunches," where freegans met to share fabric, food, and sewing tips, provided a chance for freegans to break out of this "narrow box." As Anna told me after one sewing event:

> We're so used to not doing anything with our hands, we're reminding ourselves that we have those skills. It's something that's always been done, that we can easily pick up again. It's only been one generation, and we've lost sewing. Our mothers could sew. So, there, it's not a huge difference.

Anna's ideal of "reskilling" did not require harking back to primeval foragers but to the more recent, if equally romanticized, thriftiness and independence of freegans' parents or grandparents.

Madeline once explained to me that freeganism was not "pie in the sky" but about "making use of the resources at hand"—which, in the city, usually meant waste. During one trash tour, it began to rain. Christian fashioned a makeshift umbrella out of a piece of Styrofoam and a metal pole he found on the sidewalk while the rest of the group and, of course, a few cameramen clustered around to offer their praise and take photos. These skills were not just about showing off or creating distinctions from the mainstream but had real and material impacts on freegans' lives. Lola explained how learning how to sew contributed to withdrawing from capitalism:

> I don't even remember the last time I bought clothes. That's something that people just assume you have to do. If you have a hole, you buy new pants. If your shirt is too short, you buy a new shirt. A lot of people see that I wear really ratty and crusty clothes and so they assume they have to give me clothes. At first I thought that was

generous. But now I've realized that's just another crutch, because I'd rather just learn to make my own.

Alongside learning how to sew, for Lola, one of the most important ways to express her simultaneous commitment to reskilling and reducing consumption was bicycling. When she first became involved in freeganism, she recovered a few abandoned bicycles, but they were all "really, really crappy," and she lacked the knowledge to fix them up. When I met her, though, she proudly showcased the fixed-gear bike she built, noting, "I know every part of it and understand why and how everything works. And to do that, I had to learn where every one [of the parts] came from, how it developed." For her, understanding the material properties of her bicycle was crucial: it allowed her to maintain it without paying for repairs while providing a way to actualize her commitment to self-sufficiency and sustainability.

What's more, bicycling through Manhattan provided another way to transcend the city's unnaturalness:

Bicycling is such a freeing feeling. You're in direct contact with nature. The physical aspect of it is amazing. It feels to me like breaking through some kind of invisible barrier.... You can't fall asleep on a fixed gear [bicycle]. You can't just ignore things that are going on. You can't just look up at the stars; it's actually being in contact and being directly involved with what is happening.

When Lola spent a stint housesitting in a luxurious apartment on the Upper West Side, she confided to me, "It felt really weird, so I brought my bike into my bedroom with me, just as a reminder." Lola's bicycle functioned as a personal icon of her commitment to freegan values—despite the contradiction that staying in the apartment of an affluent family friend represented.

Lola was not alone in seeing bicycling as a central freegan activity. Other participants came to the group through their involvement in direct-action bicycle groups like New York's Time's Up, and freegan.info scrupulously avoided scheduling conflicts with Critical Mass and its monthly take-back-the-streets bike rides through Manhattan. Most notable, however, was the freegan bike workshop, a project founded by Christian in 2007. Initially, the project was housed in a space on the Upper West Side of Manhattan, where, according to one account, it primarily attracted "bike aficionados."[38] When it lost its lease later that year, though, the bike workshop moved to the basement of 123 in Bedford-Stuyvesant.

Like every freegan.info project, the new bike workshop was riven with inconsistencies. Although Wendy described the workshop's $600-a-month rent as an "absolute bargain," coming up with the funds was a constant problem. The first thing I encountered on entering the "free" freegan bike workshop and asking about building a bike was a request for a twenty-five-dollar donation—although the mechanic added that I could volunteer a few hours in lieu of a payment. At times, the group debated whether the bike workshop could even be considered "freegan": first, because the various collectives at 123 threw fund-raisers and parties that charged admission and sold alcohol, and second, because some mechanics began selling bike parts off-site to cover shortfalls. Eventually, the workshop filed for nonprofit status so that it could give donors a tax write-off, giving it a level of formal legitimacy that some in the group disdained.

Despite these external problems, the inside of the bike workshop was an oasis of careful resource use, waste recovery, and personal empowerment. A tall, thin freegan in his midtwenties, with shoulder-length curly red hair, Quinn came from a well-heeled background. He offered a "recycling, reduce, and reduction" narrative, telling me, "Growing up, consumerism was gross. Freegan.info was just a mature version of me when I was younger." That said, Quinn went to an elite university and studied computer science. Quinn met Christian at the National Conference for Organized Resistance, an anarchist event in Washington, D.C., and Christian convinced him to come to the freegan bike workshop.

Quinn spent six weeks building his own bike from scratch, starting from just the triangle in the center of the frame. Quinn found this manual work far more rewarding than programming: "It was the first time I felt like I could do whatever I wanted without spending six years training for it." Wendy, who along with Quinn was one of the workshop's "bottom-liners" in 2009, expressed a similar sense of exhilaration about her first experience with bike repair: "I realized that I could build and create things—figure out how to do stuff, solve problems, use tools."

The two also realized that they could share those skills with others. One night, a man came down the stairs into the basement and asked, "Hey, can I buy a bike?" to which Jason replied, "No, but I'll show you how to build one." For Wendy, Jason, and Quinn, focusing on their own personal development would have been impossible even had they wanted to: on the nights I spent at 123, the space was overrun with local children who came to socialize, play, and—at least sometimes—learn about bikes. Quinn spoke with pride about how the bike workshop provided an egalitarian and unpoliced space for neighborhood youth:

> Part of the space was this idea of nonhierarchy and anti-oppression, horizontality. There weren't teachers and students permanently. If you knew how to do anything, you became a teacher of that skill. So if a kid learned something, they were given a status upgrade, and they could start teaching. It was decentralized. People were getting things done, but not from a center.

Visitors to the bike workshop could work for five minutes or six hours, and could complete a bike from scratch in a few weeks or leave it half-completed for months (which helped explain why the space was so cluttered).

When I reinterviewed Quinn in 2012, he had taken a job as a teacher at a public school, an environment he saw as far less conducive to effective pedagogy than the bike workshop: "Working with your hands is, it's like, so critical to being a human being. Being able to manipulate your environment and physical things—kids are not taught that at school. If they are, it's an elective thought to be a lesser subject." I cannot evaluate whether attendees who used the bike workshop left with these freegan values or just newly built or repaired bikes. Nevertheless, it was clear that a significant number of people of color from the surrounding community felt comfortable coming to the bike workshop, even though nearly all the regular mechanics were white.

Predictably, waste was instrumental in the workshop's functioning. Although the bike workshop did pay rent, freegan activists recovered most of their parts and tools from dumpsters and abandoned bikes in the street. As Wendy explained, the freegan approach meant that, compared with other community bike workshops in the city, they were "way less organized—and way cheaper." The availability of ex-commodities also meant that Quinn and Wendy could

"*Some see a mess, others see a new bike*": ex-commodified, scavenged, and salvaged parts allowed the freegan bike workshop to operate on a shoestring. Photograph by Alex Barnard.

decommodify some time that would otherwise have been sold on the labor market and put it toward helping others. At the same time, by using once-discarded bike parts rather than store-bought ones, freegans had to rely on their own knowledge and one another to determine if they were still usable. On one trash tour, we encountered a few bicycle rims in a trash can. Jason pulled one out and spun it between his hands, as each of us speculated as to whether the wheel was salvageable. The bikes that came out the other end of the bike workshop were representative of how resources deemed valueless under capitalism could provide sustainable transportation for years.

Although freegans were far from being able to provide for all their material needs through skills like bike repair or sewing, small-scale prefigurative experiments like the bike workshop suggested that they *could* do so in a way that was egalitarian, nonhierarchical, and ecologically sound. While these activities may not look "political" by a conventional definition, their broader implications should not be missed. After all, as Emily Sullivan writes in her study of well-educated youth who choose to work as manual laborers, "It is difficult to run a capitalist economy if people believe they are naturally equipped with all of the tools necessary for their own fulfilling survival."[39]

Festivals of Use Value and the Gift Economy

Published accounts from first-time dumpster divers often enthusiastically describe the value of the goods they find in terms of their price—that is to say, their *exchange* value.[40] In these narratives, the hauls from dumpster dives are tabulated like the takings from a shopping spree at an everything-must-go closeout sale. Yet even though freegans often found items with price tags attached, I could not find a single instance in my field notes where they actually talked about value in these terms. In fact, freegans actively refused to think of these items through the market language of price. Instead, they focused on objects' use value, or their capacity to meet human needs. As Maximus, the dumpster diver from Boston, summarized: "The capitalist system we live in insists that for something to have value, it needs to be sellable. We believe that in order for something to have value, it need not be sellable, only usable."

Often, freegans' attempts to rethink the value of commodities started with small, isolated attempts to conserve resources. Janet, for example, talked about rescuing paper from the recycling bins at her school and using junk mail envelopes to write her lesson plans. At meetings where we discussed the events for the upcoming month, Janet brought the pages of old wall calendars that she had retrieved and laboriously renumbered to correspond to the correct month. For Janet, avoiding waste required thinking in terms of goods' material condition and serviceability rather than their aesthetic qualities (or, in the calendar's case, the year for which it was actually intended). As she told the attendees at one session of freeganism 101, displaying a woven pink glove and a synthetic black one:

> *I have mismatched gloves myself. These are really good gloves, good for this weather. You know, they're really warm. I think people find it odd if your gloves don't match, but why? What I do is I find one— you can find a glove almost every day if you look for it—and you pick up a glove and then you wash it, it becomes just part of your wardrobe. I carry a bunch around.*

Enthusiasm for finding less-than-obvious ways to recover use value was something Janet shared with many others in the group. Leia, for her part, told me how she delighted in recovering single earrings that women had dropped or discarded after losing their match: "I love finding use in things and value in things that other people think of as garbage."

Yet for freegans, use value could not be defined solely in individual terms. There was no way Janet could eat in any reasonable time period the dozen jars of $4.99 vegan mayonnaise she found on one expedition, so she distributed them among people who could. Such actions were small steps toward implementing a "gift economy," an economic vision in which goods are neither sold nor bartered but shared freely.[41] As Adam saw it, "Capitalism measures success not in terms of whether people's needs are met. They measure it in terms of profit. As such, sharing is a frontal assault in a society based on greed."

At one gathering in Grand Central Station, Evie opened her bag and pulled out some dumpstered sunflower-seed crackers and past-date hummus her parents had given her ("They figured, 'It's expired, but Evie eats garbage'"). Zaac added some Odwalla bars, and Quinn contributed several bottles of fancy pomegranate juice. Adam simply walked around the nearby garbage bins, pulled out takeout containers with leftover food, and brought them to the table. As any newcomer no doubt found, freegans will quite literally shove prefigurative politics on them in the form of freely gifted food. The quasi-ritualistic sharing of recent dumpstered finds with which nearly all freegan meetings began also has a practical function. Vegan sources of protein like tofu, dried goods such as pasta, and olive oil are not as abundant as vegetables or baked goods and constitute some of freegans' infrequent food purchases. When freegans do find them, though, they typically find them in bulk and distribute them at meetings.

Freegans occasionally took their attempts to enact a gift economy onto a more public stage. Once a year, freegan.info organized a "Dorm Dive" on the Lower East Side to gather items discarded by NYU students leaving for the summer. In 2012 I arrived early, but Marion was already there, barely visible over the lip of a huge open-top dumpster parked by the side of the street. The dumpster's rim was lined with items that she didn't need, but figured someone else might: a half-eaten jar of peanut butter, a single leather boot, and some notebooks. I climbed in. Aside from bedding, there was a smorgasbord of half-empty cereal boxes, a huge number of mesh laundry bags, cardboard boxes, loose paper, and appliances. I found some coffee filters: "Want this?" I asked.

Marion replied, "I'm waiting to see if we can find the coffeemaker that goes with it. I think I saw it in there."

Another diver, a younger white man wearing a bike messenger hat and with large plugs in his ears, then joined us. He saw the cell phone on the edge and said to me excitedly, "Check this out."

I replied, "It's probably dead."

"No, man, it just needs a charger. Let me know if you see one," he responded.

As the two of us worked, we called out items that might be of interest: "There are all kinds of spices over here!" he exclaimed, and "I could totally use this canteen!" before adding, "I love this time of year." Down the street, two young women were going through black bags piled on the curb. "Anyone have a hamster?" one asked as she pulled out some pet food. She added after an audible sigh, "It looks like a lot of people just put all the stuff they didn't want in their laundry hampers and chucked them out. It's ridiculous. There's a thrift store two blocks from here."

The NYU Dorm Dive was a festival of use value. No one came with a particular idea of what he or she actually needed, except for one man who said he was hoping to find a pen. Instead, the focus was on retrieving wasted goods and envisioning how they might be useful to someone. The event had a carnivalesque air as we playfully imagined how torn posters could be taped together into works of art or half-eaten food could be turned into delicious meals. While it's certainly possible that someone would want to exchange or resell the things we found, I didn't get the impression that anyone was intending to do so: instead, as the "anyone have a hamster?" query indicated, the focus was on connecting use values to users. Such connections didn't always happen immediately. When I talked to Janet the next week, she said that she had come home from the dorm dive with far too many towels. "I don't really have any use for them," she explained. "But they're more useful with me than in the trash. I hate to think that they were all produced just one year ago, and they've already been thrown out." No doubt she would be redistributing them at freegan events for months to come.

The ultimate festival of use value, however, was the Really Really Free Market, a monthly event that freegan.info helped organize alongside other New York anarchist groups like the In Our Hearts collective. Really really free markets (RRFMs) emerged in the early 2000s in cities across the United States as antiglobalization movement activists began applying their models of consensus-based organizing and mutual aid to more routine aspects of social life. As the New York website describes it, "The Really Really Free Market is a bazaar & celebration, where capitalist notions of interaction are discarded. No Money. No Barter. No Trade. Try a new economic model: sharing!"[42]

During the summers, RRFMs were outside in lower Manhattan; in the winter, inside left-wing churches. Before the events, an eclectic group would turn up, from punks with dyed Mohawks and studded jackets carrying excess finds from recent dives to white-haired church patrons with unneeded apartment clutter. At one RRFM in winter 2008, there were tables heaped with books, appliances, and clothing. There were also services on offer: free advice, basic dental work, tarot card readings, portraits, and guitar lessons. Madeline sat behind two boxes labeled "singles"—right- and left-handed gloves without a partner—while her partner, Michael, gave lessons in darning socks. Janet, Cindy, and Evie were in the back kitchen, preparing a spread of dumpstered fruit, iced tea, salad, bread and hummus, and pasta. As one bearded punk exclaimed when he approached freegan.info's table, "I feel as lost here as I do in the supermarket. There's just too much selection!"

RRFMs facilitated a minimal-purchasing lifestyle for freegans and other activists who took part in them by circulating ex-commodities to those who needed them. Jason explained how the RRFM brought a gift economy into being:

> It's just the idea of utilizing things that aren't for sale. Finding things that have been discarded and collecting them together and sharing them, and creating networks not just for yourself but around that— sharing.... There really is just all this free stuff, and why can't we have access to it? We can use it to better ourselves. It allows people that aren't rich to have this community wealth.

With participants in a wide range of collectives and movements gathered in the same place at the same time, RRFMs also disseminated information about New York's anarchist scene. But the events drew a much wider audience, whether measured in terms of race, age, or gender. While many participants may not have been inspired by an anticapitalist ideology, they were nonetheless at an event that subverted capitalism's insistence that commodities should be exchanged for money, not shared based on need.

We live in an era where the market is expanding to new reaches of social life, and things that have historically *not* been commodified, such as the "ecosystem services" provided by wetlands that purify water or forests that sequester carbon, now have exchange value attached to them.[43] Even in the face of the neoliberal onslaught, though, the spaces between the moments in our lives where money changes hands are filled with moments and activities we would never think to trade on a market. As one freegan pamphlet pointed out, "We freely offer rides in our vehicles when family members need to go someplace; we don't charge for washing dishes after a meal; and we counsel grieving friends without sending a bill."[44]

What freegans did through activities like RRFMs and Dorm Dives was expand this already existing gift economy to arenas of economic life that have long since been brought under the market. Most of us are so accustomed to the idea of buying food that we forget that for most of human history food has *not* been a commodity. The norm has been for households or small communities to gather or produce food for their own consumption, not buy it. Even as capitalism spread in eighteenth-century England, people still saw food as something that had to be protected from the market and rioted when they were forced to buy bread at market prices.[45] With RRFMs and other festivals of use value, freegans attempted to return to a natural moral economy in which excess goods and unmet needs could be joined together, free from the mediation of money.

Back to Nature in NYC?

This chapter has gone beyond freegan.info's polemics to the group's attempts to construct a "new society in the shell of the old," as Adam so often said. As should be clear, freeganism was not poised to supplant urban capitalism. Prefigurative politics had its limits, not least of which being that the new society was being built with the cast-offs of the old one. Discourse about "reskilling" aside, freegans lacked the time, resources, and skills to actually produce the goods they shared with one another. It was only by taking advantage of the failure of the waste fetish to keep ex-commodities fully hidden that they could develop new ways to distribute use value.

Together, these practices were an experimental play on "nature" and the values surrounding it. In Western countries, we are prone to think of nature as something "primordial, autonomous, and mechanistic," an immutable thing that exists "out there."[46] By this definition waste is eminently natural (producing one form of waste is a biological certainty for anyone who is alive, after all).[47] But under neoliberal capitalism, waste has been naturalized to an even greater extent. It's not just that creating waste seems so normal—who thinks twice about throwing out a candy wrapper?—that it fades into the background of our lives. It's also that when we are confronted with waste that cannot be blamed on consumers or the government, we assume it's just a natural cost of doing business. During my research, I've been assured—assured, mind you—that supermarkets *absolutely* would not waste anything unless they really had to. This is, of course, the fetish of waste at work: the deeply internalized notion that markets are optimally efficient, so that if they do produce waste, it is either unavoidable and therefore natural *or* a product of *unnatural* distortions introduced by the state or civil society.

Yet, as environmental sociologists show, our ideas of what constitutes nature, and even our beliefs as to whether there is even such a thing as nature at all, depend on culture and context.[48] What freegans expose is a variation on this point: that waste is not an inherent, natural quality of certain objects but a product of the particular social arrangements surrounding those objects.[49] Thus far, I've presented a fairly stark division between a capitalistic valuation of things based on exchange value and a freegan valuation of things based on use value. These former schema lead to otherwise serviceable commodities being discarded as waste and the latter to those very same objects, suddenly, ceasing to seem like waste at all. Under capitalism, being designated as "waste" is intended to mark the termination of the "social lives of things."[50] It is not a natural death, however. As freegans show, through the labor that goes into sewing skill-shares, bike repair workshops, or really really free markets, the use value of ex-commodities can be recovered and recirculated.

The logical extension of the idea that waste is not natural is that, under different social arrangements, there might not be so much waste. But freeganism, perhaps inadvertently, demonstrated that reducing waste is more complicated. For one thing, ex-commodification already creates value in the form of profits along the commodity chain. But it also creates other kinds of value that most of us would be reticent to relinquish. Convenience, abundance, choice, and hygiene are all seemingly positive elements of our food system, yet also dependent on ex-commodification through constant culling, overordering by stores, stringent aesthetic standards, use-by dates based on worst-case scenarios, and long supply chains. We could, of course, rearrange our food system and decide that we care more about carbon emissions than having asparagus flown in from Peru during the winter; more about how potatoes taste than their shape and appearance; more about cutting down on excess than on having every imaginable flavor of bagel available to us at the bakery's closing time. But it's more complicated than just saying that we need to "value" our food more.

Even as freegans deconstructed the naturalness of waste, they were reconstructing nature in another way. Commenting on his own shifting ideas of nature, Zaac observed, "We're not just reusing nature but thinking about how we define it. We're tearing the whole idea of nature apart and putting it back together in a way that has more validity." On wild food foraging tours or in their work in community gardens, freegans tapped into the pockets of nature wedged between skyscrapers and concrete. But they also brought their lives into line with their vision of nature in less overt ways, every time they shared a find from a windfall urban foraging expedition, repaired a pair of pants rather than bought new ones, or ate an over-the-hill apple most of us would throw out. Ironically, the same ex-commodities served as proofs of the unnaturalness of capitalism's waste and, once repurposed, as symbols of freegans' more natural lifestyles.

Freegans would probably not deny that their vision for a future utopia, as enacted through everyday practices of recovering, revaluing, and sharing objects, was unsophisticated—in fact, they might very well embrace the label. Most freegans would likely roll their eyes at Adam's reiterated insistence that humans should consume only what they're "supposed to," which, in his eyes, included "food, food, water, food, maybe some medicinal plants, and food." But as Leia once remarked during a freegan feast held amid the 2008 financial crisis:

> *I heard people on CNN talking about how complicated banking systems are, how the public can never understand what policies we need. But economies shouldn't be that way. Economies should be something that everybody involved can have direct understanding of and connection to. If it's too complicated, that means there's something wrong.*

The prefigurative politics of freeganism hinged on the idea that if only we got the basic values right, and implemented them in our daily lives, the rest would fall into place. The remainder of this book looks at the limits of that strategy.

The Ultimate Boycott?

Marion was one of only two informants I interviewed who asked that I use a pseudonym for her. Unlike many of freegan.info's spokespeople, she kept a low profile, even as she gradually accumulated acute observations of freegan.info. Some elements of Marion's story sound familiar. She told me that she was "well educated" and "grew up in suburban comfort and affluence." Her family life gave her "full training in shopping skills—I was like people who study the Talmud for years and walk out of the room having never seen the light of day, except with the mall." She said that she had been involved with a handful of environmental and animal welfare causes, but insisted that they were "nothing particularly radical."

In stark contrast to most of my other interviewees, Marion avowed that she was "diving for her life"—that is, out of necessity. A few years ago, in a state of growing deprivation, the origins of which she would not explain, she began to recover wasted goods:

> I just noticed that when I went to throw things away [in my apartment building], there were perfectly usable items peeking over the top of the garbage. I don't know. It might have started when I was throwing away recyclables and one was right next to the other, and the thought crossed my mind that there were people who collected recyclable bottles to collect the deposit, and I was like, "This is an effortless resource, right here."

She first heard about freeganism, she said, when a "free rag newspaper" delivered to her building put a picture of Adam on the cover, describing "crazy people who eat out of the trash." In justifying her decision to attend a first trash tour, she elaborated, "During wars, people have to align themselves with things in order to preserve themselves that under ordinary circumstances they would have nothing to do with. It [freeganism] was like that for me."

Politics occasionally crept into our conversations, but Marion was not one to go out of her way to push her beliefs on others. When I asked her to define freeganism, she spoke only of practice, not ideology: "I consider myself one [a freegan] because I do these activities on my own, I gather the best part of my food, I'm pretty loose and flexible in terms of my fearlessness in salvaging. I'm not insane, but I'll go outside the box, let's say." Motivations aside, Marion was a skilled forager and an invaluable part of any "trash trail blaze" in an unfamiliar neighborhood. She often performed a great deal of "advance work" before tours by going to stores and checking which items would soon expire. "It's better to reduce it to a science, rather than leaving it up to chance," she told me.

Unlike some other freegans, though, she was remarkably candid about the limitations of dumpster diving. As to hygiene, she expounded:

> I've always been fairly adventurous in terms of taking things out of a bag of slime and eventually eating it. This has not always been good: I want to emphasize that. Despite what everyone tells you that "No problem will ever arise from this," that's not true.... Every once in a while, it's like, "Maybe there's some correlation between my [poor] health and the fact that I eat garbage all the time."

Dumpster diving was a year-round activity, she noted, but "in the summer it's complicated, because you do have to make a judgment about what's fermented already." While eating from the trash might have been the "least heinous" of her options, then, it was still pretty heinous.

Marion brought a critical eye not just to the practices of freeganism but to the internal dynamics of freegan.info. When I asked her, "Is there something everyone in freegan.info shares?" she replied, "I doubt it." She went on to characterize what she perceived as the two main currents within the organization: those who were "willing to live in misery and filth because they think it enhances or promotes their ability to change the world" and those who "have not totally lost their minds and are not going to do that 'for the cause.'" The latter, exemplified by Janet or Madeline, were individuals with "total safety nets" who were unwilling to cut their ties with capitalism and thus "overlapped into hypocrisy." Both groups, she noted, were overwhelmingly white and came from affluence. For those with more humble backgrounds, "This [dumpster diving] is just totally obscene, revolting, [and] unacceptable."

I asked her if she thought that the group had an impact during her five years of observations, and she laughed: "In the media group, they think they're spinning this in the political cause sense." But, she added, "when people see a story about us, I think people come away thinking, 'I just saw people eating garbage.' You can't put a political message to that visual." She did credit the media for inspiring more and more people to come up to her during her dives and ask her if she's a freegan. "They just think it means dumpster diving, though," she added.

There was one change she could point to that was connected to freegan.info's actions, however. By 2012 stores were taking steps to guard their garbage. As she observed:

> I've seen changes in specific stores, and some of these changes I attribute directly to freegan.info bringing tons of new people. The D'Agostino [in Murray Hill] used to be pretty much one-stop shopping. I would go there with a couple of people, and they would look out the windows and see what we were doing. I remember a specific incident where it was a freegan trash tour, and the manager just flipped out. He came out and he was ranting and raving about pouring bleach on the food—and that didn't actually happen because of course he'd have a severe liability problem there—but shortly thereafter, they refused to put it out at all.

The response, to her, was not particularly surprising: "If you're the owner, how do you explain that people are going through the trash and getting five hundred pounds of food while customers are still coming in and out of the store?" For her, "This, by definition, needs to be an activity in which one does not bring much attention to what one is doing."

Marion painted a darker portrait of freegan.info's activities and participants than I would. Nonetheless, she raised nearly all the issues with which the remainder of this book deals: the limits and contradictions of freegans' politics of waste (this chapter) and the backlash it provoked (the next). Within the space of two hours, she had articulated some of the weaknesses of prefigurative politics, the racial and class barriers to freeganism, and the response that freegan.info drew. In effect, she sketched a framework for how ex-commodities were reclaimed and the fetish of waste reimposed, which helps account for the decline that I observed after 2009 in freeganism as an organized force in New York City.

The Limits of "Dropping Out"

This section takes up where chapter 2 left off: with the process of becoming freegan. The *Why Freegan?* pamphlet defined freegans as people engaged in a "total boycott" of capitalism, and the same rhetoric about "dropping out" circulated within freegan.info. When I spoke with Jason in 2009, a few months into his process of becoming freegan, he told me:

> *I don't buy any of the stuff I used to buy. I make half of what I used to. I don't go to cool parties. I've definitely changed my consciousness in terms of what my life is about and where I'm headed. I don't envision myself doing any of the things I used to think I would. I actually see myself trying to earn* less *money.*

Jason told me this inside his apartment in Brooklyn, a locale that offered few hints of his hardline politics. Instead, a pile of Coors Light beer cans, guitars and amplifiers, and a pile of GRE study guides suggested that Jason and his two nonfreegan roommates were just three among the thousands of young professionals trying to make it in the city.

But Jason was insistent: "If you take it [freeganism] far enough, it's a critique of everything. It's totally revolutionary." And Jason *did* take it farther. I caught up with him in the winter in 2012. He told me that his work in the freegan.info bike workshop led him to the In Our Hearts collective, an explicitly anarchist group, and then Surrealestate, a warehouse in Brooklyn that freegan.info participants converted into a communal living space for nearly fifty activists and artists. His goal, he told me, was to "transform every aspect of my life at every level, so I can totally eliminate money, be outside of the system, [and] create something else." But to what extent was this actually possible?

Without a doubt, many freegans got most of their food without purchasing it. Madeline told me that she acquired 95 percent of what she ate through scavenging, gardening, and foraging, and bought only cooking oil. Wendy said that she purchased just flaxseed and nutritional yeast, which she saw as the "bare necessities" of a vegan diet, and dumpster dived the rest. At one freeganism 101 in an atrium at Columbia University, a participant asked Janet, "Is it possible to get *all* your food from the garbage?" to which she replied, "I don't get *all* of my food from the garbage, but I know I'm able to. Every once and a while, I'll buy soy milk or something like that, and then the freegan gods will punish me and the next time I'm out, I'll find a whole crate of it."

Others, like Adam and Jonathan, insisted that they never bought food under any circumstances.

But the possibilities for meeting individual needs through ex-commodities did not stop just outside the grocery store. Between individual consumers and retailers, America produces 68 pounds of textile waste per person per year, encouraged by constant changes in fashion and sweatshop production that makes replacing clothes cheaper than repairing or maintaining them.[1] Estimates suggest that 25 percent of books that get printed go unsold and are either ex-commodified or pulped.[2] Three *billion* magazines are sent yearly directly from retailers to the landfill without ever being read.[3] The freegan website presents a (slightly dated) partial inventory of what can be found in the trash outside retailers:

> *Freegans are able to obtain food, beverages, books, toiletries, magazines, comic books, newspapers, videos, kitchenware, appliances, music (CDs, cassettes, records, etc.), carpets, musical instruments, clothing, rollerblades, scooters, furniture, vitamins, electronics, animal care products, games, toys, bicycles, artwork, and just about any other type of consumer good.*[4]

Of course, the most common finds were relatively cheap, nondurable goods, such as the plastic costume pieces freegans regularly retrieved outside Party City or the Tupperware at the Container Store. But, on one storied occasion, we found a working iPod; I once dumpster dived two six packs of beer.

Housing, on the other hand, was more challenging. On paper, freegans had a clear method for acquiring housing without purchasing (or renting) commodified space: squatting. Yet there were very real barriers to squatting in New York City. Although the city had a vibrant squatters' movement in the 1980s, under the Giuliani administration the city adopted a "stern ... anti-squatter policy" that contrasts sharply with the relative leniency toward squatters in European cities like Barcelona or Berlin.[5] While, according to David Graeber, activists founded an "archipelago" of squatted spaces in New York in the wake of the antiglobalization movement's mass demonstrations,[6] they were nowhere to be found by the time my research started.

Despite the inauspicious conditions, some freegans did experiment with occupying unused property in New York. Christian told me that he managed to go rent-free for a few months by sneaking into apartment building utility rooms. But when he attempted to create a more permanent squat by opening up an abandoned building with bolt cutters, he was caught and spent the night in jail for trespassing. Sasha, for his part, told me that he squatted "now and again," but admitted that "the last squat I was in was raided and all our stuff got thrown out."

Some freegans were more successful in finding free space. I first met Jonathan when another researcher told me that I needed to meet a "really hardcore freegan" who was squatting on the Lower East Side. She buzzed me into a high-end, well-maintained building. As we walked up a few floors, she explained that the current residents had gained access to the building from someone they met at Occupy Wall Street, who opened up his apartment to dozens of activists when the movement's encampment was shut down. The activist left, but Jonathan and two of his friends stayed—albeit without the rent payments. When I walked in, Jonathan gave me a quick tour: the three-bedroom apartment had fresh paint, hardwood floors, stainless steel appliances ("Check it out: washer and dryer!"), and an array of dumpstered furniture.

Because they had managed to stay in the apartment for a month and established residency, the trio were sure that the process to remove them would be long and drawn out. Settling in, they had even started to pay for electricity and water. One of Jonathan's roommates was an ex-convict who had come to New York from San Diego to be part of Occupy. He proudly told me: "Everyone is always talking about

"Unsafe and unstable": a New York squatter speaks with police officers (including a SWAT team and hostage negotiator) sent to evict him from an abandoned, unused building. Photograph courtesy of Jonathan Friedman.

'eating the rich.' We're the ones actually doing it—taking money from the corporation that owns this building." Nevertheless, "the rich" were not willing to stand idly by and be eaten: the trio had received an eviction notice and gone to civil court the week before, and they were now slated to be kicked out by the end of June.

When I spoke to Jonathan later that year, he had moved on to a more remote abandoned house. The project of making the structure habitable, Jonathan noted, was taking most of his time: "Squatting isn't just living in a place where you don't pay rent. Squatting is a project in itself. It's not for someone who has a job and just wants to come here and sleep and go back to work." He envisioned the building becoming a community center with a library, tool lending services, free event space, and "free store" of dumpstered goods. But the "community" itself was skeptical about his project: one neighbor, he told me, had come over and screamed, "I've worked my entire life to buy a house, and you're just living in one for free. It's immoral." It is true that amid the economic crisis, more low-income people around the United States, supported by activist organizations, are squatting in foreclosed homes.[7] But when I asked Jonathan if the movement was taking off in New York, he said, in a word, no.

Jonathan's story, in effect, was the exception that proved the rule. As Quinn summarized, "Squatting in New York is unsafe and unstable." To forge a better alternative, in 2008 Quinn, Wendy, and several others founded "Surrealestate" in a postindustrial neighborhood of Brooklyn. With over fifty occupants, Surrealestate, which hosted the freegan.info office downstairs, operated in a manner consistent with key elements of freeganism. Quinn reported that decisions about the use of the space were made based on consensus, most of the food eaten there was dumpstered, and tenants were expected to volunteer several hours a week to activist projects.

Yet the housing project was very unfreegan in at least one sense: renting a communal loft in Surrealestate, according to Quinn, cost between three hundred and four hundred dollars a month. As he divulged, "Anarchist spaces are either bankrolled by someone or they have to take a more capitalist approach." Lacking a benefactor, Surrealestate had no choice but to charge rent and eject delinquent tenants. Quinn and others had to make significant compromises to collect each month's rent, turning parties initially intended as fund-raisers for activist groups into benefits for Surrealestate itself, for example. The space struggled with repeated attempted evictions from the city. More than that, though, the project suffered from an inability to find enough people seriously practicing its communal ideals. As Jason, who lived a year in Surrealestate, told me:

> Sure, there was FNB, bike-building, every kind of building going on, there was just a lot of general ferment, people having conversations.

But at the same time as it was a bunch of anarchists, it was also a bunch of young kids who didn't know what they thought about anything yet, and were just poor and wanted to do something. And they might have never encountered anything coming close to a radical political point of view before—ever. And some of them left without ever knowing what that means.

When Marion referenced the "misery and filth" of some freegans, she was definitely referring to Surrealestate, where a mixture of conflict, free riding, and pests led to steadily deteriorating living conditions.

Attempting to get more like-minded people to join him, Quinn once advertised over the freegan e-mail list that he was renting out "freegan" rooms. Adam was irate. To him, a place that required rent could not call itself "freegan," and he continued to "block" any freegan .info events from taking place there.[8] The debate became even more divisive when Adam declared that Surrealestate was a form of first-wave gentrification. Based on my own observations, Adam had a point: despite the founders' best efforts, most of the residents of Surrealestate were white and educated, in a neighborhood traditionally populated by working-class African Americans. Jason and Quinn moved out in 2011, and Wendy told me later that year that Surrealestate could no longer call itself an "activist"—much less "freegan"—space.

As a result, even though in Quinn's words "true freegans don't pay rent," the reality was that nearly all of them did. Some had eliminated rent payments, but only by buying a home outright, as Madeline and Janet had. In December 2011 I attended a "freegan feast" in Madeline's apartment in Brooklyn, which she bought shortly after quitting her job. Her neighborhood was modest, but her building had a doorman and her apartment a spacious living room, filled with slightly tattered but still high-quality couches, chairs, and cabinets. She avowed, "I got a lot of the furniture right off the street," but divulged that she bought the bookshelf off Craigslist, before quickly injecting that "someone was going to get rid of it, and I'm finding a use for it." She also pointed to the trees, lights, and poinsettia flowers she used as holiday decorations and told me that she found all of them in the garbage. Our discussion about which items were and were not purchased, though, never came around to the more obvious incongruity: that we were holding a freegan event in a bought-and-paid-for apartment.

This narrative of freegans' struggles to find space highlights a broader point. Just because something is being ex-commodified doesn't mean people have access to it. Despite a large homeless population and a near universally acknowledged lack of affordable housing, New York City in 2008 had over sixty thousand vacant rental units.[9] Some of these units, according to one report, were deliberately being withheld from the market to raise prices, particularly in gentrifying neighborhoods where speculators anticipated that rents would soon rise.[10] Insofar as they *could* be used by someone but for financial reasons *weren't*, these spaces were ex-commodities. Yet they were *not* ex-commodified in the same way as food in a dumpster in one important respect: while the latter's owners have relinquished any future claim to it, the former saw ex-commodification as only temporary, until their property could be *re*-commodified and turned once more into profit.

Working through Contradictions

In keeping with a totalizing view of freeganism as "dropping out" of capitalism, the freegan.info website was replete with statements about the destructiveness of wage labor and conventional employment. Indeed, the freegan.info home page insisted that *all* workers, not just employers, owners, or managers, are morally accountable for the abuses of a capitalist system.[11] At least in its idealized form, freeganism provided an escape route from these nets of culpability, because, through recovering waste, "freegans are able to greatly reduce or altogether eliminate the need to constantly be employed."[12] As Sasha told me:

> *For an activist, for someone who is working against capital, the question, "What do you do for money," becomes a really funny thing. What do I do for money? As in what do I do to get money? Or what do I do to help the inflationary state bank get money out of my dollars? The answer is "nothing." I don't want to do anything for money, I don't like money. And when you don't believe in the capitalist system it's nearly impossible to get a job.*

For Sasha, in an economy founded on the constant ramping up of production and consumption, idleness was a form of resistance. It prefigured a society with a paucity of physical goods but an abundance of leisure.

Yet my research found that voluntary unemployment was at best a transitory phase that eventually ran up against the hard realities of urban life. Even Sasha confessed, "It's way too idealistic to expect that you will never need money so long as you have to pay rent," and as a consequence, despite a stint of unemployment in the summer of 2008, work remained for him an "unpleasant reality." Similarly, Jason avowed, "Money is the fuel for global destruction, so any job for money *is* the problem," but he continued to work as a documentary film editor. He expressed his complex sentiments toward his situation at one panel discussion on freeganism, noting, "It depends on what kind of work people are doing. Some things are actively harmful, actually destroying the planet. Even investing in the stock market, you're buying into the slipping away of everything in the world." Yet, he continued, "we can't get money out of our lives yet, and it'd actually be pretty foolish to try to do that."

In some cases, freegan.info activists found paid employment that they saw as consistent with freegan objectives. Jonathan, for example, made ends meet through freelance design for activist newsletters, while Sasha got a job at a left-wing environmental press. Janet and Evie were unabashed about their work as a teacher at a public high school and speech pathologist at a public hospital, respectively. Others, however, coped with obvious tension. As Cindy confided:

> For three days a week, I teach as an environmental arts instructor in after-school programs. It's work I would be doing whether or not I'm being paid for it. But I also do two days a week of product packaging design. That's an absurd contradiction. I do periods of wage-slavery type stuff, so the rest of the time I can do something else.

However they justified it, the key takeaway was that nearly everyone in freegan.info was engaging in paid labor.

So were *any* freegans living up to the rhetoric about a complete withdrawal from capitalism? Certainly, Adam appeared to come close, insofar as he spent very little, never bought food or clothes, and was unemployed. But even Adam readily admitted that his lifestyle was not an autonomous one: he depended on external support from his parents, who paid the rent for the freegan office where he slept and covered his medical bills.

Some, however, seemed to come closer to the "total boycott." When I spoke to Gio, a self-described "pacifist Christian anarchist freegan," he was trading housework for a tiny room on the Upper West Side. I asked him if he bought anything, and he thought for the better part of a minute before replying, "not really." What limited funds Gio did spend he got from busking on the subways, which, as he explained, was "not what some people pejoratively refer to as 'wage slavery'" because "I'm not selling my time or even my energy and my effort. It's just, 'I'm here, I'm here freely, but if someone wants to contribute to my livelihood, they can put it in my little jar.'" Instead of doing his part to raise America's GDP, Gio spent much of his time volunteering at Word Up, a community bookstore.

After an hour of interviewing, I began to think that I had at last found someone who fit the freegan archetype. When I asked him whether he had time to keep talking, though, he did something I did not expect: he took an iPhone out of his pocket to check the clock. "I guess we all have contradictions," I remarked, to which he quickly responded, "Yes, thank you. That's what I've always been trying to say. Yes, I own an iPhone." He noted that he got the phone used and that his sister was paying the phone bill, but made no attempt to convince me that this changed the fundamental disjuncture between values and practice. As our interview came to a close, Gio disclosed that his barter-for-space living arrangement was not working out, and so he needed to find a regular job to pay his share of the rent for the communal apartment he was moving into.

In short, freegan.info was riddled with inconsistencies: its manifestos abounded with commitments to escaping from capitalism, but all its participants lived in ways that were deeply imbricated with the capitalist system. This is not to deny the ingenuity that freegans deployed every day to limit their participation in the mainstream economy. I saw this creativity when the group came together to research herbal remedies for Tate's pink eye, or through Janet's frequent distributions of toilet paper and shampoo thrown out by hotels. Nevertheless, many freegans would likely empathize with Evie, who told me, "I'm freegan in a lot of little things in my life, but at the end of the day, I have a job and a home so I'm paying taxes and funding a couple of enormous wars and pretty much everything that goes bad in the world." Such a finding is clearly a disappointment to many reporters. One journalism student describes the anticlimactic realization that, during her "search for the freegan ideal," freegans "had for the most part gone to school, had jobs, paid rent," all of which were clear signs of hypocrisy.[13]

There are, of course, more nuanced points to be made. One, already mentioned, is that just because under capitalism everything gets "wasted" doesn't mean that freegans can find everything they need in a dumpster. Food is, in some ways, unique in its perishability. Excess food cannot just be hoarded but must be disposed of somehow. The more distant the commodity is from food, though, the fuzzier the notion of "ex-commodity" gets. Certainly, other low-price commodities, from clothes to party supplies, get pitched out with regularity. But while high-value goods like cars may be ex-commodified in the sense of going unused, though, their owners are nonetheless reluctant to part with them.

And there *are* some things that don't get thrown out at all. According to the Environmental Protection Agency, "A great deal of what is labeled as 'e-waste' is actually not waste at all; rather, it is whole electronic equipment or parts that are readily marketable for reuse or can be recycled for materials recovery."[14] Only a tiny proportion of the 125 million cell phones discarded per year are recycled.[15] Yet no one has ever found a cell phone activation plan in the garbage, even though all the freegans, other than Cindy and Adam, had phones. Similarly, we could talk about the wastefulness of much medical spending, but that doesn't mean we can find surplus CAT scans in the trash can.

Freegans, of course, are not oblivious to these contradictions. Indeed, my second point is that there is an openly acknowledged tension between the project of building *alternatives* to capitalism and the simultaneous desire to *challenge* capitalism. As numerous interviewees observed, if they were single-mindedly concerned with not participating in capitalism, they would move to an autarkic rural commune. Freegans justified what some saw as hypocrisy by claiming that they were more concerned with collective efficacy than individual lifestyle perfection. This was a point consistent with the motivations that drove them to become freegans in the first place. "I'm not attached to being perfect, I'm about changing in a good direction rather than being perfect," one explained. Leia was particularly dismissive of a fixation on minimizing individual carbon footprints or avoiding making any purchases at all at the expense of political action: "It's selfish to say 'Fuck everybody, I just want to live in a cave.' There's so much work that needs to be done in this world."

There *are* people in modern America, like Daniel Suelo, described in *The Man Who Quit Money*, who really *do* live in caves and really *don't* spend anything.[16] But while these people offer a model from which freegans draw inspiration and feel solidarity, the reality is that most freegans are more concerned with having an impact than living blameless lives. As Keith McHenry told me, in all his travels, "Honestly, I've only met ten to fifteen people total—anywhere—who consciously never buy anything and see themselves as freegans."

Isolation and Alienation

Since the 1960s, building "community" in the face of perceived cultural atomization and fragmentation has become a core part of radical politics in the United States.[17] For their part, freegans explained that the "community" that came from routine interactions with other freegans was necessary for keeping to the strictures of their lifestyles. "If you're not part of a community, you might use mass transit or grow your own food, but it's so ingrained in our society to buy things that it takes a lot of retraining of your brain to actually consider whether or not you need to," explained Cindy. In the medium-term, freegans frequently articulated building a small-scale, self-sufficient community that could meet the full range of activists' needs outside capitalism as a central goal of their prefigurative politics. Because, as Adam told one rapt group of listeners, "capitalism tries to convince us that we're all in this alone," the very act of building community was a "huge threat" to capitalism, at least in freegans' eyes.

The conviviality of community could be seen on the trash tours themselves. In my time with the group, I noted that many people would come without collecting any food. As one middle-aged man in a sports coat offered, "This is a great way to meet radical people without going to bars." For anarchists, the local dumpster can fill in for an infoshop or squat as an informal social center. As one diver happily recounted, "I go and find people already there, putting their food out and trying different things, laughing and having a beer. More people are joining, and we'll discuss, 'Try this, try that.' Half the time I'll find some friends at my favorite dumpster when I go there." Dumpster diving thus resocialized the acquisition of food, offering a stark contrast to the highly individualized actions of most "ethical consumers."

Monthly freegan feasts represented more deliberate attempts to create a sense of solidarity within freegan.info. Cindy justified the value of forging links through food by critiquing the way that, in cities, "people aren't treating food as social glue which sticks community together. People lack that. People see that [sociability centered on food] is very valuable." One wintry night, I attended a feast at Madeline's flat in Brooklyn. When I arrived, she and her partner were brainstorming a menu for the evening based on the haphazard collection of vegetables and packaged beans and pasta they had found on the tour two days prior. Slowly, other members of the group dribbled in, each bringing their own eclectic ingredients. As new contributions piled up, the menu changed: an Italian dish turned into curry when no one brought eggplant as expected, and avocados meant for a salad became guacamole when someone announced that she had found tortilla chips.

Feasts gave freegans not just a community in the broad sense but also spaces in which they could construct the principled, nonoppressive relationships that they felt other movements lacked. In August 2008 the menu at one feast in Leia's Brooklyn apartment included broccoli rabe, vegetable stew, bread with hummus, stir-fry, and, for dessert, a fruit smoothie. One vegan attendee approvingly noted, "It's pretty rare to have a meal where I can eat everything on the table." The conversation eventually turned into a strident debate over the efficacy of animal welfare legislation. When I mentioned that I had taken a class with Peter Singer, an animal rights philosopher, Cindy called out from the kitchen with a tone of scandal, "Wait, isn't he the guy who says it's okay to eat mollusks?"

Jason, on the other hand, raised the argument that early hunter-gatherers showed that some forms of meat eating could be ethical. His proposition quickly became contentious, as Sasha countered:

I feel one hundred times happier when I'm not eating animals because I know my biology is not set up for being an animal eater. I don't want to kill any animals, and I don't really want to eat them. That's just how I am. I feel like it's a better life to be more at peace with nature.

The freegan feast: a classic American potluck, albeit with ingredients taken from the garbage and discussions of animal liberation and gift economics. Photograph by the author.

When the argument became heated, Jason backpedaled, stating that, "To a large degree, my belief is that what we did before civilization was pretty much the right thing. But in the case of hunting, maybe we don't just have to revert to a precivilized way of life." He then sat back and laughed and said that it was nice to be able to debate this sort of "minutiae."

Yet freegan community had its limits. Sewing skill-shares or foraging tours were what anarchists often call "temporary autonomous zones" where freegans could, for a moment, feel what it would be like to live in a postcapitalist society. But they were just that—temporary—and as I show in the next chapter, often fractured by conflict. Freegans thus spent much of their time not with other freegans but with coworkers, roommates, and nonfreegan friends. As a result, even the most basic dimensions of everyday interactions could be ethically problematic. In a society where many social situations involve buying something like a beer or a movie ticket, being a freegan could be profoundly isolating. As Janet told me, "You can sit in a room of five or ten people, and they're talking about bargains and sales and 'Where'd you buy that?' and what the latest technology is, and you can really feel like you don't want to participate at all, or that you have to guard it [your freeganism]." Jonathan elaborated how the ideology behind his freeganism fed into a feeling of alienation and disaffection: "I always stand around in a room full of people and think, 'Oh my God, no one is an anticapitalist here.' I feel so alone, I feel so out of place.... It's so lonely. It's depressing as hell to live here [in New York]."

Becoming freegan did not just isolate the group's participants from the city's residents writ large but also from their friends and families. In our interview, Jason mentioned a conversation he had with a close friend from college the previous night:

> He was talking about how he loves Obama but he thinks that it's not a good idea to raise taxes on the upper class because it's going to hurt small businesses, and he's a pretty wealthy person, and I was just like, "Oh my god, let's just not even talk about this." My old liberal democrat self would disagree with you, but my new radical self, I don't even want to bother having this conversation. Where do I even begin? I don't just disagree with you, but on top of that, I reject the whole argument in the first place.

Gio told me that every time he went home, his mother would embark on another attempt to convince him to follow a more "normal" life course: "She'll tell me, 'You're so smart. You have all these skills. You could get a job.' And I'm at a loss for words because I don't know how to comfort my Mom and stay true to my values and the way that I feel I have to live." Although freegans wanted to "unplug" from capitalism, they didn't want to sever ties with everyone happily participating in capitalist society.

Cities like New York concentrate diverse lifestyles and fringe viewpoints in a small area, and it is therefore possible that freegans could find community in any one of the city's abundant subcultures. Yet many freegans also described feeling alienated from other nonfreegan activists. Freegans critiqued other radical and anarchist movements for being insufficiently committed to living out their principles and more focused on partying than achieving social change.[18] Sasha was both witty and scathing when he told me that, "with most anarchist groups, everyone wears black and is, sort of, nothing." As for squatters, "Half the time, the goal is to find a wasted space and get wasted."

Indeed, in the group's ongoing collective struggle to find a free, public place to meet, it often seemed as if the entire city were conspiring against it. When I returned to freegan.info in 2011, a significant portion of a planning meeting was taken up by trying to find a new location. A few weeks prior, an irate grocery store manager had threatened to call the police and eject the freegans from his store's seating area (since, unsurprisingly, no one had bought anything). Madeline shared her fear that clashes like this were preventing erstwhile participants without a background in confrontational politics from becoming involved in the group.

This particular evening, we were sitting in a Starbucks ("Seating is for Customers Only") inside a bookstore. When we sat down, we chose a table behind a column, but Madeline decided it was best to purchase a cup of coffee and display the receipt on the table. When Janet arrived, she started unloading some premade stir-fry and leftover Halloween candy while Madeline built a wall with discarded cups from the waste bin to obscure them. At other times, the group met in public–private atriums: lobbies that private corporations are required to open to the public in exchange for tax breaks from the city.[19]

Freegan.info's struggles were microcosmic of the decline in public space in America. Over time, town squares are being replaced with shopping malls, parks closed to the homeless, and those who can afford it retreat to gated communities and country clubs.[20] The bulldozing of community gardens in Manhattan or the recent arrest of elderly Korean men for lingering too long in a McDonald's in Queens are just two examples of these trends.[21] In many ways, then, freegans were right to think that the main currents of American society flowed strongly against them.

During one December meeting in the back of one of the few grocery stores that had yet to kick the group out, the loudspeakers began blaring "Silent Night." Janet interrupted the conversation to announce, "I really hate it this time of year, when I can't even walk down my street without hearing Christmas music piped out into the street. It's almost like a mandate to go out and buy stuff. I think it's offensive." Ron went to the front of the store and returned to tell us that he had asked them to turn down the music but that "they can't even control it. It *is* a mandate—they have to listen." Cindy turned to me and joked, "Isn't it funny that a song about the baby Jesus makes you want to buy stuff?" Although, in this moment, freegans could revel in their mutual disaffection, most of the time their anticonsumerist sentiments were lonely ones.

Left Out from Diving In

Although with ample caveats, I have argued that freegan.info's message proved surprisingly appealing. Whether drawn by the tangibility of direct action, the appeal to traditional values of nonwasting and thrift, or the practicality of free stuff, a steady stream of newcomers, usually numbering a dozen a night, came to freegan.info events during my research. But who, exactly, was this "public" to which freegan.info was appealing? And who was excluded from it?

The group was relatively successful in attracting and engaging individuals from across the age spectrum. Freegan.info involved a fair share of older individuals: half my interviewees were over thirty, and one-fourth over forty. This contrasted sharply with similar movements in New York. Commenting on the age range at one trash tour, one person involved in Manhattan Food Not Bombs noted, "Over there [at FNB], there's no one over thirty." Similarly, the "Grub" community meal—a dumpster-dived feast hosted by In Our Hearts—stubbornly drew a younger set.

Similar observations could be made with respect to gender. In the FNB chapter I was involved with at Berkeley, participation was so heavily skewed that some joked that they were "man-archists." A study of freegans in Australia describes freegans as "predominantly male."[22] In contrast, two-thirds of my interviewees self-identified as women, and trash tour audiences were often largely female. Some freegans speculated that the group drew larger numbers of women because it appealed to innate gender roles. Whether we put stock in this essentialism, survey data make it clear that women are more likely to voice concern about waste, the environment, and animals than men.[23] It certainly helped the group that some of freegan.info's prominent spokespeople were women like Janet, Cindy, and Madeline.

The class backgrounds of freegan.info's trash tour attendees were difficult to assess, but most core freegan.info activists came from comparative privilege. On the whole, freegans were reflective about the way social class facilitated their participation in freeganism and differentiated them from those who adopted waste recovery out of necessity. As one former freegan articulated:

> The fact that I was choosing to live that lifestyle [freeganism] meant that I never really learned what it meant to have to. I recognize that my privilege was always there. I don't want to pretend that I've experienced living minimally, because I've never had to really do it without a choice.

Cindy pointed out how the stigma attached to dumpster diving was easier to ignore for someone not facing other forms of social censure:

> Certainly people who have grown up with privilege, it's a lot easier to break taboos and to be seen out digging through the trash for your food. That's very basic: if you're at the bottom of the economic heap it's not as easy to say, "Oh yeah, I'm going to be voluntarily poor" because you're not voluntarily poor, you're involuntarily poor. Economic privilege is pretty specific to freegan stuff in that we're talking about voluntary poverty, and that is a pretty hot-button issue for people who are being forced into that kind of a situation.

As freegans recognized, the idea of recovering ex-commodities had a different meaning in communities that lacked the resources to purchase those commodities in the first place. Adam put it tersely when he remarked, "For some people, the message 'Stop buying so much' is inane and offensive, since they can't even provide for their basic needs."

The basic daily routines of being a freegan, too, created barriers to participation that fell along class lines. Dumpster diving, bike repair, or community gardening were all time-consuming. Freegan .info events were always scheduled around the assumption that attendees would have middle-class or professional work hours. Even as the group was constantly making its members more informed about environmental and social issues, participation in freegan.info presumed a baseline political vocabulary closely tied to a formal college education (or, at least, a lot of free time spent reading critical theory). As other research points out, the individualistic, horizontal, and prefigurative approach to politics taken by anarchist-influenced groups like freegan.info can be intensely off-putting to those who have fought tooth-and-nail for the right to engage in "conventional" tactics like voting or petitioning elected officials.[24]

An overrepresentation of upper-middle-class individuals was not a problem specific to freegan.info. Indeed, similar criticisms have been leveled at Occupy, the antiglobalization movement, and Food Not Bombs. To its credit, freegan.info's central practices at least had the potential to bridge the class divide by simultaneously seeking structural change *and* trying to address the real, immediate needs of lower-class individuals. In a city with over one million food insecure individuals, trash tours provided at least some with quality food.[25] The value of the practical skills taught by freegan.info became apparent in late 2008, as the economy went into free fall. Just as New York City began to shed jobs at every step of the economic ladder, freegan.info's events were flooded with newcomers.[26] Of course, long before the economic crisis, rescuing discarded food or redeeming recyclable containers was already a widespread, but deeply stigmatized, survival strategy among the poor in the United States. What freegan.info added was the legitimization and valorization of these practices, which some self-described "low-income" attendees greatly appreciated.

The role of race in the freegan movement, on the other hand, was more clearly problematic. At least in principle, freegans were deeply concerned about structural racism and oppression in American society. As one e-mail of group principles firmly stated:

> *Freegan.info is a non-hierarchical organization that strives to be respectful and anti-oppressive.... We see it as necessary to address power dynamics within our group and consider the impacts of our privileges (such as race, class, gender, sexuality, culture, age,*

ability, and species). We want to create a positive atmosphere that encourages and supports sustainable living, and we strive to meet people where they are and reject exclusion, judgment, and self-righteousness.

Putting these principles into practice, however, was more complex. For example, when Sasha spoke about his "squat tour," he claimed that in many buildings "antiracism was a real focus point for the whole project."

At this point, a middle-aged African American woman in the audience stood up and challenged him: "If antiracism is so important to freegans, how come everyone you've talked about is under thirty, no kids, and white? All these squatters sound like they have no one to take care of but themselves."

Initially, Alex stayed away from the question of race, replying, "No, no, no. There was a kid who was being raised by a bisexual couple, both of them from Norway."

"OK," the woman replied. "Still sound under thirty, white."

"Well, some of them were not white they were, I guess, brown," Sasha responded. "As far as identifying as white, that's something that a lot of people don't like to do. There's a lot of connotations of norms and things that you're automatically thrown into if you're identifying yourself as white.... It wasn't really an issue where 'I identify as that color, I identify as this color.' It's about 'I identify as this person.'"

The woman sat down, clearly dissatisfied.

As the anecdote implies, freegans reacted to the frequent characterizations of their movement as overwhelmingly white by oscillating between denial and concern. The anthropologist who studied freegan .info prior to my research, Kelly Ernst, reported that, by 2007, some in freegan.info were fretting that media coverage invariably depicted freegans as white.[27] Yet for once, the media were on the mark: the core members of freegan.info *were* almost all white. Of my interviewees, only three were people of color.[28] When Leia queried the group if there was interest in starting a "Freegan Women's Caucus," the reply was enthusiastic. No one responded when she proposed a caucus for freegans of color.

All freegans trespass a social norm when they go into the trash to find food. People of color, however, face an added burden: that their contact with waste reinforces a "globally ubiquitous racial construction" of entire races as "polluted" or "diseased."[29] This representation contributes to explaining why, as critics have pointed out, the organic and local food movements' celebration of "getting your hands dirty" in community gardens or farms (or, for that matter, dumpsters) is singularly unappealing to people who have long been forced to "get their hands dirty" to survive and/or produce food for white people.[30] Indeed, in interviews, residents of inner-city ghettos often describe themselves as literally "left to waste" by economic abandonment and the withdrawal of the state.[31] By associating themselves with waste, then, people of color risk reaffirming a long-standing conflation of "wasted" objects with "wasted" people. As one commenter on a free-gan forum explained, as a black male he was "extremely embarrassed for people to see me diving, because I can tell that I'm not just me, I'm also a representation of black people in general."[32]

One night, on the subway after a trash tour, I had a conversation with Stacey, an African American woman in her late twenties who worked in alternative medicine. During the evening, I noticed that she stayed at the periphery of the group and, as far as I could tell, didn't gather any food. The idea of reducing waste appealed to her, but she told me that she was worried the entire trash tour that one of her corporate clients was going to walk by, adding, "I've worked too damn hard to be seen digging through the trash." She then tentatively broached the issue of race, saying, "I think it's a lot easier for white people to do that. People almost expect you to be doing something like that [referencing my appearance]. When white people do it, everyone just assumes 'Oh, it's a project.'" To her, to be white and dumpster diving suggested a deliberate and adversarial action; to be black and dumpster diving was a marker of desperation or criminal activity. The same black diver quoted above observed, "I got harassed by security several times while diving on my own campus, until my white friends pop their heads out of the dumpsters."[33]

I don't want to suggest that "waste" is a peripheral issue for people of color. In contrast, nationwide, an outgrowth of the civil rights movement usually labeled the "environmental justice" movement is at the forefront of challenging the production and unequal distribution of wastes.[34] In New York, in the 1980s, for example, activists from black neighborhoods joined with Hasidic Jews in contesting the placement of a toxic incinerator at the Brooklyn Naval Yard.[35] But the *types* of waste confronted by the environmental justice movement and freegan.info are quite different. Although ex-commodities may be an important part of the municipal waste stream, municipal waste is itself only a small fraction of the material excess produced in the United States.[36] Much of the rest consists of industrial by-products like mining tailings or ash, which analyses of "environmental racism" show are disproportionately dumped in minority communities.[37] Many people of color don't need the "fetish of waste" exposed to them, since they are already living with waste and its harmful impacts daily, and the waste with which they are confronted cannot be recovered and reused.

There are clear potential points of solidarity between environmental justice movements and freegans, given that both are deeply concerned with the waste of capitalism. In my time with freegan.info, though, such linkages were rarely drawn, partly because "race" was an infrequent topic of conversation. Ernst attempted to arrange a meeting on racial dynamics in freegan.info, but only Adam attended.[38] In his words, the group never got beyond "having conversations about not having conversations on race." I have no doubt that freegans were sincere when they listed racial domination as one of the social ills that they opposed. But to treat racism as just one of many forms of oppression misses that American capitalism was built on the backs of people of color.[39]

Scavenging for Survival, Scavenging as a Statement

There was one sort of cross-racial interaction that did occur with regularity at freegan.info events: encounters with the city's homeless population. During one tour, an apparently homeless black man walked up, carrying a few ragged bags and mumbling. Someone declared, "He's hungry," and the group leaped into action. Sasha started explaining some basic tips for dumpster diving. Jason filled up a bag with bagels for him. When the man himself was goaded into going through the garbage, however, I saw him handle a few pieces of produce but immediately put them back. He didn't accompany us to our next stop, and left the bag of bagels behind. Why wouldn't a needy person take free food, even it came from the garbage?

The answer is certainly not that harvesting the excesses of the rich is an unfamiliar activity to marginalized people. In response to claims that dumpster diving is exotic or strange, freegans often note, "Freegans aren't the first people to do this. There have always been people who have lived off the waste of society." The practice of "gleaning" surplus crops left behind from the harvest was for millennia an important safety net for the rural poor, so much so that the Bible enjoined it.⁴⁰ In eighteenth-century Europe, gleaning rights were hotly contested as early capitalists sought to force peasants seeking to stay on their land to move to cities and sell their labor by denying them access to unharvested food.⁴¹ The pattern continues around the world today: the advance of markets and wage-labor are closely coupled with attempts to curtail the rural poor's access to excess crops.⁴²

Gleaning crops was never a widespread subsistence strategy in the United States, but the cast-offs and leftovers of the well-to-do have still frequently served as a resource for impoverished Americans. Ragmen and collectors of surplus household metals were an important, if largely unappreciated, part of the American landscape up through the beginning of industrialization. Until 1878 New York City actually paid scavengers for their recycling services, and up to 1910 there were sorting plants built specifically for gleaning from rubbish.⁴³ At the turn of the twentieth century, though, progressive reformers sought to eliminate informal scrap collectors, who as members of minority and immigrant groups were seen as "dirty" and "unruly."⁴⁴ In the ensuing decades, the face of waste collection in the United States changed from an informal scrap collector focused on reusing excess materials to a municipal garbage man whose job it was to keep trash out of sight and out of mind. After a several-decades hiatus, though, across the United States, "the trash pickers are back," owing to a rise in homelessness and the disappearance of blue-collar manufacturing employment.⁴⁵

How do freegans position themselves with respect to other trash pickers? One of the "rules" of freegan.info events was that individuals diving "out of necessity" take precedence. While this rule is arguably problematic in itself—how can freegans tell who's diving out of necessity versus choice, other than by skin color?—it's also largely irrelevant. Although I've come to think that practically every garbage bag in New York gets handled once or twice before getting picked up, my sense is that homeless people, by and large, aren't looking for unprocessed, unprepared food.⁴⁶ There are some obvious practical reasons for this: by definition, someone who is homeless doesn't have a place to clean, store, or cook food, so all they can take from the average supermarket is premade sandwiches or pizza.

One elderly woman who frequently attended freegan.info tours on the East Side asked me and Janet during the walk between stops why we thought so few homeless people joined our dives. As she contemplated:

> *Indigent people don't do this [dumpster dive for food]. I always see people like me doing it, but I never see homeless or starving people doing it. I used to feel guilty for taking it [food] from the homeless starving people, but the homeless starving people don't do it. We do it because we know we don't have to.*

To this, Janet replied, "It's easier for someone who is educated or well-off to not mind the funny looks of strangers walking by."

Not all freegans were as reflective as Janet about how issues of necessity, choice, and stigma play into people's decisions to access or not to access ex-commodities. One person writing from a freegan viewpoint, but not part of freegan.info, for example, claims that "a simple lifestyle is more in keeping with our origins as human beings ... the less privileged people on our planet just naturally fall into a 'freegan' pattern of living."[47] This statement misses the obvious rift between voluntary and involuntary nonconsumption. While some homeless scavengers may offer up a critique of the excesses of consumer society, the reality is that many of them are trying to eke out a place within capitalism, not found a utopia outside it.[48]

Indeed, the (presumably) homeless individuals who came up to freegans during meetings in public places or trash tours to ask for money were rarely enthused when they were offered food instead. What seems empowering to freegans is a mark of extreme disempowerment for others. As Leo, a New York panhandler, told one ethnographer, "I think it's degrading to go through trash. I would never go that low."[49] My own assessment is that even most homeless people who do engage in scavenging would rather redeem a few cans or resell some discarded household items to buy something to eat than take food directly from a bin. I thus think there's little substance to the criticism that freegan dumpster divers "take" food from the homeless.[50]

Freegans like Janet and Cindy told me that they had repeatedly tried to donate recovered items to homeless shelters. Even though their efforts were invariably unsuccessful, the group occasionally gave it another try. Still, no one at freegan.info saw himself or herself as a provider of social services, and many bristled when told they should become one. One night, a few freegans were discussing the calendar for the upcoming month when Ron, a muscular middle-aged white male wearing a bandana and motorcycle jacket, attending his first freegan.info meeting, butted in: "Why don't you get some people to get all the food? I see this place on Sixth Avenue, and it's just throwing out loaves of bread, packaged stuff. You guys could go and get it and take it to the homeless shelter."

Cindy replied, "I think there are two different answers. One of them is that we're a very small group of people and we're not really set up for something like that. We're focused on rescuing food rather than redistributing it ourselves. You're not going to do much effective food redistribution with a granny cart and three people."

Before she could get to the second reason, Ron began talking animatedly over her: "But you could buy surplus federal vehicles in Pennsylvania for $300!"

Cindy continued, "Our focus isn't on reducing food waste, it's on dismantling capitalism. We're not here to give stores an easy out and so that they can feel good about continuing to waste, because we're doing the work for them to make sure it gets used. Food not going to waste is a good thing, but giving Trader Joe's a way to up their green check mark and improve their public image, that's not necessarily so good."

As the interchange revealed, for many people, there is a reflexive assumption that "surplus food" should go to feed "surplus people." This is partly a result of campaigns by the food banks and soup kitchens that haphazardly fill in for the void of government programs in the United States, which often appeal more to concerns about food waste than about poverty.[51] Never mind, as Adam claimed to have calculated, that New York City alone wastes enough calories to meet the baseline needs of all the food-insecure people in the United States. In attempting to turn food waste into a political issue, freegans were running up against the presumption that the crumbs of capitalism belonged to the poor, a demographic that—far from being victimized by the historically specific way our economy and society are configured—will "always be with us."

As with the environmental justice movement, there were potential political alliances that could have been developed, but weren't. Following the more general neoliberal trend, waste itself is becoming increasingly commodified, threatening those who survive off it.

Global garbage is big business, not just in the sense that the economy as a whole depends on producing waste but also insofar as waste management itself is a $1 trillion industry.[52] Worldwide, governments under pressure from institutions like the International Monetary Fund have turned previously public municipal garbage and recycling services over to private corporations.[53] Despite the rhetoric behind it, privatization has almost nothing to do with increased efficiency, since private companies rarely deliver better services or cost savings, and everything to do with ideology that offers commoditization as a universal cure for all ills.[54]

Wherever "garbage" has become a new profit-generating opportunity, people eking out a meager subsistence through scavenging are even further marginalized. For the *zabaleen* in Cairo, the *recicladores* in Bogotá, or the veritable army of 150,000 trash pickers in Delhi, the grim consequences of privatization have been largely the same.[55] In New York, Sims Municipal Recycling wails that "thefts" of recyclable materials by scavengers cost it between $2 million and $4 million per year (its contract with the city is worth $1.5 billion).[56] Partly under industry pressure, New York City recently passed Local Law 50, which makes it illegal for anyone but the Department of Sanitation to remove or transport recyclable materials from residential stoops.[57]

While in the next chapter I describe how freegans' own attempts to recover discarded food came under assault, their situation was only a continuation of a broader process by which capitalism has perpetually tried to squeeze those trying to make a living, whether willingly or unwillingly, outside the market economy. A broader anticapitalist politics would recognize homeless scavengers not as protofreegans but as potential allies with their own complex relationships to waste and grievances against capitalism.

Profligacy and Parasitism

Freeganism, as should be clear by now, had its limits, both in terms of the people it appealed to and the extent to which freegans themselves could apply it to their own lives. On top of that, though, there were some profound contradictions within those activities that freegans actually *could* engage in.

Freeganism is ideologically closely related to movements that seek to "downshift" consumption or adopt "voluntary simplicity."[58]

Unsurprisingly, freegans were often as scathing in their denunciations of "consumption" as they were of capitalism as a whole. One interviewee told me that "consumerism victimizes everybody in every direction," while another freegan's essay observed that "consumption and waste are linked by very similar meanings. To 'lay waste to' something is to completely destroy, or consume, it."[59] Freegans' visions for the future, too, hinged on drastically restricting consumption. From this perspective, freeganism really did look like a form of deliberate poverty or, as one academic puts it, "an expression of scarcity and denial."[60]

But freegans' relationship to consumption, scarcity, and self-abnegation is, in practice, more complicated. Neoliberal capitalism asks us to accept "scarcity" created by limited public services, inequality imposed by the market, or tax dollars diverted into financial speculation today in the name of future, market-provided abundance.[61] Freegans, on the other hand, call for a future of scarcity, in which people acknowledge the limits of the biosphere and adjust their consumption accordingly. Yet, precisely because capitalism produces so many ex-commodities, freegans could live in abundance in the present, at least with respect to goods like food. Freeganism may sound like voluntary poverty, but, as one freegan put it in an interview, it's a "decadent poverty."[62]

That freegans are able not just to live but to live extraordinarily *well* off the fruits of a system they claim to despise has, unsurprisingly, led to allegations that freegans are "parasitic." Janet parried the claim at one freeganism 101 event:

> People comment, "Aren't you freeloading? You criticize the capitalist system but in the meantime you're living off the fat of it?" And yes, right now we are, because there is the fat of it…. It's not our ultimate goal to continue living off this horrible system. But in the meantime while this horrible system exists, we remove ourselves from it and we're not participating in it, we still do need to eat. As long as it's there [waste], it should be rescued.

This paradox of waste as both something "horrible" and something to be "rescued" played constant tricks on my mind as I took up diving. I would often engage excitedly in conversations before expeditions over what I hoped to find, only to catch myself and realize that, no, I didn't want to find anything, because I wanted capitalism to stop ex-commodifying so much. Freegans simultaneously wanted the dumpsters to be full and empty: full, to support their prefigurative projects, and empty, to show that those projects were having the desired effect. As Janet verbally seesawed, "That is the beauty of New York: pretty much anything you want you can get it here. But you can also get it here [waving to the trash]. I wouldn't call *that* the beauty of New York. It's cheaper for us, yes. It's easy. It's convenient. But it's really a tragedy."

Janet's compulsion to "rescue" ex-commodities often went far beyond any plausible political justification. Later that night, Janet picked up a broken shoe rack next to a trash can. She asked me if I needed it; when I said no, she told me, "Me neither, but I can't just leave it there." As she herself disclosed:

> I've been doing this for seven-and-a-half years, and things just start to accumulate. I can quit my job, and quit sleeping, and spend all of my time fixing what people have done wrong with the things they throw out, sorting through their recycling, and finding homes for all it. But it's burdensome to keep on taking charge of the world.

Janet's basement was cluttered with found things, including hundreds of dumpster-dived Hallmark cards, dozens of messenger-bag straps, and a packet of inflatable cactuses for party decorations, among others, all in various states of disrepair and decay. Strangely enough, by spending so much time collecting, repairing, and redistributing goods in the name of honoring the resources and effort that went into producing them, freegans gave consumer goods an inadvertently central place in their lives.

Some freegans enthusiastically embraced how, by appropriating ex-commodities, they could absolve themselves of the guilt they would otherwise feel purchasing them while still engaging in consumption. One study noted that dumpster divers were able to consume fancier items from the garbage than when buying food: as one interviewee put it, "I can't afford to buy organics at Safeway, but I can afford to take it out of their bin."[63] Leia told me she thought that she should probably be more involved in gardening, since that offered a more positive vision for the future of the food system, but that she found it hard to be motivated because "dumpster diving has tastier food." Christian summarized the attitude that a handful of freegan.

info participants had toward consumerism when he explained, "I've dedicated myself to having pretty much the same lifestyle [as I had when I made $300,000 a year], just without the money."

Few freegans were quite so extreme, but there were moments where freegans engaged in normative consumer behavior, albeit swapping commodities for ex-commodities. At one winter freegan feast, the group held a holiday gift exchange. People unwrapped with glee and laughter dumpster-dived and recycled colognes, soaps, fancy French pens, kombucha, dresses, candy, body oil and a garter, VHS tapes, Christmas lights, and pagan novels. The most communal moment of the evening, during which all our attention was focused on a single activity, revolved around one-time commodities. One first-time feast attendee even asked, with genuine confusion, "Is this about consumerism or anticonsumerism?"

Some freegans recognized this dangerous appeal. As one e-mail sent to the freegan-world e-mail list observed:

Realizing that shopping had become a form of entertainment spurred me in my own life to adjust my views on consumerism and eliminate shopping. I eventually made myself stop dumpster diving for similar reasons. I tended to dive and recover things for entertainment rather than the purpose of getting useful things, and my apartment was cluttered up to boot.

Gio, too, cautioned against "just showing up [at a trash tour] and taking food," which to him was "another form of consumerism, not really taking responsibility for yourself." He thus strove mightily to "give back" through volunteering, activism, and music. Undeniably, however, an element of not "taking responsibility" for consumption was inherent in freegan practices. In fact, some would say that this was the entire point: freegans, like everyone, have needs, but they don't want to take responsibility for the production of commodities under capitalism to meet those needs. Dumpster diving allowed freegans to wash their hands of guilt for consuming the things they needed—and some they did not.

Diving also freed some freegans from contrition over what ultimately happened to ex-commodities. During my research, I came to a strange realization: I actually wasted *more* food as a practicing dumpster diver than as a normal grocery store shopper. Partly, it's because the food I found, while still edible, tended to be near the end of its life and thus went bad quickly. Moreover, when I dove, I didn't worry about taking more than I needed, since there seemed always to be an abundance (and, some might point out, because I wasn't paying for it). The result was a surprising amount of waste.

While some freegans deliberately took more than they could eat in order to share it or at least put it in the compost, others just didn't worry. Because ex-commodities were free and had been destined for the landfill anyway, some freegans felt comfortable throwing dumpster-dived food out. One resident of Surrealestate disclosed that "because we're diving, there's way too much food [and] people aren't worried about leaving it out or throwing it away."

One evening, while hanging out at Jonathan's squatted apartment, Lucie opened the cupboard and declared, "This bread is getting stale."

Jonathan replied dismissively, "Just throw it out—we'll get more tonight."

Lucie hesitated, and Jonathan added, "You're just *re*-wasting it!"

Unconvinced, Lucie defiantly took a bite with a loud "crunch" and declared, "Don't waste the waste!"

Adam, for his part, was never particularly enthusiastic about consuming anything, whether or not it came from a dumpster. As he cautioned in one essay:

> *Freegans rescue capitalism's castoffs from the jaws of the garbage truck compactor, defying capitalism's definitions of what is valuable and what is worthless. Since the goods are salvaged and therefore do not support the destruction behind the market, freegans can have a clear conscience about enjoying these goods. But we need to be mindful not to be too charmed by their allure. We know the history of what we consume and always remember the ravages of the culture that produced them.*[64]

Yet at times, freegans clearly *were* enchanted. Ex-commodities became oddly refetishized as the dumpster scrubbed the objects inside clean, allowing freegans to forget about where their products came from or where they went.[65]

In another essay, Adam argued that, in the absence of "real demands," capitalists had to constantly "invent desires, manufacture demand, and fabricate need." The flaws of freeganism, in a sense, confirmed the truth of their own critique of consumer activism. On their own, even "anticonsumers" struggled to break free from the "invented desires" and "fabricated needs"—much less the wasteful practices—of advanced capitalism.

Backlash, Conflict, and Decline

Freegan.info's greatest strengths and most intractable internal challenges stemmed from the range of people it pulled together under the freegan banner. I have already introduced Leia, a Latina mother in her midtwenties, whose clothing of ripped fishnets, black hoodies, and piercings announced her connection to punk and goth subcultures, and Janet, a white high school Spanish teacher in her early fifties. A closer look at their pathways into freeganism, living situations, preferences for political action, and visions for a postcapitalist future speaks to some of the fault lines within freegan.info that eventually cracked open.

Janet came to freeganism through her long-running fixation with eliminating waste and antipathy toward consuming useless commodities, which to her ranged from ninety-nine-cent shower curtains to iPods. The paradox of her thrift, as she told one group of newcomers, was that "I haven't bought crap all my life, so now I have a lot of money." Striking a defiant note, she continued, "I own a house. I guess that's not really freegan, but I've got a good job and I've made money and eleven years ago I decided to buy a house. And I wasn't going to get rid of it just because I became a freegan." Janet's house in Queens was nestled in a middle-class neighborhood of white clapboard residences, many sporting American flags. In 2013 Janet completed her teaching obligations and told me that she planned to retire with a full pension to her second home in Pawling, upstate. There, she said, she envisioned holding really really free markets and swaparamaramas to share the practices of recycling and reuse that brought her to freegan.info.

In contrast, Leia confessed to me that even with her job as a campaigner for the New York Public Interest Research Group, she struggled to make rent for the cramped Brooklyn apartment she shared with the father to her baby and her grandfather. Although Leia had been involved in activist causes from a young age, she came to dumpster diving out of necessity. Leia initially joined freegan.info when she stopped paying rent to an abusive landlord, declaring, in her words, a "rent strike." Christian helped her get legal assistance, and she subsequently became more deeply involved in freeganism, both to provide for her family and to continue her long-running resistance to capitalism.

These women's divergent pathways *into* freeganism were mirrored in their practice *of* freeganism. For Janet, "my activism is my lifestyle, and telling people about it, rather than in protests." Janet's commitment to an ethical regime posed its own dilemmas, given her continued connection to the accoutrements of the middle class. She mentioned, for example, her uncertainty about whether to occasionally go out to dinner to avoid alienating her nonfreegan friends. When it came to transportation to work, it was easiest for her to drive her car, because she would have to take three buses otherwise. Balancing convenience and ecological concern, she told me that she often drove her car halfway and then took a bus.

Some of these ethical impasses would likely strike Leia as distractions. Leia was militantly anti–private property, and occasionally used this to challenge the sincerity of the political commitments of other freegans. She was well-versed in revolutionary doctrine, thanks to her prior involvement with communist groups, and talked about "turning the tables of power" to immediately create a "postcapitalist society." When Janet described freeganism as "an environmental movement, a social movement, and a community-building movement," she left out what to Leia was the most important descriptor of all: "revolutionary."

These differences carried into their respective postcapitalist visions. When I asked Janet about her "utopia," she articulated the need for "lots of community while still respecting privacy." She envisioned parks, community centers, places for "sitting and talking," excellent public transportation, mandated recycling, and a "new type of supermarket that doesn't waste as much." I queried whether she identified as an anarchist, and she hesitantly replied, "I haven't read enough to say, but maybe if I read more, I wouldn't be [an anarchist] because I'm not sure if anarchists can truly create a world that is respectful."

For her part, Leia talked about a horizontal and egalitarian economy, "based on satisfying actual needs and not abstract numbers,"
in which production would be "geared toward community, people's
real needs." She added that her utopia would be a "direct" democracy,
because "I don't believe in representative democracy. I don't see anyone as able to represent me as an individual other than myself." While
Leia hoped that people would rise up to bring this world into being,
Janet preferred strict government regulation. In the fall of 2008, Leia
won a scholarship for registering the most voters of any volunteer
in a nationwide contest—but she averred that, as an anarchist, she
would never vote herself. Janet, on the other hand, wore an Obama
'08 button to freegan events before the election.

It is hard to avoid the observation that, absent their shared
involvement in freegan.info, these two women would be unlikely
to ever meet. Nonetheless, both Janet and Leia worked together
frequently on freegan.info projects from 2007 to 2009. During this
period, freegan.info pulsed with ideas and energy for freegan projects
and actions, pushed forward by a steady and diverse stream of new
activists.

How did such an eclectic set of individuals pull together to form a
"movement"? Sociologists have shown that movements are organized
around cultural "anchors" that are powerful enough to elicit a degree
of consensus while broad enough to accommodate debate.[1] What
made collaboration between Janet and Leia possible was agreement
on some basic anchors. When I asked Janet, unsure of the response
she would give, if she were an anticapitalist, she replied:

> *There's no question among normal intelligent people that this capi-
> talist system is destroying our planet. And it's appealing to find that
> there's a practical activity that people can do [in response]. Free-
> ganism is an anticapitalist movement that encourages people to
> find alternatives to supporting corporations and buying and using
> crappy things once to discard.*

Using her own preferred terminology, Leia defined freeganism as a
"strategic boycott of exploitative industries" that sought to "reinforce
communities that stand in opposition to class society and the state"
by "getting creative about resources, mutual aid, and redistribution."
In so many words, both united around a belief that ex-commodities

exposed the ills of capitalism and should be used to contest it and build alternatives.

Leia and Janet shared one other thing: when I revisited New York in 2012, both had ceased to identify as freegans. Leia had left freegan .info and soured on the label "freegan," having encountered too many self-described freegans who believed that freeganism was just about getting free stuff. She seethed, "Not helping out with somebody is anticommunal, it's not mutual aid, it's destructive, and it's freeloading." Janet used the same term to explain why, despite still rarely skipping a trash tour, she had disassociated from the term *freegan.* "For a lot of people," she told me, "freegan has a negative connotation, like 'freeloading.' Often I just tell people I'm an environmentalist." Both continued to hold anticapitalist beliefs and engage in waste-recovery practices, but they had ceased to see freeganism as a way to pull these two together. How did that happen?

Garbage-Bag Backlash

At least as of 2009, dumpster divers in New York had a distinctively easy time recovering ex-commodities, partly because they were confronted with bags, not dumpsters, and partly from the benign neglect of the stores whose garbage they targeted. Most stores had minimal policies for dealing with food waste, so managers had little reason to deter divers.[2] And, of course, my occasional conversations with store employees confirmed that many felt bad about what they were ex-commodifying and thus were happy to turn a blind eye to urban foragers. As Janet observed, "We have stores where we see that the guys who are throwing out the food; they're not looking at us funny. They know it's good stuff. But they're not allowed to take it. They know they're throwing out good food. They almost sometimes set it up for us, so that it's easy to take."

Within the freegan community, and the broader milieu of dumpster divers, there was a sense that this relatively easy access to free food was too good to last. A famed anarchist travelogue from the late nineties opined, "There was a clear trend toward the obsolescence of dumpster diving, disquieting reminders that one day we might all have to get jobs and start paying for things. One by one, slowly, the dumpsters were becoming trash compactors."[3] Yet despite widely shared stories about locked dumpsters, garbage doused in bleach or mop water, and police ticketing trespassers, there was little indication during my research that stores in New York were acting to deter dumpster diving—at least, until I returned in 2012.

As dumpster diving became more popular and publicized, stores began to take notice. One indication of this was that some of freegan.info's more aboveboard strategies for rescuing food evaporated. Once, Janet had been caught dumpster diving at a health food store in Queens, but rather than shoo her away, the employee told her, "Don't do that, we'll just give it to you." So every Monday Janet picked up between thirty and fifty loaves of bread for a local homeless shelter. Eventually, as she explained it, "someone in the store got upset. They [a customer] saw that I was walking off with the same things that they were buying, and they decided they weren't going to let us do it anymore." She added, "Now I just get it from the dumpster, again," although, as a result, she could no longer donate the food.

Janet offered another example: a hot-food buffet in the West Village that would let the freegans come in fifteen minutes before closing time to take what was going to be thrown out. "It was always awkward," she noted, "because there were still people shopping. They didn't want people to realize what we were doing, so they insisted that we use their containers, not bring our own, and pretend like we were going to buy it." Eventually, however, "they realized how absurd that was" and told the freegans the deal was off. While some store employees might have found it ridiculous to throw away good food, in the end it was even *more* preposterous for a capitalist enterprise to give some people in stores free commodities and then expect others to buy them.

Specific chains of stores also began taking explicit steps to deter diving. Trader Joe's has long had a reputation for "the most abundant and consistent chain of dumpsters in the world" thanks to its heavy dependence on packaged precut salads and ready-to-eat meals.[4] The Lower East Side Trader Joe's dumpster was also a favorite spot for freegan.info, which led the broadsheet *AM New York* to publicize the store's food waste exposed during a trash tour. The store subsequently claimed that it donated all its "good" excess, but Trader Joe's continued to waste so much that it became the object of a 2010 documentary by a group of divers in Southern California.[5] Although Jeremy Seifert, the filmmaker, did not succeed in getting the company to adopt any policies to reduce waste or increase donations—or even talk to him about the possibility—my conversations with divers around the country confirmed that the attention did contribute to one change: locks. As Seifert told me:

> I've found a lot of locked dumpsters, for sure. I think they are quietly doing that to avoid more films and videos being put out. They refuse to adopt a corporate-wide policy, which means that they allow each individual store to determine their giving. Some stores might give some of the food, but don't want to deal with fruits and vegetables, so they're going to throw that away.... There's probably still significant waste happening, so they're locking dumpsters to avoid the scandal of it.

Cindy recounted that, in New York, some dumpster divers who were driving into Brooklyn from outside the city to partake of the Trader Joe's ex-commodity cornucopia had even been ticketed by police.

As of 2012 it was still possible to dive at the Trader Joe's in lower Manhattan, but more complicated. Jonathan explained the new "tactics" being used: "Now, they're waiting until the last possible minute until they put it out—usually like 10:30, right before the [garbage] trucks come." This store was thus no longer amenable to the slow, educational format of a trash tour. When I accompanied the group to the store one night, Cindy explained that we were only going because there were no media along and so no risk of creating a "scene." The group seemed both excited and nervous as we walked up, grabbed the bags, and rushed off unseen.

Another example of the growing backlash against waste reclamation came from the two practically adjacent D'Agostino stores in Murray Hill. In 2011 they abruptly switched from putting out their garbage at 10 p.m. to 5 a.m. As one disaffected diver wrote over the freegan.info e-mail list:

> Did we really think that there would be no discernible response to the activities of Freegan.info from the businesses whose food and material waste we salvage? Here are a few things that might have grabbed their attention: crowds, blocked entrances/exits and sidewalks, strewn garbage, media attention and dramatic denunciations.

Although the sidewalks outside these stores abounded with nonfreegan divers on nights where there were no trash tours—and freegan .info often arrived to find those sidewalks a mess, covered in smashed food and torn bags—many of the local divers blamed freegan.info for the change.

In response to these complaints, the group sent Janet to talk to the stores to convince them to revert to their old disposal practices, and I tagged along. At the D'Agostino on Thirty-Fifth Street, we introduced ourselves as "the freegans" and the manager nodded sternly. He told us that the new policy came from the store's corporate office. When we asked if it was related to the freegans bringing cameras outside his store, he said it was. Freegan.info's "dramatic denunciations" of waste became little more than plaintive supplication: we appealed to him to consider changing back to the old timing, promising not to bring cameras back. He said that we would have to speak to corporate and that there was virtually no chance of such a change happening. He added that the store donated "all" its edible food to charity.

From one perspective, it seems absurd to deter dumpster diving. After all, by putting food in the garbage, stores clearly indicate that they no longer see any value in it. As one outraged dumpster diver exclaimed, "It's really obscene, I mean, totally paradoxical; people starting to guard their garbage!" Yet according to the most basic prerogatives of capitalism, the amicable entente between freegans and stores should never have existed in the first place. Grocery stores exist to make money: every time someone dives food rather than buys it, potential profit is lost.[6] More importantly, large groups of divers publicly gathering good food—rather than, say, a few homeless people taking leftovers—threatens the carefully cultivated image that stores use to distinguish themselves in a competitive market. This menace was significant enough that one business journal actually advised managers to begin reading freegan forums to identify potential "branding problems."[7] (The article added, as an afterthought, that reducing waste might also help stores protect their image.)

These experiences aside, I had always thought that stories about stores putting bleach on their dumpsters were apocryphal, until I encountered it myself. I was going through a dumpster in Paris, chocked full of hundreds of yogurts, artisan cheese, and choice cuts of meat. Each of them had been individually cut and, wafting above

Ex-commodities outside a store in Paris, which did not have time to donate its food but did have a chance to individually cut open dozens of items and pour bleach over them. Photograph by the author.

it all, was the unmistakable smell of bleach (I eventually found the bottle, left, presumably, to drive the point home). I recently spoke to some freegans who said that they had encountered destroyed food and bleach in New York, too. Both newspaper reports, freegans' testimonials, and my own personal experience find, moreover, that other kinds of ex-commodities, like clothes, are increasingly being destroyed as well.[8]

My anecdote from Paris also hints that the pushback against waste reclamation in New York was part of something broader. One researcher in Seattle, writing in 2012, concluded, "The proliferation of locked Dumpsters, then, may be proportional to the growing public profile of Dumpster-divers' cultural and political activities in general."[9] Recently, dumpster divers have been prosecuted for theft in the Netherlands, France, and the UK, with the Crown Prosecution Service declaring that it had a "significant public interest" in pressing charges against three individuals accused of taking tomatoes, mushrooms, and some cakes from a supermarket bin.[10] Freegans in Sweden and Germany report growing problems with the police over the freegan-world e-mail list. One Hungarian diver I talked to summarized, "You hear the same thing everywhere: it [dumpster diving] is getting harder."

The coherent logic behind stores' actions was visible in other moves they have made to deflect attention to food waste brought, at least partly, by groups like freegan.info. Statistics on waste are maddeningly unreliable in no small part because the actors that actually know how much waste there is refuse to share the data. One activist contacted retailers in an attempt to access their statistics on wastage, but every single supermarket denied his requests.[11] When food manufacturers and retailers do depict their waste stream, it's often a distorted portrait: one report by the industry-funded Food Waste Reduction Alliance claimed that 95 percent of food manufacturing waste gets diverted to "higher uses," which it later mentions consists largely of feeding animals and spreading excess onto fields.[12]

Lately, supermarkets have responded to heightened scrutiny by evoking another aspect of the fetish of waste: that, in the end, *anything but* free markets should be blamed for waste. While retailers in Europe have accused government aesthetic criteria of causing waste—even though nearly all supermarkets have stricter criteria than those mandated—the main whipping boy has been the consumer. One spokesperson for the British Retail Consortium told the BBC, "Most of the wasted food that we have actually comes from domestic waste, so it comes out of homes rather than out the back of supermarkets."[13] When activists strong-armed supermarkets into signing the Courtauld Commitment to reduce waste, they pledged only to help in "identifying ways to tackle the problem of household food waste."[14]

They have a point, of course: consumers do appear to make a major contribution to food waste.[15] This doesn't necessarily make them "responsible," however. Indeed, across the food supply chain, powerful actors like large, multinational supermarket chains and agribusinesses push the wastes (and attendant costs that come along with their business models) onto weaker entities farther upstream and downstream. For example, supermarkets impose contracts on farmers and processors that obligate each to overplant and overproduce, respectively, to avoid substantial penalties for undersupply.[16] Supermarkets also get around the problem of inelastic demand for food through strategies that push consumers into buying unneeded, excess calories. Promotional offers, like "buy one get one free" deals or bulk discounts, have received the most attention in this respect, but the problem is endemic.[17] Research on food waste shows that waste in households often comes from a mismatch between the quantities people actually want and the quantities in which items are sold.[18] After all, has *anyone* ever used an entire bunch of cilantro from the supermarket before it went bad? In other cases, consumers in focus groups note that it is virtually impossible to get all the food out of yogurt pots or jam jars as they are currently designed.[19] Companies have known this for decades—the designers of the first aerosol cans in the 1950s were aware that there was no way to get all the whipped cream out of them—but, unsurprisingly, have not acted to rectify the situation.[20]

These actions are not necessarily a symptom of some worldwide antifreegan conspiracy but instead a product of individual companies doing what is, in a capitalist economy, rational (even if the consequences are insane). Grocery store employees, of course, might see through the fetish of waste and recognize that the food they bin is good, which is why stores punish such salvaging by their employees.[21] But when individuals *outside* stores' purview become aware of this same fact, there is little for the store to do other than lock up its garbage. By doing so, however, stores put pressure on the very ex-commodities that were the "anchor" of freegan.info's politics. It thus exacerbated other conflicts by making accessible waste scarcer and, in turn, rendering the divergent meanings and uses freegans attached to ex-commodities mutually exclusive.

Waste(d) Celebrity?

Even as stores began to protect some of their ex-commodities, the mass media played their own part in containing freeganism. One simple way was by making a sport of identifying disconnects between freegan practice and ideology. A 2007 *New York Times* article on freegan .info glibly noted, "Despite their earnest efforts to separate themselves from the capitalism system, freegans aren't able to avoid it entirely" and, in fact, when it comes to cell phones or computers, were "dependent on the things they are critical of."[22] Three years later, another *Times* piece, "The Freegan Establishment," mocked a group of squatters who "worked their butts off and paid the back taxes and utilities" to get their house, ultimately proving that "they are more conformist than they want you to think they are."[23] In each case, contradiction was portrayed as evidence of freegans' insincerity, rather than the inevitable compromises that came from living in a capitalist society.

At the very least, though, to report on contradictions required the media to acknowledge that freegans had *some* ideology. Far more common, however, were stories that ignored the political element of freeganism entirely. As sociologists observe, for the media "purposes are not photogenic, [but] tactics may be."[24] Without question, dumpster diving was freegan.info's most visible and photogenic tactic, and many media stories began and ended with trash tours. The result, as Quinn fumed years later, was a conflation of freeganism with dumpster diving:

> For the media, it was a freegan freak show. That's why we got on the media, and then we would take that opportunity to try to show them the bike shop, and they wouldn't come. And we tried to show them that freeganism isn't just about recycling garbage, it's recycling everything, but freeganism wound up equaling dumpster diving to everybody except the members of freegan.info, sadly.

In reports, dumpster diving itself was gradually divorced from any conception of the multifarious political ends for which it served. Reflecting on how the words *freegan* and *dumpster diver* were becoming synonymous, Cindy angrily observed:

> I think that's the fault of a lot of the media stories that have happened over the years. If you're digging through the trash in New York, people will come up behind you and say, "Hey, you're the freegans!" and they have no idea what that means except that freegans are people who dumpster dive.

My own experiences confirm Cindy's statement: more and more often, when I tell people I study freegans, the assumption is that I study dumpster divers. While freegan.info itself is partly to blame, given that dumpster dives were their signature event, there's no doubt media accounts drastically oversimplified freegan practice.

The particular ways the media portrayed dumpster diving only made this conflation more problematic. In effect, the media worked tirelessly to stitch back together the waste fetishism that freegan .info had been trying to rip apart. The media framing that Adam described as "weirdoes with garbage" proved to be a consistent one. Once, an NYU student followed the group for several months, claiming to be preparing a documentary on freeganism. When he screened the film, however, it quickly became apparent that the student had created a short parody of the movement, splicing together clips of freegans performing strange or disgusting acts. Janet recounted, "You could almost hear the audience going 'Ewww' when Wendy ate a rotten-looking strawberry straight from the trash."

Occasionally, the media added expert testimony to discredit freeganism. One reporter for ABC News interviewed a spokesperson for the New York Health Department, who stated:

> *There are too many uncertainties involved about what the food in the dumpsters have been exposed to.... We have concerns about the practice [of dumpster diving] mainly because anything that goes into trash has exposure to any sort of food pathogens, including rat droppings, pesticides, or household cleaners that can be a potential health risk.*[25]

For Marx, a "fetish" was an irrational fixation that obscured a broader truth. The media's obsession with (admittedly not entirely invalid) concerns about food from a dumpster never turned into a more circumspect analysis of health and safety in our food system. They left out the thousands of Americans who die each year from food-borne illnesses spread partly through the negligence of the very corporations freegans were protesting.[26] And they sidestepped how other practices from food service companies, such as denying 90 percent of restaurant workers paid sick days, create risks that vastly outstrip those from dumpster diving.[27] These representations distracted from the more germane question—should otherwise edible and safe food end up in a dumpster?—to reinforce the cultural trope that anything labeled "waste" is intrinsically contaminated.

These inclusions and omissions are far from politically neutral. In recent years, dozens of municipalities have justified the criminalization of Food Not Bombs' group feedings of the homeless and (violent) evictions of Occupy encampments by claiming that they pose hygiene concerns.[28] I found records for dozens of arrests of dumpster divers looking for food starting in 2008, but virtually none before. They included a sixty-three-year-old woman in Delaware looking to feed feral cats and a homeless veteran in Houston, who were evidently putting themselves and society at risk by dumpster diving (but not, apparently, by going hungry).

By 2012, when I returned to freegan.info, those still in the group were worried that the quality of the media coverage was tumbling farther. Most major outlets—from CNN to Al Jazeera to the *Colbert Report*—had already done a basic segment on freeganism, and the group had no new projects to regain their attention. Those stories that did come through the pipeline thus portrayed freeganism almost exclusively as a moderately amusing and easily mocked subculture. One *Wall Street Journal* piece dispensed with freegan ideology quickly.[29] As the reporter recounted:

> *"I'm not participating in a wasteful system," she [Janet] says.*
> *That's all very noble, but I'm interested in the whole eating for free angle. Can you really live decently on food found in the trash?*

The story then went on to play up the dirtiness of food waste, which my own experience suggests reflected a mix of sheer incompetence as a diver and deliberate exaggeration:

> *I made a recording of my search through the garbage at my favorite produce stand. Here is a brief transcription: "Gross … Oh god, this is horrible … Cauliflower! My favorite! … Arrr, I can't stand this … Huh, a potato … Oh nooooo … Disgusting … What the %$!# is this? … Hey, raspberries!"*

The report concluded by stating, "You know what's really fun? Slime-free shopping. I'll leave the garbage grub to the freegans."

Indeed, dumpster diving became something of a running joke, associated with deviants, hipsters, and nutcases, but not participants in serious political movements. In one episode of the show *Portlandia*, two self-described dumpster divers announce before entering a supermarket bin, "I don't know why people live any other way." Their finds include baby food, which they claim could be used as a sauce, a "perfectly good" rotting watermelon with a hair on it, a piece of metal pipe that the female diver claims she can use as a sleeve, and a tiny, hideous sweater. The next scene shows the two cooking a meal while flies buzz through their kitchen, and then follows them as they discover that all their friends have canceled on their dinner party (for unstated but obvious reasons). In the end, the male diver states to the camera, "To my friends I say this: 'OK, you guys win, but who saved more money?' And the answer is really, they did, because all of the energy and work, but still..." While the clip certainly put its fair share of emphasis on the "ick" factor of dumpster diving, it also reinforced the fetish of waste by negating the idea that the objects that get disposed of could ever be *actually* useful, at least to anyone in full possession of their mental faculties.

The one genre of media that seemed to have become more enamored with freeganism was reality television. Madeline even showed me a stock response the group had prepared to reject such requests, convinced that semifictional shows looking to include a freegan character couldn't possibly be interested in doing the movement justice. They were probably right. Freegan.info turned down a request from a TLC show, *Extreme Cheapskates,* but the producers found another dumpster diver anyway. As the profile emphasizes, the woman "dumpster dives for all her food, doesn't use toilet paper or do laundry, and hasn't bought toiletries in 10 years."[30] While the piece does not use the word *freegan*, it does conflate people who dumpster dive with filth—in this case, dramatized by the woman's decision not to use toilet paper, an ex-commodity most freegans can easily find outside hotels.

Once again, we do not need to believe in a secret cabal to see how this happened. The basic pressures of selling stories, appeasing sponsors, and winning favor with politicians lead journalists to offer satire and ridicule rather than complex political critiques and alternative viewpoints.[31] Movements, of course, can push back by attempting to shape their own coverage or creating new forms of media themselves. For freegan.info, though, the avalanche of stories and limited size of the group itself meant that it had little power to shape how it was portrayed beyond simply saying no to some outlets, which went on to do stories anyway. While freegan.info's successes are hard to imagine without the publicity its engagement with the media generated, its failings—and the shifting public understanding of freeganism that accompanied them—were equally difficult to disassociate from media misrepresentations.

Naming and Shaming

The attempts by stores to restrict dumpster diving highlighted the extent to which freegan.info's core critique of capitalism depended on ex-commodities produced by capitalism itself. Media critics, unsurprisingly, loved to make this point. As one *Times* piece commented:

> [There is] a quandary inherent in the freegan movement. Freegans maintain that by salvaging waste, they diminish their need for money, which allows them to live a more thoughtful, responsible and deliberate existence. But if they succeed in their overriding goal, and society ends up becoming less wasteful, the freegan lifestyle will no longer be possible.[32]

Again, this critique rests on collapsing freeganism into dumpster diving. While some of freegan.info's activities used ex-commodities as resources, the values and practices with which they were experimenting were, in their own eyes, trial runs for a world *without* ex-commodities. Certainly, no freegan I ever spoke to thought that dumpster diving had any place in their postcapitalist utopia.

But freegans never had an effective response to the claim that what they were doing was self-defeating partly because they, themselves, could never quite agree on what ex-commodities should actually be used for. For freegan.info, the media circus began swirling immediately after its formation, before the group had defined its goals or decided on strategies to achieve them. While the group was anchored by a commitment to contesting capitalism and using waste to do so, much of the rest was left ambiguous, despite numerous failed attempts to come up with a clear mission.

Many anarchists saw ex-commodities as a rare bit of beneficence from the capitalist system, a boon that allowed them to survive on the system's margins. Consequently, some politically motivated dumpster divers—including some self-identified freegans—rejected and opposed exposing this waste to a broader audience. One how-to guide for dumpster diving, under the heading "Don't Spoil Sites," cautioned, "We don't want to bring unwanted attention to dumpsters. The more people you tell, the more likely it is that someone will go there and fuck things up. Use discretion when telling people about the places you frequent."[33]

Some in freegan.info, however, had no qualms about sharing spots, to the extent that the group eventually posted a dumpster directory on its website. More than that, over time, the group turned dumpster diving from a survival strategy into a public act of protest. This decision earned the group significant criticism. As Janet admitted:

> There have been freegans who object to this and say "You're ruining this for us." There have been issues with them saying, "What are you doing? You're messing it up! They're going to ruin our garbage. They're going to ruin our source." Not all freegans want to talk to the public about it.

This debate about whether dumpster diving ought to be public came to a head over the question of whether freegan.info should publicly shame the particular stores that produced waste. In doing so, the group would aim to get stores to reduce their waste output, as opposed to a single-minded focus on overthrowing "the system" as a whole.

The issue was long on the group's agenda, and when it came up for discussion, Cindy led off by explaining that, in her view, "given what we're trying to do as an organization, which is not just promote free living but also target corporations for being so wasteful, maybe naming the companies … would be a good thing."

Janet responded, "Theoretically, I totally agree," but that she was concerned about antagonizing other dumpster divers, who had been incensed after freegan.info called out Trader Joe's. She added:

> They [Trader Joe's] didn't appreciate that their name was in millions of homes as wasteful. It was after that they have security guards at their dumpsters. Those of us that call ourselves "freegans"—not just "dumpster divers"—want to draw attention to these corporations, but we do have to consider the backlash against fellow dumpster divers and on ourselves.

Leia was even more skeptical of outing wasteful stores. She insisted that "if we decide to start naming the names of corporation, I think it should be part of a comprehensive strategy." Leia seemed particularly concerned about the impact that the freegans' decision could have on those people who dumpster dive out of necessity, and the loss of a "resource" that could be used to lure people outside capitalism.

From 2007 to 2009 the group never managed to agree on whether to name and shame stores. The debate did not break down under clear radical-versus-reducer or anarchist-versus-nonanarchist lines. Wendy and Adam, who were often on the more extreme end of the ideological spectrum, were in favor of pressure campaigns of the sort they engaged in with Wetlands against particularly wasteful corporations. Others, like Jason, were frustrated with the reformist undertones of the idea. "I joined freegan.info because I wanted to boycott *the whole* system," he half-whispered in frustration.

Eventually, after I departed in 2009, the group did decide to create a campaigns and advocacy working group, which, according to an announcement e-mail from Wendy, would focus on "those companies that give no thought to throwing away more food than we can ever distribute, or those who destroy their merchandise so that it cannot be used by people who are trying to give some discarded items a new life." This focus on stores with "more food than we can ever distribute" and that "destroy their merchandise" was clearly a concession to those worried about losing ex-commodified resources. By this point, though, both the internal energy of freegan.info and media attention had dissipated. As Wendy told me with a sigh, "We've done so little with it [the media]. We've just done exposing, exposing, and exposing, and if you do that enough, people just get numb to it."

From Freeganism to Freeloading

Virtually everyone in freegan.info agreed that the combination of intensified media coverage and the economic downturn led to a major bump in attendance at trash tours starting in 2008. In a moment of deepening economic need and want, there was a growing public awareness of the free use value that ex-commodities represented, and freegan.info was drawing thirty to forty people weekly to every event. Some of these newcomers, however, were clearly attending to get free food, not to participate in political action.

One night, a well-dressed NYU student told me that she had come because she had just started college and couldn't stand the food in the dining hall. She enthusiastically grabbed meat and dairy products, stuffing them into a designer handbag. She never offered to share her finds with the group, even after Janet politely admonished her to do so. As I walked with her between diving spots, she declared, "I'm only interested in environmental things because they save me money. I'm a tightwad. If I turn off the lights or something, it's just because I'm cheap." I offered her a flier for an upcoming series of movies put on by freegan.info's Films and Forums working group on corporate globalization. She waved me off: "I'm an economics and finance major," she told me.

Similar "freeloaders" began attending freegan.info events, undermining the group's sense of shared purpose and the very notion that trash tours and other events were political. At the start of one summer meeting held in Union Square Park in 2012, Madeline introduced herself by stating that she was interested in freeganism as a strategy for "social revolution." A young black woman sitting next to her spoke next, declaring "I've been doing this for years, but when I found out about this group, I thought it was really revolutionary." Madeline perked up at another declaration of revolutionary intent, until the woman explained, "For me, what matters is saving money and cutting corners wherever possible."

The changing mix of motives for participation was evident at monthly Really Really Free Markets. At the RRFMs I attended in 2008, the organizers were often left with *too many* goods, as people brought more than they took away. During an interview in 2012, though, Madeline explained that the challenge for organizers had shifted: "People come with a giant suitcase and fill it with the brim, or heap it up on a granny cart." Some of them were truly needy, she said, while others were "hoarders, and re-sellers" who came to "cherry-pick and high-grade."[34] Zaac complained that there had been an "onslaught" of people attending his wild food foraging tours hoping to gather and then *sell* the plants they collected, "absurd as that sounds."

At the RRFMs, freegan.info continued to provide a table of dumpster-dived food, but there, too, the group encountered problems. As Madeline explained, "We were trying to build community, but it was very individualistic. People would come to our table, take some food, and ask, 'That's all you've got?' This is something we're really fighting in NYC right now; it's hard to attract people with a more communal attitude." As a subsequent e-mail announced, the

RRFM organizers decided to ration out the goods on display, rather than put them out all at once, and markets moved from monthly to quarterly.

This freeloader attitude even undermined freegan.info's signature event: the trash tour. At one tour I attended in 2012, Janet and Madeline struggled to get people to stop combing over the display for choice items and to pay attention to the "waving the banana" speech. This ethos seemed to be the new norm throughout the growing ranks of dumpster divers in New York, as Jason described:

> I have encountered, at moments, "the frenzy." Maybe at Trader Joe's or some of the more popular spots where it's kind of really caught on at the mainstream level that you can get free food, and you can go there and you can actually see people fighting, elbowing, thinking, "How much am I going to be able to get for myself? How much do I have to give to someone else?" That breaks my heart, to see that, this thing we were gung-ho about and tried to spread, and maybe we were responsible for letting people know, and they bring that attitude of trying to get more, and that's a shame.

Others also informed me of a rise of "competitive dumpstering." One exasperated would-be diver wrote the freegan.info "ask box" to report that she knew people who dived but wouldn't share their spots. As Madeline concluded, "There are more and more people who are dumpstering out of desperate need, hoarding, or other reasons which are very much capitalist-friendly." The rising popularity of dumpster diving was problematic, too, because outside the (semi)controlled context of a trash tour, dumpster divers often left bags ripped or untied, giving stores further reason to act to deter waste reclamation.

For freegan.info, problems came not just from "freeloaders" who dropped in on events with no sense of freeganism's political content but also from "low-key" freegans who attended *many* events despite having little interest in anticapitalism. By most active members' assessment, freegan.info's trash tours were by 2009 drawing large numbers of people with "stable, boring lives" who were loosely concerned about waste and the environment and looking for a social activity or good food. One night, I managed to initiate a conversation with a frequent attendee whose name no one in the group knew. She hesitantly revealed that she taught English at a nearby university. I asked her "Where?" and she told me, "I don't really want to say." She then added, "I live in a doorman building in this neighborhood. I don't know what they think of me at night [when I'm dumpster diving], but I don't care." When I asked her why she was so secretive about her freeganism—refusing to give her name, agree to an interview, or be shown on camera—she explained that, her previous comment aside, she was afraid of the way people would judge her if they knew that she ate discarded food. Sounding almost distraught, she carried on, "I can't tell my husband, I can't tell my friends. My best friend of my life I can't tell. I can't tell my students." While most freegans would likely be sympathetic to her concerns about stigma, such attitudes did make it difficult to connect her concern for reducing waste to any broader agenda for social change.

While not as frustrating as the freeloaders, these low-key freegans made little contribution to the group's collective project. One such woman in her midforties, who had been involved in the group for over a year, explained to me:

> I'm interested in it [freeganism], but I don't need to be outspoken about it...I don't like to hear a lot about politics, which I think would put me off in a sense....I'm happy doing things in my corner of the world, partaking in what I want to partake in, but I don't necessarily want to be active in taking my freeganism to the world.

Although freegan.info had long tried to frame freeganism in an appealing way, it had always brought those framings back to an overarching rejection of the central imperatives of capitalism, like endless growth or commodification of needed goods. This woman, though, found the rhetoric problematic: "You'll get more people involved if people just get involved slowly, rather than being scared into something. I guess that's why I'm more for the low-key approach." She thus filtered freeganism through a widely diffused cultural lens that limits "politics" to personal lifestyle decisions and views confrontational claims as inappropriate.[35]

These participants' ideological and practical orientations changed the group's tone in a way that drove off rebels and radicals. Jonathan, a consummate rebel who described himself as an "anarchist-nihilist," talked about attending a freegan.info action in 2012:

I was so disappointed! It started with, "We're against capitalism and we're going to show you this waste," but then, in two minutes, everyone forgot about that first part and it was just about getting free stuff. Everyone was grabbing things as quick as they could [and] no one was sharing.

When I asked if he planned to go back, he said, "No. No one is an anticapitalist there. Like, there are *no* radicals. When I told people about my lifestyle, they were like, '*whoooooa.*'" These frustrations extended to those who had already been involved in the group for a long time. Madeline announced that she would be taking a break from involvement in the group after one feast where several "regulars" showed up only after the meal had already been cooked and failed to bring any of the items they had collected with the group the night before.

If anything, this section on freeloaders and low-key freegans is a reminder of the powerful hold that the individualistic and acquisitive spirit of capitalism maintains even within a nominally anticapitalist movement. In a culture that glorifies consumption as the pinnacle of political engagement, it is little surprise that some would flock to trash tours as others might stampede at Black Friday sales. Madeline was circumspect about this, but also acknowledged that it created real limits to the impact of prefigurative politics: "It's the problem of any of these mutual-aid activities within a capitalist society. Everyone is trying to do the best they can within a capitalist society, and for some people that means getting one-up on other people who are around."

Stealing the Meaning of Waste

The purpose of cultural anchors in social movements is to provide shared points of reference that prevent debate and disagreement from spiraling out of hand. Part of why freegan.info could have sprawling, often heated, discussions of weighty topics like whether the group should seek to overthrow civilization (i.e., primitivism) or the state (i.e., anarchism) was because there was still a sense that everyone was on the same page when it came to using waste to both critique and develop alternatives to capitalism.

During my time with the group, though, one issue proved so divisive that some even suggested that I keep it out of this book:

shoplifting. I include it, though, because it highlights the grossly different understandings that people held of freeganism. These conflicts, often sparked by individuals who had never been to a freegan .info event and were sending e-mails from far-flung parts of the world, called into question whether freeganism had any "anchors" at all and set the stage for the departure of many of the group's key players.

Shoplifting is normalized in certain segments of the anarchist community.[36] In the East Bay Food Not Bombs community I studied, activists casually talked about stealing commodities ranging from toothpaste to washing machines. When Sasha returned from his "squat tour" in Barcelona, he spoke of shoplifting as if it were an obvious choice for those unwilling or unable to work:

> There was like a family of four in one of the squats we were at that had like a two-year-old and a ten-year-old, and the parents weren't making money. They needed dairy, bread, and lentils that weren't dumpster-able. So they would go to the store and steal because they needed to support their family.

For some, the justification for direct action actually makes shoplifting more intuitive than purchasing. As Jason explained:

> If you want it, that's your license to take it. It's what we need to live. There should be free food. We die if we don't have it. So what reason should there be that we have to pay into this complex system where we're working for these tokens that we exchange? That doesn't make any sense at all.

Indeed, some activists even see shoplifting as a *doubly* effective tactic because it meets material needs while cutting into capitalists' profits.

Shoplifting's place within freeganism is, however, ambiguous. The pamphlet *Why Freegan?* raises shoplifting as one possible way to get off the grid, but—unlike *every* other tactic it mentions—is equivocal about whether it "counts" as freegan:

> Shoplifting: There is some debate over how freegan this really is because you are still creating an empty shelf that must be restocked, but it is more freegan than forking over big bucks. This is a more

> direct attack on the store selling the goods, not the producer … so
> you should consider if you are putting a ma & pa organic veggie
> stand out of business or just chipping away at a corporate giant.

Freegan.info's own literature makes no mention of shoplifting, even among the thirty-nine different strategies highlighted by the group's pamphlet "Freeganism in Practice." I've never heard stealing raised in a "waving the banana" speech.

In 2009 Adam—in his capacity as "moderator" for the "insane asylum" that was the freegan-world e-mail list and its several thousand subscribers—posted an e-mail from a student looking to gather different viewpoints on shoplifting. Both Adam and the researcher were clear that they weren't endorsing shoplifting, just asking for opinions on it. These qualifications were quickly drowned by scores of hysterical messages on the topic that flowed through the list over the ensuing week. Many expressed immediate and unequivocal condemnation of any discussion of shoplifting being associated with freeganism:

> I will be unsubscribing [from this e-mail list]. Shoplifting is steal-
> ing, plain and simple. And it does not contribute to a "free" or "free-
> gan" lifestyle. It is simply wrong. You made a poor judgment call by
> including this request in the list. It negates all the effort done by free-
> gans to have their lifestyle accepted and even honored in some cases.

E-mails such as these expressed a reflexive condemnation of stealing, apparently on the assumption that it was wrong to violate private property. The response from some of the list's self-styled anarchists was sparse in nuance:

> As far as I'm concerned there is no argument to be made that steal-
> ing from a bunch of murderers and con artists is immoral. One can
> make an argument for how functional it is and to what purpose it
> serves, but not that it is immoral. To say that it is immoral to steal
> from them is to say that you uphold the structure of class society
> and you think it is justified for [the] bourgeois class to steal from
> the masses but not for the masses to take back what was rightfully
> theirs. And I think that's an inherently unfreegan argument.

As the last line suggests, this single tactic raised profound questions about what freeganism was and was not, clear boundaries that the group had fairly deliberately avoided clarifying.

Among the activists actually involved in freegan.info, the debate was more considerate. Many perceived shoplifting as problematic because it was a "faulty tactic, both lazy and ineffectual." Stealing, one freegan explained, creates a "demand for products that are made by sweatshop workers on stolen land from mismanaged resources that destroy the environment or are tested on tortured animals." As another added, shoplifting puts "hypocritical blood on your hands" because it leads individuals to possess "products you claim to hate." Madeline told me about a discussion she had with a much younger anarchist who had just shoplifted a blouse: "I told her, 'Maybe just wear an old one, and make it more your style. Altering it.' For this person, that was like, 'Hah!' There is still a mind-set that, all this stuff is being dangled in front of our faces, direct action means just going ahead and taking it." For her, the debate captured some of the enduring challenges of escaping capitalist patterns of consumption:

> Shoplifting is like waste, in that it starts with overconsumption, and starts with a sense of entitlement and deprivation. What does it mean to actually be deprived? If you feel deprived of that new fashionable blouse, are you really deprived? Or is this something akin to racism telling you black people are inferior to you, or homophobia, saying that you are less worthy as a person if you're gay? It is that kind of feeling that we hear in ourselves, that, I have to have this, and I have to have it or I'm deprived. Isn't that capitalism talking to us, not our own feelings?

Others, despite their own misgivings about shoplifting, felt that the debate was a disturbing example of how "moderates" and "liberals" were co-opting freeganism. Adam, while noting that he himself did not shoplift aside from occasional scams he used to copy freegan literature, pointed out to me that "you can't have a revolution without stealing."[37] For him and others, like Jason and Leia, the acrimony among supposed "freegans" for merely raising the idea of shoplifting revealed that many people attracted to freeganism were unwilling to endorse a truly radical transformation of society.

Their frustration grew when some self-styled freegans of the low-key variety began claiming that being against waste did not entail being against capitalism. As one e-mail at the tail end of the debate articulated:

> *I see now that I have to state my reason to call myself a "Freegan," I just hate waste. That is why I want to be a Freegan, because I am quite willing to dumpster dive to stop things being wasted. I think that about covers it. Not to take what is someone else's property. I therefore, obviously believe in owning property. I value mine and look after silly things other people would think of as rubbish, but in my eyes I see value and use.*

Leia was furious: "The real tragedy is the waste? Say nothing of the exploitation of workers and resources that went into making the product?" Another e-mail list subscriber, though, was encouraged by the first e-mail and responded:

> *I am affluent and own several businesses (all successful) but get most of my stuff for free and never hesitate to stop and trash pick or jump in a dumpster to hunt down items to keep out of the land-fill. I am very in favor of capitalism, just not corporate or business irresponsibility to the communities in which they operate and supposedly serve.*

"If you are looking for a pro-capitalist hang-out, go to some sports bar," one person shot back.

The issue grew more complex when, with the proliferation of locks on dumpsters, making use of wasted resources increasingly and undeniably meant violating private property. When one message came across the list mentioning that a favorite dumpster had been chained shut and put behind a fence, one freegan replied, "I've got two words for you: BOLT CUTTERS." The resulting condemnation from proproperty, antiwaste freegans led to one pedantic excursus on the real meaning of freeganism:

> *When a store locks their dumpster, they don't want people to take things from the dumpster, they want people to go inside the store*

and buy things. Taking things from an unlocked dumpster may seem free, but it isn't because it costs the store money from the profits they would make if people bought things instead of diving. If the goal is to respect private property and corporate profits, and to seek respect from capitalists, then the best way to do that is to buy things instead of diving. Capitalists will have much more respect for you if you buy things than if you dive.

A similarly heated argument opened up over a related issue a few years later, train hopping. This time, though, it drew in heavily involved freegan.info activists, reflecting the growing unmooring of any kind of consensus within the group. One participant proposed via e-mail that the group delete the website's reference to train hopping as a freegan form of transportation, implying that it was a form of "petty theft" that entailed avoiding fares for public transportation. Some quickly pointed out that train hopping typically meant jumping on *freight* trains, taking advantage of their excess, unused capacity to carry people. As Gio enumerated, train hopping was "trespassing, maybe, definitely illegal, not very reliable, and pretty dangerous. But freegan nonetheless, whether you like it or not."

Cindy attempted to calm the discussion down by reverting to freeganism's antiwaste anchor, reassuring the original sender that "train-hopping… is the same, basically, as squatting, guerrilla gardening, dumpster diving and any number of other ways freegans use resources that would otherwise go to waste." She added that freegan .info took no official position on shoplifting and pleaded, "Can we agree that making use of wasted resources is a good thing? And agree to disagree on the rest?" The problem, however, was that by the time of this debate, the meaning of "making use of wasted resources" had already become contested.

Discarding Freegan.info

As conflicts within the group grew, various individuals floated proposals to resolve them. Some wanted to break freegan.info into autonomous projects, so some could hold trash tours, others could pressure corporations to reduce waste, and still others could focus on prefigurative projects like gardens or squats—with all three calling themselves "freegan" at the same time. Adam repeatedly implored for a moratorium on trash tours and on interactions with the media until the group took the time to articulate its long-term goals and strategies. Jason proposed different strategies for limiting the attendance of freeloaders at freegan.info events. In the end, though, none of these proposals came to fruition, partly because many participants had begun to abandon the very label "freegan" itself.

A major blow to the group came in 2009, when a landlord hoping to cash in on Bedford-Stuyvesant's rapid gentrification evicted the 123 Community Center and the freegan bike workshop.[38] For a short time, Wendy and Quinn shuttled the bike parts between activist houses and cooperatives, but they could never find an affordable space. Wendy woefully explained that, with the closure of 123, "We really lost our sense of community," as well as freegan.info's most frequent recurring activity that was not dumpster diving. Madeline, too, commented on how "having the primary activity have something that can be one-off for participants"—that is, trash tours—meant that "we're not really building community." The comparison was stark: "To build a bike workshop, you have people committed to taking shifts, gathering parts, maintaining a stock of parts. You can drop into a trash tour and never come again, that's the thing." The bike workshop had given freegan.info a plug-in point for activists with a particular set of skills and interests, which it lost with its closure. It had also given them the credibility of being associated with an openly anarchist space in a low-income community. As the group's scope narrowed, so did the range of people involved in it.

Another key source of frustration that several freegans cited as their reason for departure was the sense that, as the debates over shoplifting suggested, freeganism was increasingly severed from its roots and devoid of political content. Speaking about his disillusionment with cooperative "freegan" living in Surrealestate, Quinn told me, "You really do have to find people who have a mature understanding of capitalism, and an analysis of the way it works, and that can envision a different way of functioning. There are only so many people who have that vision and have that commitment." He paused a few seconds and added, "And if you don't have that, you just become a mooch." The increasingly individualistic and reformist orientations of the people coming to freegan events showed that freeganism itself had become exactly the kind of atomized consumer activism they thought they had rejected.

Despite this, all but one of the one-time freegan.info participants I reinterviewed in 2012 was still heavily involved in politics. Some had moved even farther toward direct action and anarchism. Sasha, for example, spent time in Tucson with a pirated radio station and anarchist infoshop before moving to Portland to work for an ecological press. Jason continued to dumpster dive on his own and with his roommates, explaining how he was building on what he saw as the "kernel" of freeganism: "I like the idea of setting up networks of mutual aid, figuring out, literally, physically, how to do this simple idea, which is reclaiming waste, and using it for the benefit of everyone, outside of capitalism."

Freegan.info as an organization continued, at the time of writing, to hold twice-monthly trash tours, monthly freegan feasts, and occasional wild food foraging tours or reading groups. It had been sustained primarily by the strong commitments of Janet and Cindy. Cindy commented, during our second interview, on what kept her engaged as well as her own frustrations:

> We consistently get thirty people coming to our events, and maybe one-half of them are new. They're interested and they're learning and they're having their eyes opened. I understand the frustration that the same three people shouldn't be doing trash tours for seven years, that there should be new people who are leading them. I don't think that's a fault of the trash tours, maybe it is a fault of outreach skills and people skills. It's just been unfortunate that there hasn't been the energy level to do other things.

At the meetings I attended, I could see myself that the group persisted in attracting new people, but struggled to find anyone with the drive to organize skill-shares or restart the bike workshop. Although the media coverage had tapered off, there was still an uneven inflow of journalists. Moreover, by Cindy's assessment, the group had "sharpened its political criticism" by coming to a consensus on advocating for a reduction of waste: "We're not a pro-dumpster diving group, we're an anti-capitalist, anti-waste group. So now we agree that if waste is reduced and people can't dumpster dive anymore, that's a victory, not a loss."

That freegan.info persevered in being at least loosely connected to the anticapitalist scene in New York was confirmed when, in the summer of 2011, the initial organizers of Occupy Wall Street got in touch with freegan.info. Jason described how OWS was rooted in anticapitalist movements that freegan.info had played a small part of keeping it alive during a nadir of mobilization in the late 2000s, explaining, "Occupy didn't come from the mainstream. It came from the fringes.... it was used as a leverage point for anarchists to have an event, try to get people to organize. Lots of people that were involved in Occupy were people that also used to come to freegan.info."[39] Gio, who claimed to have been one of the first campers in Zuccotti Park near Wall Street, also saw a connection between freeganism and Occupy, noting, "I think in many ways freegan.info, maybe along with all those other little activist factions and issues that people have been talking about for years, contributed to this 'bang bang,' where it all just kind of coalesced at once."

Freegans were attracted to both the tactics of OWS and the message. Janet noted the affinity between their critiques of capitalism: "Occupy Wall Street isn't about waste per se, but it is about excess: excess bonuses, excess profits."[40] Others perceived it as a far more successful instance of what freegan.info had been trying to do for years, which is engage in very public anticapitalist direct action. Jason cited the encampment's utopian aspirations as a major draw:

> What were the occupations themselves but big camps of mutual aid networks, people setting up free everything—free food, free books, free clothes, free housing? It was all just a big free place to live. In Zuccotti they didn't have infinite resources and room, but for the people who were there, it was an outpost of mutual aid. What happened inside—aside from the spectacle of it, the news story—was a freegan paradise, a utopia. Maybe not really a utopia, but that's what they were trying to make.

Indeed, OWS expressed its prefigurative vision partly through waste. In its heyday, "Zuccotti boasted a greywater system as part of the People's Kitchen, a bike-powered composter whose compost was cycled to several nearby community gardens, a recycling depot and a refuse station to fuel the movement's cardboard aesthetic."[41] Jason, Wendy, and Madeline all said that they helped dumpster dive supplies for the occupation before donations rendered doing so unnecessary.

While freegans, ex-freegans, and freegan practices all played a

significant role in Occupy, freegan.info itself did not. Madeline admitted that, with respect to Occupy, "I don't feel like there was a 'we'"
that got involved, even though she and Cindy both were arrested at
an Occupy demonstration. Cindy herself lamented:

> *Freegan.info in New York was pretty isolated by the time Occupy
> came around. There were some people in the group who were very
> involved in Occupy and a lot of people who weren't. We talked about
> making those connections, but we didn't have the energy to make a
> concerted group effort to connect.*

As I observed, the newer constituencies involved in freegan.info outside the core organizers were not people for whom Occupy was particularly interesting. These were individuals interested in personal,
small-scale action around waste; Occupy was a large-scale, collective
challenge to global financial capitalism. While the old anchor of free-
gan.info made seeing the connection between the two easy—which
is why so many former freegan.info participants got involved in
OWS—the group no longer had the shared sense of purpose that
made involvement in the upwelling an obvious choice.

As Keith McHenry from Food Not Bombs pointed out in our
interview, freeganism was, at its inception, just a joke. One group
of people in New York, taking advantage of a particularly favorable
urban environment and drawing on diverse histories of activist
engagement, tried to turn it into something else. All things considered, they were remarkably successful: they used ex-commodities to
expose abuses of capitalism that often go unremarked, even among
anticapitalists. At times, they even repurposed these ex-commodities
to experiment with alternatives. But this small group was always
arrayed against much bigger forces, which I have characterized as
combining to reinforce the fetish of waste: stores with the power
to lock their dumpsters, media that could misrepresent or trivial-
ize them with impunity, and cultural norms that led many people
to either actively imagine waste away or see ex-commodities as a
bonanza of free stuff to be voraciously consumed. Combined with
contradictions and conflict within the group, these forces eventually
left freegan.info unanchored and adrift.

Freeganism has largely returned to where it started: a set of diffuse
practices with no clear meaning or strong organizations to promote it.

But most freegans themselves remained politically engaged, regardless of the labels they chose. This finding should not be surprising. Freeganism resonated at a particular moment in time, but the commitments of activists themselves were always fluid. As Lola reflected to me, "Realizing what you believe and trying to live that is very complicated and something that a lot of people—especially myself—are going to spend the rest of our lives trying to figure out." Becoming a freegan, as Sowmya explained, was a "wonderful journey," but for most, it was more of a step along the way than a final destination.

Conclusion

Salvaging Sustainability

When Adam had finished his encyclopedic recounting of the injustices that went into the individual commodities we had encountered on that cold December night in 2008, he switched into a more contemplative mode. Usually when he "waved the banana," Adam looked away from the cameras, but this night, he addressed them directly:

> What we are doing is building up an extensive global archival record, documenting the enormous waste of resources in the U.S. that is being beamed all over the world. Being that this probably will be the record for some time, I have a question: when we think about people in twenty years, and in forty years, looking at this footage, we wonder, "What will they think of all of this needless waste of resources?"

He then switched from a pensive message to one reminiscent of a doomsday sermon. He questioned whether *anyone* would be able to look at the footage at all:

> We know that global industrial economic capitalism is on the verge of total collapse. We are in fact in the final days of Rome. While there is still bread on the shelves, and our newspapers are still filled with the idiot circuses of Paris Hilton and Britney Spears, all of these distractions are frankly failing to keep people from realizing that the end really and truly is near.

Later that night in the privacy of the Surrealestate basement, I asked Adam if he was serious. He nodded, "It's time for us [humans] to pack our bags and go, and I don't mean colonizing the stars." He probably could tell that I looked skeptical, and added, "Now, how practical is that?" before answering, "Well, very. Because barring a miracle we're not going to see the end of the twenty-second century, and quite possibly [not] the end of the twenty-first."

Although it's difficult to capture in retrospect, within a particular place and historical moment, what Adam told me felt entirely plausible. In the ideological soup of freegan.info, talk of climate change, biodiversity loss, peak oil, and even avian flu melded into one dire appraisal of humanity's present course. The economy was in the worst downturn since the Great Depression, and New York was the epicenter of a crisis that seemed to be deepening with no end in sight. Back at my university in New Jersey, where I was writing the senior thesis that became this book, graduates who previously would have walked effortlessly into jobs as investment bankers were suddenly confronted with the possibility of unemployment. With even Princeton students taking an interest in freeganism, I thought I was describing reality, not an aspiration, when I wrote, "Freegan values and practices are exploding *everywhere* right now." Caught up as I was in a host of freegan projects, and enthralled by the ineffable charisma of freegans like Adam, I really did believe, as Jason avowed to me, that we stood at the "fulcrum of history."

But given that I've finished this book without having had to forage edible greens amid postapocalyptic ruins, it seems that Adam's predictions were off the mark. In fact, within a few months of his speech, Adam was gone. He stepped back not just from freegan .info but from the very word he was so instrumental in popularizing, *freegan*. To him, freeganism had turned into a list of "fifty little things you can do to save the environment," a "political veneer on a money-saving hobby."

Often, when I talked about my research with people who had only a cursory knowledge of freeganism, I was assured that, by the time they hit thirty, freegans would be driving Saabs and shopping at Whole Foods.[1] Now in his midthirties, Adam is like most of my informants in showing no signs of abating in his activism. Instead, when last we talked, he was organizing furiously against the Trans-Pacific Partnership, a trade agreement that he saw as a harbinger of intensified animal abuse and environmental destruction. "It's depressing work, honestly, fighting to keep things from getting worse with little hope of success," he told me. Then again, a belief that he could actually *stop* injustice was never a precondition for Adam's attempts to do so. He had backed off some of his rhetoric about "dropping out" of capitalism, having concluded that he was "way too much of a privileged motherfucker to be preaching to anyone about how they should live." But he certainly wasn't shopping at Whole Foods.

The sociologist Kai Erikson once suggested that the first aim of any ethnography has to be to "get the story straight," and that is what I have tried to do: to offer a nuanced and sympathetic, albeit incomplete, picture of a largely undocumented and misunderstood social movement.[2] I'm not convinced, though, that "getting the story straight" is, in itself, enough. Freeganism still crops up occasionally—when, for example, a hacker with the anarchist group Anonymous was arrested and identified as a "freegan,"[3] or the Hollywood drama *The East* linked freeganism with eco-sabotage—but the deluge of media coverage of the phenomenon has slowed to a trickle. When I mentioned to Janet that I was still working on my "freegan book," she said that she worried that the moment "had passed." She might be right.

That said, freeganism does offer some insights into something bigger. Upon his departure, Adam lamented that too many freegans were unwilling to name the root of the problem: capitalism. When I asked him if conceivably not mentioning capitalism was strategic, he replied, "Can you be antiracist if you avoid saying you are antiracist? If you really think capitalism is a life-destroying, soul-crushing, planet-killing system, there's no reason not to say so." His admonition could, in its own way, apply much more broadly. The word *capitalism* has almost completely disappeared from much of sociology, including the study of social movements—even when describing anarchist-influenced phenomena like the antiglobalization movement.[4]

If the persistence of anticapitalism has been hard to see in the new millennium, it may be because movements like freeganism don't look or sound like the anticapitalists of yore. In their exhaustive chronicle of the ongoing dance between capitalists and anticapitalists, Luc Boltanski and Eve Chiappello show that critiques of capitalism have transformed in tandem with changes in capitalism itself. In the 1930s a "social critique" of capitalism centered on the exploitation of labor and the growing inequality created by industrial capitalism. By the 1960s the focus had shifted to an "artistic critique" that lambasted the "dehumanization," "loss of autonomy," and "absence of creativity" endemic to mass production and consumption.[5]

Freegan discourse is emblematic of a third kind of a critique—an ecological one.[6] I mean this not just in the sense that environmental issues are front and center in current radical analyses of the shape of our economic system. In "ecological critiques," issues of scale, size, and sufficiency are now articulated as among the unavoidable downsides of capitalism. While quite literally waving a banana during one trash tour, Sasha cried out, "We are the ones shouting 'stop.' We represent the void in the system. It's like a credit card being declined. We say, 'No more.'" In a sense, while the "social critics" were concerned with *how* things were being produced, and the "artistic critics" with *what* was being consumed and produced, "ecological critics" like Sasha were above all worried about *how much* is being produced, consumed, and wasted. As such, shouting "stop" was a political program in and of itself, one centered on a single word: *less*. This critique engages with capitalism on its chosen battleground, mirroring the centrality of discourses of "waste" in justifications for neoliberal policies and threats of "scarcity" if the market's dictates are not heeded.

To be sure, freegan.info is not the only movement offering an ecological critique of capitalism. Quite the contrary: I believe freeganism is one expression of the general zeitgeist of contemporary anticapitalism, as manifested in the cries of "enough" from the Zapatistas in Mexico or the graffiti declaring "the world is full" left behind after antiglobalization demonstrations.[7] As one dumpster diver playfully asserted, "The real freeloaders and scavengers . . . are the people who . . . choose to compete and fight over it [the earth's resources], rather than sharing their time and possessions with others in need."[8] The unveiling of waste fetishism could thus continue to play a powerful role in anticapitalist politics, as there is no better evidence that capitalism produces way too much than the fact that many things are disposed of without ever even passing into a consumer's hands.

There's another lesson about contemporary anticapitalism that freeganism can teach us. Sociologists still tend to think of social movement "politics" as being expressed through symbolic events like marches, demonstrations, or rallies, which are intended to dramatize some position and spur politicians to take action.[9] It would not be entirely inaccurate to view trash tours through this lens: as attempts to call waste to the attention of the public and media, with the hoped-for ultimate effect of getting elites to pass legislation to address the problem. This is the lens the public, too, tends to apply to movement, asking, "What are the demands?," "Where are the banners and chants?," or "How will this turn into legislation?"

But this approach offers a one-dimensional view of freeganism, one that overlooks entirely how freegans *also* see themselves as achieving social change through "prefigurative" acts like building bikes or eating over-the-hill produce. The vision is not one of sweeping change coming in one fell swoop but a gradual—almost invisible—accretion of the institutions, practices, and values of a new society over time.[10] Although the specifics of freegan practice may seem eccentric, they are responding to much bigger challenges: disillusionment with elected leaders, the absence of convincing blueprints for alternative social arrangements, and the growing power of nonstate actors like corporations or international finance. Other studies affirm that freegans are not the only ones who are "disavowing politics" in their traditional form and turning toward more community-level, bottom-up, and direct strategies for social change.[11]

The study of freeganism offers additional insights for those who have *already* recognized the contemporary salience of prefigurative politics. Research on the prefigurative aspects of the antiglobalization movement or on Occupy has typically focused on organizational structure, democratic decision making, and use of information technology.[12] While I could have touched on these themes, the real center of gravity of freeganism lay in its grittier, material side. Freeganism highlights the day-to-day processes through which activists are rethinking how to provide for mundane necessities like food, shelter, clothing, and transportation. In a neoliberal era where cuts to social services, widespread unemployment, and criminalization of homeless have put certain populations' very survival into question, it's unsurprising that movements are addressing not just how to govern financial capital but also how to eat, sleep, and stay warm.

If examining freeganism has analytic value for scholars, it also has strategic value for activists. The "fetish of waste" and "ex-commodities" are not just ideas intended to meld into the academic rhetorical mush: they each point to how freegans' politics could be further developed and spread. Ex-commodities are a powerful tool for dispelling the fetish of commodities that tells us we can save the biosphere by switching detergents. Unveiling the fetish of waste, on the other hand, is a simple yet powerful way to undermine some of the foundational justifications for capitalism. It doesn't require evoking complex Marxist concepts like the labor theory of value or alienation. It draws, instead, on the nearly universally shared belief that "waste" is a bad thing. Ex-commodities can also enable activists to experiment with how to organize a postcapitalist economy without moving to the countryside and free up time for political action that would otherwise be spent on wage labor. Of course, each of these openings for challenging capitalism has to be defended. Future struggles will have to protect ex-commodities from being (literally) fenced off and counter the (figurative) blinders that insist all waste comes from distortions of the market imposed by governments or consumers.

Even those with little interest in "anticapitalist critiques" or "prefigurative politics" might have something to learn from freeganism. When I first began my research in 2007, it was safe to say that, when it came to food waste, the freegans were a voice in the wilderness. In 2011 the U.S. Department of Agriculture could confidently state, "Currently, in the United States, there is no widespread or visible political or social momentum to reduce food loss and waste."[13] By the agency's own reckoning, though, the situation has rapidly changed.[14] In 2013 the USDA and Environmental Protection Agency launched a "Food Waste Recovery" challenge, to which 210 organizations—including universities, professional sports teams, and one petroleum-refining company—signed on. In advance of a 2015 meeting at the United Nations on sustainable development, the two agencies declared that the United States would aim to reduce food waste by 50 percent by 2030.[15] These national initiatives grew out of a multiplicity of grassroots initiatives, from smartphone apps for sharing leftovers to state-level bans on landfilling organic waste.

If anything, though, the United States is a laggard. The European Union has promulgated dozens of decrees and regulations addressing food waste, the United Nations recently unveiled a "Think.Eat. Save" campaign, the British government put millions of pounds into a "Waste & Resources Action Program," and France introduced a "National Pact Against Food Waste" and is contemplating legislation requiring supermarkets to donate excess food, granting amnesty to dumpster divers, and promoting the use of "doggie"—or in France, gourmet—bags.[16] Even Pope Francis has jumped on the bandwagon, tweeting, "Consumerism has accustomed us to waste. But throwing food away is like stealing it from the poor and hungry."[17]

On first glance, this surge in interest in food waste seems like a logical response to an objective problem. Somewhere between 12 and 15 percent of humanity's total water consumption and 23 percent of its farmland are used to grow food that no one eats.[18] If "food waste" declared itself an independent nation, its yearly greenhouse gas emissions would be third, behind the United States and China.[19] Global food prices hit an all-time high in 2012, pushing millions of people into hunger.[20] With the human population expected to surpass nine billion by 2050, reducing food waste seems like a straightforward way to meet growing need and alleviate hunger without exacerbating the grisly environmental toll wreaked by modern agriculture.[21]

But "social problems" do not just burst onto the public stage under their own momentum: it takes movements, activists, and issue entrepreneurs to put them there. So where does freeganism fit into the picture? In early 2014 I attended a conference in Belgium put on by "GreenCook," an EU-funded collaboration between governments, businesses, and nonprofits committed to reducing food waste. The keynote speaker was Tristram Stuart, a British public intellectual who, by his own account, first became interested in food waste through "skip dipping" in London. He opened his remarks by asking, "Who here has ever been dumpster diving?" My hand and that of my partner shot up: the other 250 people—mostly government functionaries, corporate sustainability officers, and high-level NGO employees—looked at us quizzically. Yet when I pulled Stuart aside afterward, he told me:

> *By taking journalists round the back of supermarkets, showing them what was there, and serving them dinner based on it, and being able to very articulately talk about how this fit into a global problem—the amount of media that generated certainly sparked a lot of interest on the part of policymakers and companies.... I absolutely think freeganism was the original instigator of this new wave of global action on food waste.*

Drawing a direct link between the stimulus from a single movement and a societal response is notoriously challenging, and becomes even more so when we consider the multiplicity of different actors making demands on our food system.[22] What we *do* know is that when movements have an impact, it tends to come through amplifying preexisting currents in public opinion and politicizing concerns previously left out of the political arena.[23] Once issues move from the margins to the mainstream, though, they quickly spiral out of movements' control.

I feel comfortable, then, stating that there is probably some connection between the *hundreds* of media stories on freegan.info in major news outlets in the United States and food waste's subsequent entrance into the public arena. Other scholars concur that freeganism, alongside the actions of NGOs, the economic crisis, and government policies, contributed to channeling preexisting concerns about the environment and waste onto excess food.[24] Nonetheless, just as sociologists might predict, these contemporary initiatives against food waste present the issue in ways that freegans like Adam would doubtlessly find alien.

Indeed, some contemporary advocates have insisted that decreasing food waste is absolutely *not* a contentious proposition. According to Stuart, "Reducing food waste … is uncontroversial [and] relatively painless and easy" compared with other reforms to address climate change.[25] His American counterpart, Jonathan Bloom, gushes that solving food waste is a "triple bottom line" solution that benefits everyday citizens, businesses, and the environment: "By trimming our waste and recovering the low-hanging fruit (literally and figuratively!), we can help feed hungry Americans, bolster our economy, combat global warming, and make our society that much more ethical."[26] All that is needed, cheers another report, is "raising awareness of the 'hidden' costs" of waste, at which point food businesses will grab at the profits they are throwing away.[27]

While food waste prevention campaigns have occasionally targeted businesses, institutions, and governments, they have overwhelmingly continued a long-running pattern integral to the fetishization of waste: namely, displacing blame from producers onto consumers. The British Environmental Secretary pointed his finger at a "culture of perfection" as the culprit for wastage.[28] In announcing the U.S. food waste reduction goal, Secretary of Agriculture Tom Vilsack mentioned *only* consumers when describing the culprits of food waste.[29] Much like campaigns that propose shorter showers and fluorescent light bulbs as a way to arrest climate change, the United Nation's Think. Eat.Save website assures us that "with relative ease and a few simple changes to our habits, we can significantly shift this paradigm [of waste]."[30] Concern about food waste is thus often channeled toward lists of strategies like planning meals in advance, making a shopping list, cutting out the rotten parts of produce, choosing portions more carefully, or freezing leftovers.[31] They thus begin and end at the individual level, despite research that consistently shows that effective waste-reduction strategies target the context in which consumption happens—by, for example, changing the size of packages of food sold in the supermarket or by taxing waste—rather than the values and practices of consumers themselves.[32] Yet even those who, like Stuart, acknowledge the need for structural transformation in our food system nonetheless see the key change makers as individual consumers. As he writes, "Consumer power is the new face of democracy... we vote every day with our money, and we can use it to bring about change, often much more rapidly than legislation can ever achieve."[33]

Even if we get over some philosophical concerns (if dollars are the new votes, do people with more dollars get more votes?), there are good reasons to doubt that changes to consumer practices, while undeniably sensible, will have much of an impact. As the freegans themselves discovered, the idea of "consumer power" rests on believing the *rhetoric* of capitalism while ignoring how it actually works. It assumes a relatively neat correlation between what consumers want and what actually gets produced, a relationship that ex-commodities themselves suggest is not so straightforward. Recent studies have lauded a 21 percent decrease in food waste in British households— partly because of the economic downturn, partly because of increased awareness—but it's unclear whether households wasting less means less waste in aggregate or simply that waste is happening higher up in the food chain as commodities that get produced fail to find buyers.[34] Just as Adam argued that going vegan means more chickens wind up unsold in the supermarket bin, the same could be true of the food "conserved" by diligent consumers.

Contemporary initiatives against food waste fail to grapple with the fundamental dynamics of overproduction and commodification that were elucidated by the two Karls, which are drives integral to a capitalist system and which bear an outsize responsibility for creating ex-commodities in the first place. Since World War II, expanding agricultural productivity has far outstripped population growth. The total global food supply is 4,600 kcal per person per day—much of which is inefficiently fed to animals, less than half of which gets eaten, and the rest of which gets wasted.[35] It seems obvious that, to reduce food waste, we will have to reduce production of food. Yet the word *less* does not exist in the lexicon of capitalism—or, it would seem, in that of most food waste campaigners.[36]

To suggest that we should reduce production is politically and economically unacceptable in a capitalist society. Stuart writes that "sorting out the food waste problem would be . . . good for business," adding that, "where waste has been cut, profit margins consistently soar."[37] Yet aside from a few anecdotal examples, this claim quickly collapses. Food corporations employ thousands of analysts, consultants, and economists whose job it is to find the most profitable conceivable business model. If it were really so easy to raise profits through eliminating waste, wouldn't they already be doing it? As none other than the U.S. Comptroller General concluded, "In the course of preparing this report, no material has been found that would indicate that opportunities were knowingly overlooked by business owners to conserve food at an acceptable cost. The profit motive should dictate against such loss."[38] While the U.S. food reduction goals include "no real plans or penalties" and thus "will succeed or fail based on whether or not the food industry opts in," European countries have recognized that changing business practices requires coercive legislation and social pressure, not faith in the inherent goodness of market mechanisms.[39]

The issue becomes even more obdurate when we move from the level of the individual firm to the entire food sector. We can see the intractable barriers that overproduction presents to reducing waste by narrowing our gaze to one of the most-vaunted solutions to food waste: charitable donations. Once again, the solution seems simple: there are hungry people, there is excess food, and there are food banks not currently keeping pace with demand.[40]

On closer examination, however, there are numerous well-documented problems with addressing hunger through private charity, including nutritional inadequacy, unstable supplies, inaccessibility, and the indignity of "means testing" and religious requirements.[41] Through no deliberate malice on their part, food banks have smoothed the transition from a public system where poor people were given money to buy food of their choice to a private one in which the poor get whatever surplus falls out of the food system at a particular moment. Increasing donations only exacerbates this trend. In fact, in a draft of the most recent U.S. farm bill, billions in cutbacks to food stamps were paired with millions for community food rescue.[42]

Freegans themselves were ambivalent toward charitable groups like City Harvest (which, it should be noted, had publicly criticized freegan.info). For one thing, freegans observed that even stores that claimed to donate "all" their food continued to ex-commodify it in enormous quantities. As Janet observed:

> It's lip service to say, "We don't throw out." We've had stores we go to regularly that say to the cameras, "We don't throw out our food, we give to City Harvest." . . . It's good what they're [City Harvest] doing, but it's just literally not enough. There are still such quantities of waste. And, meanwhile, I think it placates the companies and the public.

Lucie, who interned with City Harvest one summer, was shocked that the organization actually lauded those stores whose business models relied on overabundance and excess:

> City Harvest doesn't even see the problem. It's just something normal that there is waste. We were talking about one of our suppliers, and they said, "They're great, they give us fifty bags of bread." And I asked them if that's changed over time, and they said, "No, they're very reliable, it's always been fifty bags." There's no attempt to change the situation at all. There's no questioning of capitalism, of waste, or of the need for free food in the first place.

No doubt, donations to food bank help alleviate hunger. But they also prop up unsustainable business models by allowing stores to claim tax deductions for overproduced and unhealthy food. Sadly, much of this winds up being thrown out anyway, because it simply does not fit the nutritional needs or culinary habits of the people these institutions serve.[43] Indeed, when I worked for three months at a food bank, people often came in looking for produce or protein but left with birthday cakes or pumpkin pies frozen since Thanksgiving—a reminder that, given that 50 percent of the excess calories produced in the United States consists of "added fats and oils" and "added sugars and sweeteners," what "we" don't want is not necessarily what "they" need.[44]

But imagine for an instant that stores, manufacturers, distributors, and producers decided to donate *all* their surplus food (or were mandated to do so, as legislation in France proposes)[45] and that food banks had the capacity to share it widely. Given that the United States wastes a number of calories equivalent to the nutritional deficit of the *entire world,* it follows that the needs of the hungry in the United States would quickly be met, at least in terms of raw calories. So where would the rest of that food go? It's more a fairy tale than thought experiment, though, because there's no way that the more than 40 percent of U.S. food production currently going to waste could be decommodified and redistributed for free. To do so would challenge the basic social contract of capitalism: that, by and large, you must work to survive.[46] It follows that charity has an obvious upper bound: as soon as potential *customers*—as opposed to poor people who are presumed unable to buy food anyway—began getting food for free, the spigots of ex-commodities would be switched off. Some restaurants already admit that they don't donate for fear that potential customers might get their product for free.[47]

Under neoliberal capitalism, production, consumption, and waste are all bound together as part of a single process. You can't remove one link in the chain—like "ex-commodification"—without the whole thing falling apart. Capitalism's nonnegotiable requirement that needed goods are commodities thus presents a roadblock for some of the other designs of food waste campaigners. Stuart, for example, argues that if the rich world stopped wasting food, it would reduce pressures on food supply, lower prices, and increase access among the world's poor. It's certainly more plausible than directly redistributing the world's surplus, but it is still naive to the way markets for agricultural commodities actually work.

So long as food is a commodity, it will go to the highest bidder, and recently, the highest bidders for food have had remarkably little interest in eating it. The world food crisis of 2007 and 2008 was spurred by financial speculation and a growing demand for biofuels made from food crops.[48] Extending this trend, speculators have started to see the value of excess in its capacity to serve as fuel, not food. In Europe, alongside shaming consumers, efforts have focused on "diversion"—that is, channeling food waste toward anaerobic digesters, fertilizer, or composters.[49] Past experience with waste-to-energy incinerators shows, however, that when we create demands for "waste," perverse things happen. Municipalities become obligated through "put-or-pay" contracts to produce a certain amount of waste, stunting any impetus to prevent waste in the first place.[50] This is the case even though the evidence is unequivocal that *reducing* food waste is far more environmentally beneficial than diverting it, and anaerobic digestion is only one step above landfilling in the food waste hierarchy of environmental sustainability.[51] Far from challenging the commodification of food, waste-to-energy and other contemporary schemes actually deepen it. Whatever their other merits, they certainly don't put more food in the mouths of the world's hungry.

For his part, Bloom predicts that reducing food waste will soon become as commonplace and "second nature" as recycling.[52] On one level, it's a hopeful comparison: recycling rates have climbed steadily from 10 percent of municipal solid waste in 1990 to 33 percent today.[53] Following the pattern begun for materials like glass and plastic, nearly two hundred municipalities have started programs for curbside collection of food scraps (which are then diverted into the industrial digesters or composters discussed above).[54] The actual positive impacts of recycling, however, are dubious.[55] Much of the export of materials for recycling is actually "sham recycling" intended to avoid government regulations on production and has little ecological value. The chief "impact" of recycling has been to assuage ecological guilt, giving us a sense that production and consumption can continue to grow so long as we put our discards in the right bin.[56] I fear food waste initiatives will similarly prove to be forms of what Samantha MacBride, criticizing contemporary recycling, calls "busyness": "a fulfilling sense of work and achievement that often brings positive side-effects but fails to reach the central effect."[57]

Indeed, as freegans were fond of saying, agribusinesses and retailers are already using food waste reductions as a way to get their "green check mark" while distracting us from the fact that our entire food system needs an overhaul. As I noted in the introduction, there are two sides to the tomato's story. Certainly, eating that tomato rather than ex-commodifying it would have been a good thing. But it wouldn't magically improve the working conditions of the Mexican laborers, pull greenhouse gases from the air, or put water back into the aquifers. Ex-commodities are a symptom, but they are not the entirety of the disease. If we are not careful, addressing food waste could actually *exacerbate* other ecological problems. For example, the packaging industry has enthusiastically leapt on the food-waste-reduction bandwagon by claiming that more packaging could mean less *food* in our trash bins (never mind the plastic and Styrofoam).[58]

We thus return to the problem that tied freegans in knots for so long: if we are to withdraw our dollars from wasteful or unethical food production, where exactly should we put them? Bloom writes that, if American consumers stopped wasting food, a family of four could "save" $2,200 a year.[59] But "saving" money on food is just a way of saying "spending" on something else. And what, exactly, are we supposed to spend it on? iPhones? clothes? The former can be traced to factories in China where workers commit suicide in horrendous numbers and that contain metals from mines in Africa that employ children from war zones.[60] If we follow the latter, we might wind up in a sweatshop in Bangladesh where the lack of even basic safety precautions can lead to hundreds of deaths.[61] And, of course, both clothes and cell phones get ex-commodified in egregious quantities, too.

There are real trade-offs involved in reducing waste, which discussions of "triple bottom line" solutions breeze past. Throughout this book, I've shown how, for freegans, waste isn't really waste at all—it's actually useful and valuable stuff. Yet, in a sense, my analysis shows that waste isn't waste for capitalists either. When a distributor, retailer, or consumer buys something and then throws it out, the money paid still serves to keep the economic machine running and makes profits for the entities upstream. Ex-commodities are part of economic growth; ex-commodities provide jobs—and not just for garbage men. Little wonder that the output of trash has an astonishingly close correlation with the health of the U.S. economy.[62] The final trash tour I joined was poorly attended and moribund, but Janet still said something deceptively unpretentious yet profoundly accurate: "The sad thing is, the better our economy, the more our economy is being boosted, the worse is our ecology. They're just at odds with each other."

This might seem like an unremittingly pessimistic conclusion, but I actually believe this perspective is a liberating one. The structural approach to waste I have elaborated in this book allows us to make sense of an apparent paradox. Everyone claims that they want to eliminate waste. Consumers are better off if they don't throw out their leftovers; stores are better off if they optimize the supply chain. Yet the capitalist system as a whole is massively wasteful, and, in some ways, we are beneficiaries of this. The consumer gets better produce when the store throws out all but the best vegetables, and the store makes a bigger profit when the consumer buys more than he or she needs. Our economy as a whole thrives on waste just as it thrives on other things that we, as individuals, might not like, like financial speculation or environmental degradation.

I don't want to end with the cheap trope that only revolution can save us. The fact that capitalism has not everywhere and always been wasteful in the sense of producing ex-commodities in large quantities speaks to the potential for reform. But even "reform" of capitalism must, as Polanyi notes, be at least anticapitalist in spirit, insofar as it reins in the imperatives of endless growth and commodification. And reform involves costs. I often hear food waste campaigners saying that we "don't value food" and that this failure to value is at the root of the problem. Certainly, freeganism tells us a lot about the things we as a society devalue, such as, for a start, the workers, animals, and natural resources that make our food. But it also tells us a great deal about what we *do* value. We don't just value money. We also value convenience, abundance, aesthetics, choice—all worthy in and of themselves, but all dependent on waste. We may very well be able to give up waste; it's just that we might have to discard these values—and, far more importantly, the institutions and policies that inculcate and promote them—along with it.

I once asked Sasha what he would like to see in a book about freeganism. I expected him to suggest that I make sure to have a thorough reading of Marx, an accurate rendering of freegan.info's internal dynamics, or a careful exegesis of the use of ex-commodities in anarchist movements. Instead, he told me, "What I'd like to see is an absence of angst." As he elaborated:

> Freeganism in some ways sutures the void of overproduction and underprivilege that our society affords to its people. The community that is enabled by that suture, being one of integrity and friendship and sharing, that is built on mutual aid and conviviality, rather than this angsty feeling of unwilling engagement with a capitalist state . . . for me, it was like a shaft of life in a solitary confinement

*cell, because it showed me that there was an escape from what
seemed like a hopeless situation.*

Freeganism is not going to overthrow neoliberal capitalism. It may
not even have much of an impact where it is most needed, in contemporary debates on food and waste. We tend to judge movements by
whether they accomplish what they set out to do: in this, freeganism
is a resounding failure.

But, at least for those willing to dive in a little deeper, freeganism
offers an important reminder that, so long as we live in a capitalist
system—and so long as that system continues to bring us acceler-
ating inequality, exploitation, and environmental devastation—we
should at least recognize how that system actually works and see the
full scope of its consequences. Freegans' decisions to move beyond
"ethical consumption" (and, in the end, freeganism too) challenge
those of us who *are* concerned about those downsides to be both
creative and self-critical about our chosen strategies for addressing
them. And, at least for a short time, freeganism gave a sense of possibility and meaning to a small band of hopeful activists—including
one wide-eyed student from New Jersey—in New York City. All that
hardly seems like a waste.

Acknowledgments

I am the lucky beneficiary of various professors who supported, advised, and directed me in ways that may have contradicted accepted wisdom yet which I hope have proven sage in retrospect. For better or for worse, were it not for Patricia Fernandez-Kelly, I might be writing legal memos in law school rather than a book on anarchists from graduate school. Delia Baldassarri encouraged me to follow my instincts into the garbage of New York, despite, as I learned later, a fear that my parents would call her demanding to know why the Department of Sociology was encouraging their son to eat trash. On top of his invaluable advice and inspiration, Mitchell Duneier remarked that my senior thesis "could be a book with very little revision," which has kept me going through five years of not-so-little revisions. Michael Burawoy read that thesis and this manuscript, plus a few other manuscripts, and each time artfully convinced me I was on to something important while delivering the bad news that I had a great deal of work left to do. Mischa Gabowitsch, Colin Jerolmack, Sam Lucas, Mark Granovetter, Mike Benediktsson, Robert Wuthnow, and Marion Fourcade provided additional academic support.

This project was undertaken primarily outside the ivory towers of academe, so my thanks extend beyond it as well. Will Fisher joined me on my first dumpster dive, and without him I doubt I would have had the courage to go—much less the know-how to navigate the subway. Other groups and individuals contributed both to my senior thesis and to the subsequent book in ways too numerous to enumerate. They include Emily Sullivan, Kristen Davila, Doug Sprankling, the Princeton University Band, Courtny Hopen, the WCBC, Martino Cornelli, Charles Gillespie and the Sachs family, Lindsay Breuer (check the hyphens!), the Citadel, Tolan Thornton, the MaxPo gang, Lindsay Berkowitz, Sara Morley, and the Naturalia Dumpster Crew.

Among long lists, a few other individuals stand out. To write a book, one must be alive, and for that—and so many other things—thanks go to Jordan Bubin. Jacqueline Thomas bears a certain (if disputed) responsibility for calling my attention to freeganism in the first place, and commands an undisputed gratitude for years of companionship and support. Becky Tarlau shepherded this book and its author through an exceptionally difficult period, and I am thankful both for her intellect as a scholar and for her kindness as a human being. Manuel Rosaldo, too, has been one part incisive but encouraging colleague and one part generous and wise friend.

This book's final stretch toward publication received help from unexpected quarters. Matthew Stewart read a dense, impenetrable manuscript and counseled me that I needed to "detonate the theory chapter," advice for which all but the most masochistic reader should be appreciative. Mark Smith braved an array of technical errors to provide much-needed editorial support. Jason Weidemann from the University of Minnesota Press took a chance on an unpublished graduate student and has left me with a markedly positive view of academic publishers, our epic "title fight" notwithstanding.

While I'm not sure if my parents exactly *wanted* me to study freegans, their efforts to make me aware of my own privilege and my obligations to help others, in a way, led me to the dumpster. They offer unconditional love and support no matter what I study. I also recognize my grandfather, a lifelong Republican and banker, for providing living proof that radical left activists do not have a monopoly on the pursuit of fairness, decency, and sustainability. Regardless of our paths to pursue them, it is to the values you helped teach me that I aspire.

Marcel Mauss once likened ethnography to fishing: casting a net into the vast ocean of human experience and crossing your fingers in the hope that you catch something interesting. In the end, though, the freegans are the ones who "caught" me. Although I know some of the onetime members of freegan.info would prefer never to think about freeganism again, and certainly would rather not see a book about it in print, they have nonetheless shaped the person I am today in profound ways that extend far beyond my academic career.

I express a special gratitude to Janet Kalish, who, in addition to welcoming me to almost every freegan.info event I ever went to and inspiring me to keep coming back, held a poorly attended freegan sewing brunch that, in retrospect, has proved rather important. And then, of course, there is Marie Mourad, my coconspirator on many a dumpster-diving expedition, my solid rock of support through the ups and downs of rewrites and peer review, and my muse for turning my thesis into the book I truly wanted to write. May the "Dumpster Gods" always smile on you two—at least until you manage to convince the world to stop its wasteful ways.

Notes

Preface

1. Technically, *Dumpster* is a trademarked term, referring to the Dempster Dumpster invented by the Dempster brothers in 1935 (U.S. Trademark 71,773,015). Scrupulously capitalizing the word throughout this book to respect the patent seems not quite in keeping with the spirit of freeganism, though.
2. Michael Burawoy, "The Extended Case Method," *Sociological Theory* 16, no. 1 (1998): 4–33.
3. "What Is a Freegan?," http://freegan.info/.

Introduction

1. Between 1995 and 2011 the U.S. government gave over $81 billion to growers of corn alone. See Environmental Working Group, "Farm Subsidies Database," 2014, http://farm.ewg.org/.
2. Gabriela Pechlaner and Gerardo Otero, "The Neoliberal Food Regime: Neoregulation and the New Division of Labor in North America," *Rural Sociology* 75, no. 2 (2010): 179–208.
3. Barry Estabrook, *Tomatoland* (Kansas City, Mo.: Andrews McMeel, 2011). See also Seth Holmes, *Fresh Fruit, Broken Bodies: Migrant Farmworkers in the United States* (Berkeley: University of California Press, 2013).
4. Tracy Wilkinson, "Mexico's Tomato-Farm Workers Toil in 'Circle of Poverty,'" *Los Angeles Times*, November 11, 2013.
5. Deborah Barndt, *Tangled Routes: Women, Work, and Globalization on the Tomato Trail,* 2nd ed. (Lanham, Md.: Rowman and Littlefield, 2008), 189.
6. Estabrook, *Tomatoland*, x.
7. Thomas A. Lyson and Annalisa Lewis Raymer, "Stalking the Wily Multinational: Power and Control in the US Food System," *Agriculture and Human Values* 17, no. 2 (2000): 199.
8. Food Chain Workers Alliance, *The Hands That Feed Us: Challenges and Opportunities for Workers along the Food Chain* (Los Angeles: Food Chain Workers Alliance, June 2012), 3.
9. Although unionized employees—including those at D'Agostino—almost certainly fare better. See Saru Jayaraman, *Shelved: How Wages and Working Conditions for California's Food Retail Workers Have Declined as the Industry Has Thrived* (Berkeley, Calif.: Food Labor Research Center, June 1, 2014), 6.
10. Krissy Clark, "The Secret Life of a Food Stamp," *Slate*, April 1, 2014, http://www.slate.com/.

11. Grocery store workers were twice as likely to report food insecurity as the general population (Jayaraman, *Shelved*, 7), and migrant farmworkers in California were three and a half times more likely. See Laura-Anne Minkoff-Zern, "Hunger amidst Plenty: Farmworker Food Insecurity and Coping Strategies in California," *Local Environment* 19, no. 2 (2014): 204–19.

12. Food Marketing Institute, "Supermarket Facts," 2012, http://www.fmi.org/.

13. Up slightly from a low of 9.5 percent in 2008. By comparison, the figure for 1960 was 17.5 percent. See Annette Clausson, "Food CPI and Expenditures," *USDA Economic Research Service*, November 13, 2013.

14. For a review of contemporary food movements, see Eric Holt Giménez and Annie Shattuck, "Food Crises, Food Regimes, and Food Movements: Rumblings of Reform or Tides of Transformation?," *Journal of Peasant Studies* 38, no. 1 (2011): 109–44.

15. See David Evans, Hugh Campbell, and Anne Murcott, "A Brief Pre-History of Food Waste and the Social Sciences," *Sociological Review* 60 (2012): 5–26.

16. Alisha Coleman-Jensen, Mark Nord, and Steven Carlson, *Household Food Security in the United States in 2012*, Economic Research Report (Washington, D.C.: U.S. Department of Agriculture, September 2013).

17. City Harvest representative, interview by author, New York, March 2, 2009.

18. Although the United States is the world's largest international trader in food, imports and exports roughly cancel each other out. The last U.S. government estimate of food loss used estimates for 260 separate commodities to come to a figure of 31 percent for 2010. See Jean Buzby, Hodan Wells, and Jeffrey Hyman, *The Estimated Amount, Value, and Calories of Postharvest Food Losses at the Retail and Consumer Levels in the United States*, Economic Information Bulletin (Washington, D.C.: U.S. Department of Agriculture, February 2014). These estimates are conservative, however, because they do not include preharvest, on-the-farm, or farm-to-retail losses and leave out some commodity groups. Looking at the overall discrepancy between food consumed and food produced, Kevin Hall et al. calculate that 40 percent of the calories produced in 2003 were wasted. See "The Progressive Increase of Food Waste in America and Its Environmental Impact," *PLoS ONE* 4, no. 11 (2009): e7940. If we consider the fact that a mere 30 percent of the calories we *feed* to livestock are actually returned in meat, dairy, and eggs as a form of "waste," then the figure tops 50 percent of the available food supply. See Tristram Stuart, *Waste: Uncovering the Global Food Scandal* (New York: Norton, 2009), 139. The proportion swells even further if we consider "luxus consumption"—excess calories that we eat but for which we have no nutritional need. See Dorothy Blair and Jeffery Sobal, "Luxus Consumption: Wasting Food Resources through Overeating," *Agriculture and Human Values* 23, no. 1 (2006): 63–74. These disparities reflect not just differing measurement assumptions but fundamentally political differences over what qualifies as "waste."

19. Jonathan Bloom, *American Wasteland: How America Throws Away Nearly Half of Its Food* (Cambridge, Mass.: Da Capo Lifelong Books, 2010), ii.

20. Jean Buzby et al., "The Value of Retail- and Consumer-Level Fruit and Vegetable Losses in the United States," *Journal of Consumer Affairs* 45, no. 3 (2011): 507.

21. Kumar Venkat, "The Climate Change and Economic Impacts of Food Waste in the United States," *International Journal of Food System Dynamics* 2, no. 4 (2011): 441.

22. Stuart, *Waste*, 83.

23. Bloom, *American Wasteland*, 179.

24. Mary Griffin, Jeffery Sobal, and Thomas A. Lyson, "An Analysis of a Community Food Waste Stream," *Agriculture and Human Values* 26, nos. 1–2 (2009): 77.

25. Only 4 percent of food waste is composted or recovered for waste-to-energy plants. See U.S. Environmental Protection Agency, *Municipal Solid Waste in the United States* (Washington, D.C.: Office of Solid Waste, May 2013), 6.

26. Patrick Markee, *As Mayor Bloomberg's Failed Policies Exacerbate Crisis, NYC Homeless Shelter Population Tops 41,000* (New York: Coalition for the Homeless, November 9, 2011).

27. Derek Hall, Philip Hirsch, and Tania Murray Li, *Powers of Exclusion: Land Dilemmas in Southeast Asia* (Honolulu: University of Hawai'i Press, 2011), 60.

28. The term *disenchanted prophets* is from the late great Alberto Melucci, *Challenging Codes* (Cambridge: Cambridge University Press, 1996), 1.

29. Hernando de Soto, *The Mystery of Capital: Why Capitalism Triumphs in the West and Fails Everywhere Else* (London: Black Swan Books, 2000), 1.

30. Edward McBride, "Talking Rubbish," *Economist*, February 28, 2009, 5.

31. Wayne Glowka, Megan Melancon, and Danielle Wycoff, "Among the New Words," *American Speech* 79, no. 2 (2004): 194–200.

32. Unlike most of the rest of the developed world, in New York City, scavengers rarely encounter dumpsters, and as such, the term *dumpster diving* is a misnomer. Even though many freegans acknowledge this, *dumpster diving* is still the most common term used in freegan.info, and I follow that convention throughout this book.

33. "Freegan Philosophy," http://freegan.info/.

34. Published articles include Alex V. Barnard, "'Waving the Banana' at Capitalism: Political Theater and Social Movement Strategy among New York's 'Freegan' Dumpster Divers," *Ethnography* 12, no. 4 (2011): 419–44; Anna Lúcia Carolsfeld and Susan L. Erikson, "Beyond Desperation: Motivations for Dumpster™ Diving for Food in Vancouver," *Food and Foodways* 21, no. 4 (2013): 245–66; Lauren Corman, "Getting Their Hands Dirty: Raccoons, Freegans, and Urban 'Trash,'" *Journal of Critical Animal Studies* 9, no. 3 (2011): 28–61; Michelle Coyne, "From Production to Destruction to Recovery: Freeganism's Redefinition of Food Value and Circulation," *Iowa Journal of Cultural Studies* 10 (2009): 9–24; Ferne Edwards and David Mercer, "Gleaning from Gluttony: An Australian Youth Subculture Confronts the Ethics of Waste," *Australian Geographer* 38, no. 3 (2007): 279–96; Ferne Edwards and Dave Mercer, "Food Waste in Australia: The Freegan Response," *Sociological Review* 60 (2012): 174–91; Joan Gross, "Capitalism and Its Discontents:

Back-to-the-Lander and Freegan Foodways in Rural Oregon," *Food and Foodways* 17, no. 2 (2009): 57–79; Scarlett Lindeman, "Trash Eaters," *Gastronomica: The Journal of Food and Culture* 12, no. 1 (2012): 75–82; Victoria More, "Dumpster Dinners: An Ethnographic Study of Freeganism," *Journal of Undergraduate Ethnography* 1 (2011): 43–55; Hieu P. Nguyen, Steven Chen, and Sayantani Mukherjee, "Reverse Stigma in the Freegan Community," *Journal of Business Research* 67, no. 9 (2014): 1877–84; Sean Thomas, "Do Freegans Commit Theft?," *Legal Studies* 30, no. 1 (2010): 98–125. There are also dozens of unpublished theses and dissertations on freeganism.

35. I am deeply indebted to Zsuzsa Gille for this tripartite framework for analyzing societal "waste regimes." See Gille, *From the Cult of Waste to the Trash Heap of History: The Politics of Waste in Socialist and Postsocialist Hungary* (Bloomington: Indiana University Press, 2008).

36. My discussion of ex-commodities and the fetish of waste, drawing largely on Marxist political economy, comes to conclusions quite similar to those of David Giles, who applies post-structuralist insights to develop a theory of the production and subsequent sequestration of "abject capital." See Giles, "The Anatomy of a Dumpster: Abject Capital and the Looking Glass of Value," *Social Text,* no. 118 (2014): 93–113.

37. The dizzying proliferation of uses of "waste" in the humanities and social sciences is documented by Sarah Moore, "Garbage Matters: Concepts in New Geographies of Waste," *Progress in Human Geography* 36, no. 6 (2012): 780–99.

38. Evans, Campbell, and Murcott, "Brief Pre-History of Food Waste," 6–7.

39. Arjun Appadurai uses the term *ex-commodity* to describe "things retrieved, either temporarily or permanently, from the commodity state and placed in some other state." His formulation highlights the indeterminate status of the ex-commodity—namely, that it can at least potentially be recovered—but he does not connect "ex-commodification" to a particular phase of capitalism. See Appadurai, ed., "Introduction: Commodities and the Politics of Value," in *The Social Life of Things: Commodities in Cultural Perspective* (Cambridge: Cambridge University Press, 1986), 16.

40. Zsuzsa Gille, "Actor Networks, Modes of Production, and Waste Regimes: Reassembling the Macro-Social," *Environment and Planning* 42, no. 5 (2010): 49–50.

41. Karl Marx, *Capital: Volume 1,* trans. Ben Fowkes (London: Penguin, 1976), 125. This caricature of "capitalists" is not a reference to actual people but to social roles that, in certain circumstances, people step into. CEOs or factory owners might be loving parents, community leaders, and stalwart advocates for progressive causes, but when faced with the pressures of investors and the rigorous competition of the market, they act as "capitalists."

42. Joseph Schumpeter, *Capitalism, Socialism and Democracy,* 2nd ed. (Martino Fine Books, 1947), 31.

43. Robert J. Gordon, *Is U.S. Economic Growth Over? Faltering Innovation Confronts the Six Headwinds,* Working Paper 18315 (Washington, D.C.: National Bureau of Economic Research, August 2012).

44. Marx, *Capital: Volume 1*, 374; see also Michelle Yates, "The Human-as-Waste, the Labor Theory of Value, and Disposability in Contemporary Capitalism," *Antipode* 43, no. 5 (2011): 1679–95.

45. Marx, *Capital: Volume 1*, 303; see also Karl Marx, *Capital: Volume 3*, trans. David Fernbach (London: Penguin, 1981), 195.

46. Marx, *Capital: Volume 3*, 325.

47. See David Harvey, *The Limits to Capital* (New York: Verso, 1999), 175.

48. See Gay Hawkins, *The Ethics of Waste: How We Relate to Rubbish* (Lanham, Md.: Rowman and Littlefield, 2006); Gille, "Actor Networks"; Vinay Gidwani and Rajyashree N. Reddy, "The Afterlives of 'Waste': Notes from India for a Minor History of Capitalist Surplus," *Antipode* 43, no. 5 (2011): 1625–58.

49. Karl Marx, *Capital: Volume 2*, trans. David Fernbach (London: Penguin, 1978), 252.

50. János Kornai, *Economics of Shortage* (Amsterdam: North-Holland, 1980).

51. Andrew Abbott, "The Problem of Excess," *Sociological Theory* 32, no. 1 (2014): 1–26.

52. Karl Polanyi, *The Great Transformation*, 2nd ed. (Boston: Beacon, 2001).

53. Adam Smith, *The Wealth of Nations*, ed. Edwin Cannan (New York: Bantam Classics, 2003), 22.

54. Polanyi, *Great Transformation*, 3.

55. See Miguel A. Centeno and Joseph N. Cohen, "The Arc of Neoliberalism," *Annual Review of Sociology* 38, no. 1 (2012): 317–40; Peter Evans and William Sewell, "The Neoliberal Era: Ideology, Policy, and Social Effects," in *Social Resilience in the Neo-Liberal Era*, ed. Michele Lamont and Peter Hall (Cambridge: Cambridge University Press, 2013), 35–68; David Harvey, *A Brief History of Neoliberalism* (Oxford: Oxford University Press, 2005).

56. Polanyi, *Great Transformation*, 76.

57. Jan Breman, "Myth of the Global Safety Net," *New Left Review*, no. 59 (September–October 2009): 29–36.

58. Walter Korpi, "Welfare-State Regress in Western Europe: Politics, Institutions, Globalization, and Europeanization," *Annual Review of Sociology* 29, no. 1 (2003): 589–609; Guy Standing, *The Precariat: The New Dangerous Class* (London: Bloomsbury, 2011).

59. Zygmunt Bauman, *Wasted Lives: Modernity and Its Outcasts* (London: Polity, 2004).

60. For assessments of the increasing material outputs of global capitalism, see Fridolin Krausmann et al., "Growth in Global Materials Use, GDP, and Population during the Twentieth Century," *Ecological Economics* 68, no. 10 (2009): 2696–705; Julia Steinberger, Fridolin Krausmann, and Nina Eisenmenger, "Global Patterns of Materials Use: A Socioeconomic and Geophysical Analysis," *Ecological Economics* 69, no. 5 (2010): 1148–58.

61. For a more detailed exposition of this process from a Marxist standpoint, see Stephen Horton, "Value, Waste, and the Built Environment: A Marxian Analysis," *Capitalism Nature Socialism* 8, no. 2 (1997): 127–39.

62. Jeff Byles, *Rubble: Unearthing the History of Demolition* (New York: Harmony Books, 2005), 11.

63. An artful discussion of "abject land capital" can be found in David Giles, "'A Mass Conspiracy to Feed People': Globalizing Cities, World-Class Waste, and the Biopolitics of Food Not Bombs" (PhD diss., University of Washington, 2013), chap. 3.

64. Stephen Gandel, "Bulldoze: The New Way to Foreclose," *Time,* August 1, 2011.

65. George Henderson, "'Free' Food, the Local Production of Worth, and the Circuit of Decommodification: A Value Theory of the Surplus," *Environment and Planning D: Society and Space* 22, no. 4 (2004): 490.

66. Michael Burawoy, "From Polanyi to Pollyanna: The False Optimism of Global Labor Studies," *Global Labour Journal* 1, no. 2 (2010): 301–13.

67. "What Is a Product?," http://freegan.info/.

68. Michael Thompson, *Rubbish Theory* (Oxford: Oxford University Press, 1979); Joshua Reno, "Your Trash Is Someone's Treasure," *Journal of Material Culture* 14, no. 1 (2009): 29–46; Kevin Hetherington, "Secondhandedness: Consumption, Disposal, and Absent Presence," *Environment and Planning D: Society and Space* 22, no. 1 (2004): 157–73.

69. Mike Crang et al., "Rethinking Governance and Value in Commodity Chains through Global Recycling Networks," *Transactions of the Institute of British Geographers* 38, no. 1 (2013): 12–24; Josh Lepawsky and Mostaem Billah, "Making Chains That (Un)make Things: Waste—Value Relations and the Bangladeshi Rubbish Electronics Industry," *Geografiska Annaler: Series B, Human Geography* 93, no. 2 (2011): 121–39; Carl Zimring, *Cash for Your Trash* (New Brunswick, N.J.: Rutgers University Press, 2005).

70. Marx, *Capital: Volume 1,* 165.

71. James G. Carrier, "Protecting the Environment the Natural Way: Ethical Consumption and Commodity Fetishism," *Antipode* 42, no. 3 (2010): 672–89; Ryan Gunderson, "Problems with the Defetishization Thesis: Ethical Consumerism, Alternative Food Systems, and Commodity Fetishism," *Agriculture and Human Values* 31 (2014): 109–17.

72. Marx, *Capital: Volume 1,* 165, 169.

73. Polanyi, *Great Transformation,* 258.

74. See also Benjamin Coles and Lucius Hallett, "Eating from the Bin: Salmon Heads, Waste, and the Markets That Make Them," *Sociological Review* 60 (2012): 156–73.

75. Sherry Olson, "Downwind, Downstream, Downtown: The Environmental Legacy in Baltimore and Montreal," *Environmental History* 12, no. 4 (2007): 845–66.

76. Samantha MacBride, *Recycling Reconsidered: The Present Failure and Future Promise of Environmental Action in the United States* (Cambridge, Mass.: MIT Press, 2012), 57, 75.

77. Katie Kelly, *Garbage: The History and Future of Garbage in America* (New York: Saturday Review Press, 1973), 77.

78. Edward Humes, *Garbology: Our Dirty Love Affair with Trash* (New York: Avery, 2012), chap. 10.

79. On the possibility of waste being "fetishized," see Risa Whitson, "Negotiating Place and Value: Geographies of Waste and Scavenging in Buenos Aires," *Antipode* 43, no. 4 (2011): 1414.

80. Edd De Coverly, Lisa O'Malley, and Maurice Patterson, "Hidden Mountain: The Social Avoidance of Waste," *Journal of Macromarketing* 28, no. 3 (2008): 295.

81. Jennifer Clapp, "The Rising Tide against Plastic Waste: Unpacking Industry Attempts to Influence the Debate," in *Histories of the Dustheap: Waste, Material Cultures, Social Justice,* ed. Elizabeth Mazzolini and Stephanie Foote (Cambridge, Mass.: MIT Press, 2012), 212.

82. Andrew Szasz, *Shopping Our Way to Safety: How We Changed from Protecting the Environment to Protecting Ourselves* (Minneapolis: University of Minnesota Press, 2007), chap. 3.

83. Gille, *From the Cult of Waste,* 6–7.

84. "Ideology of the Product," http://freegan.info/.

1. Capitalism's Cast-offs

1. For a longer discussion of "direct action" and how it differs from other forms of political action, see David Graeber, *Direct Action: An Ethnography* (Oakland, Calif.: AK Press, 2009).

2. Verta Taylor, "Social Movement Continuity: The Women's Movement in Abeyance," *American Sociological Review* 54, no. 5 (1989): 761–75.

3. Some claim freeganism had earlier origins. See Stephen Kurutz, "Not Buying It," *New York Times,* June 21, 2007. In October 1966 a group calling themselves "the Diggers" (after a seventeenth-century English peasant movement) began distributing free food to the hippies and homeless congregating in the Haight-Ashbury district of San Francisco, as well as creating "free stores" and offering medical care and housing. See Warren James Belasco, *Appetite for Change: How the Counterculture Took on the Food Industry,* 2nd ed. (Ithaca, N.Y.: Cornell University Press, 2007), 18. While the affinities with freeganism are clear, I have never heard anyone in freegan. info mention the Diggers.

4. Barbara Epstein, *Political Protest and Cultural Revolution: Nonviolent Direct Action in the 1970s and 1980s* (Berkeley: University of California Press, 1991), chap. 2.

5. Sean Michael Parson, "An Ungovernable Force: Homeless Activism and Politics in San Francisco, 1988–1995" (PhD diss., University of Oregon, 2010).

6. Quoted in ibid., 74.

7. Ibid., 151.

8. A listing of cities in which FNB has had chapters can be found at www.food notbombs.net, although many groups appear dormant.

9. Janet Poppendieck, *Sweet Charity? Emergency Food and the End of Entitlement* (New York: Penguin, 1999).

10. Tilly provides a thorough discussion of this modern, state-centered "repertoire" of collective action in *Contentious Performances* (Cambridge: Cambridge University Press, 2008).

11. Even though I juxtapose this "new" prefigurative emphasis against the more "traditional" focus on seizing power among socialist revolutionaries, even "old left" movements—like the Knights of Labor in the 1880s—have had prefigurative dimensions. See Kim Voss, *The Making of American Exceptionalism* (Ithaca, N.Y.: Cornell University Press, 1993), 83.

12. Jeffrey Jacob, *New Pioneers: The Back-to-the-Land Movement and the Search for a Sustainable Future* (University Park: Pennsylvania State University Press, 1997); Belasco, *Appetite for Change*; Francesca Polletta, *Freedom Is an Endless Meeting: Democracy in American Social Movements* (Chicago: University of Chicago Press, 2002); Joshua Bloom and Waldo E. Martin, *Black against Empire: The History and Politics of the Black Panther Party* (Berkeley: University of California Press, 2013).

13. See Epstein, *Political Protest and Cultural Revolution*; Ben Holtzman, Craig Hughes, and Kevin Van Meter, "Do It Yourself . . . and the Movement beyond Capitalism," in *Constituent Imagination*, ed. Stevphen Shukaitis, David Graeber, and Erika Biddle (Oakland, Calif.: AK Press, 2007), 44–61; Ryan Moore and Michael Roberts, "Do-It-Yourself Mobilization: Punk and Social Movements," *Mobilization* 14, no. 3 (2009): 273–91.

14. Williams and Lee find a 43 percent increase in the number of anarchist organizations worldwide between 1997 and 2005. See "'We Are Everywhere': An Ecological Analysis of Organizations in the Anarchist Yellow Pages," *Humanity and Society* 32, no. 1 (2008): 57.

15. Centeno and Cohen, "Arc of Neoliberalism," 312.

16. Kim Voss and Michelle Williams, "The Local in the Global: Rethinking Social Movements in the New Millennium," *Democratization* 19, no. 2 (2012): 352–77.

17. Graeber, *Direct Action*; Jeffrey Juris, *Networking Futures* (Durham, N.C.: Duke University Press, 2008); Georgy Katsiaficas, *The Subversion of Politics: European Autonomous Social Movements and the Decolonization of Everyday Life*, 2nd ed. (Oakland, Calif.: AK Press, 2006).

18. Some participants in these movements might nevertheless not recognize themselves as being "anticapitalist" or "anarchists," owing to the label's pejorative connotation.

19. Juris, *Networking Futures*, 14.

20. Given their affinities, it is little surprise that FNB helped serve activists at virtually all the AGM demonstrations and that "many of the principal organizers in the movement against neoliberalism [the AGM] had their start as Food Not Bombs volunteers" (Holtzman, Hughes, and Van Meter, "Do It Yourself," 52).

21. David Graeber, *Fragments of an Anarchist Anthropology* (Chicago: Prickly Paradigm, 2004), 2.

22. Ibid., 60.

23. Chris Carlsson, *Nowtopia: How Pirate Programmer, Outlaw Bicyclists, and Vacant-Lot Gardeners Are Inventing the Future Today!* (Oakland, Calif.: AK Press, 2008).

24. Ibid.

25. Infoshops and community spaces are among the most common anarchist organizations, with scores in the United States alone (Williams and Lee, "'We Are Everywhere,'" 51).

26. Jeff Shantz, "One Person's Garbage, Another Person's Treasure," *Verb* 3, no. 1 (2005): 12.

27. Katsiaficas, *Subversion of Politics,* 112, 168.

28. Paul Baran and Paul Sweezy, *Monopoly Capital* (New York: Modern Reader Paperbacks, 1966).

29. For such histories, see Heather Rogers, *Gone Tomorrow: The Hidden Life of Garbage* (New York: New Press, 2005); and Susan Strasser, *Waste and Want: A Social History of Trash* (New York: Holt Paperbacks, 1999).

30. Susan Archer Mann, *Agrarian Capitalism in Theory and Practice* (Chapel Hill: University of North Carolina Press, 1990).

31. Deborah Kay Fitzgerald, *Every Farm a Factory: The Industrial Ideal in American Agriculture* (New Haven, Conn.: Yale University Press, 2003).

32. Stuart Chase, *The Tragedy of Waste* (New York: Macmillan, 1929), 193.

33. Kenneth Finegold and Theda Skocpol, *State and Party in America's New Deal* (Madison: University of Wisconsin Press, 1995).

34. Bill Winders, *The Politics of Food Supply* (New Haven, Conn.: Yale University Press, 2009), 52–53.

35. Poppendieck, *Sweet Charity?,* chap. 5.

36. Harriet Friedmann, "The Political Economy of Food: The Rise and Fall of the Postwar International Food Order," *American Journal of Sociology* 88 (1982): S261.

37. Winders, *Politics of Food Supply,* 136.

38. Marjorie L. DeVault and James P. Pitts, "Surplus and Scarcity: Hunger and the Origins of the Food Stamp Program," *Social Problems* 31, no. 5 (1984): 545–57; Poppendieck, *Sweet Charity?*

39. Raj Patel, "The Long Green Revolution," *Journal of Peasant Studies* 40, no. 1 (2013): 1–63.

40. Environmental Working Group, "Farm Subsidies Database."

41. Lyson and Raymer, "Stalking the Wily Multinational."

42. Winders, *Politics of Food Supply.*

43. Ron Nixon, "Crop Insurance Proposal Could Cost U.S. Billions," *New York Times,* June 6, 2012, http://www.nytimes.com/2012/06/07/us/politics/bill-to-expand-crop-insurance-poses-risks.html.

44. Frederick Kaufman, "The Food Bubble," *Harper's,* July 2010, 32.

45. Ibid., 34.

46. Eric Vanhaute, "From Famine to Food Crisis: What History Can Teach Us about Local and Global Subsistence Crises," *Journal of Peasant Studies* 38, no. 1 (2011): 47–65.

47. Poppendieck, *Sweet Charity?*, 3.

48. Dorothy Rosenbaum, *Families' Food Stamp Benefits Purchase Less Food Each Year* (Washington, D.C.: Center on Budget and Policy Priorities, March 9, 2007), http://www.cbpp.org/.

49. Mark Nord, *Effects of the Decline in the Real Value of SNAP Benefits from 2009 to 2011* (Washington, D.C.: U.S. Department of Agriculture, August 2013), http://www.ers.usda.gov/.

50. Bloom, *American Wasteland*, 95.

51. "Dump Your Milk: California Dairymen Say Two-Day Dump Would Help Market," *Farm and Dairy*, May 27, 2009, http://www.farmanddairy.com/.

52. Buzby, Wells, and Hyman, *Estimated Amount, Value, and Calories of Postharvest Food Losses*, iii.

53. Economic Research Service, "Food Availability per Capita," *U.S. Department of Agriculture*, 2013, http://www.ers.usda.gov/.

54. Stuart, *Waste*, 174.

55. Hall et al., "Progressive Increase of Food Waste," 1. This is a low estimate for the number of calories per day wasted in the United States, because it excludes all waste before food reaches retailers and doesn't include food that could feed humans but that is instead fed to farm animals.

56. Stuart, *Waste*.

57. Institution of Mechanical Engineers, *Global Food: Waste Not Want Not* (London: Institution of Mechanical Engineers, 2013). For the consequences of developing-world dumping, see Zsuzsa Gille, "From Risk to Waste: Global Food Waste Regimes," *Sociological Review* 60 (2012): 27–46.

58. Gross, "Capitalism and Its Discontents," 69.

59. Ibid., 61.

60. Edwards and Mercer, "Gleaning from Gluttony."

61. Dylan Clark, "The Raw and the Rotten: Punk Cuisine," *Ethnology* 43, no. 1 (2004): 28, doi:10.2307/3773853.

62. Anon., "Extreme Happiness: Essays by Freegans," n.d., 53, http://www.antifa.ca/.

63. Laurie Essig, "Fine Diving," *Slate*, June 10, 2002, http://www.salon.com/.

64. Benji and Kaylan, "Dumpster Dive: A Zine Guide to Doing It and Doing It Well," *Seattle DIY Collective*, n.d., 1, seattlediy.com.

65. Mara Loveman, "High-Risk Collective Action: Defending Human Rights in Chile, Uruguay, and Argentina," *American Journal of Sociology* 104, no. 2 (1998): 479.

66. *Wetlands Preserved: The Story of an Activist Nightclub* (dir. Dean Budnick, 2008).

67. "Home Page," wetlands-preserve.org/.

68. Christopher Manes, *Green Rage* (Boston: Little, Brown, 1990).

69. "Past Campaigns," wetlands-preserve.org.

70. "Home Page," http://freegan.info/.

71. Anon., *Evasion* (CrimeThinc Ex-Workers Collective, n.d.), 25.

72. See introduction, note 34.

73. Anna Davies, *The Geographies of Garbage Governance: Interventions, Interactions, and Outcomes* (Aldershot, U.K.: Ashgate, 2008).

74. For a discussion of "gleaning" in France and Italy, see Rachel Black, "Eating Garbage: Socially Marginal Food Provisioning Practices," in *Consuming the Inedible: Neglected Dimensions of Food Choice*, ed. J. MacClancy and J. Henry (Oxford: Berghahn Books, 2007).

75. Strasser, *Waste and Want*, 125.

76. Robin Nagle, *Picking Up: On the Streets and Behind the Trucks with the Sanitation Workers of New York City* (New York: Farrar, Straus and Giroux, 2013), 96.

77. Sarah Brannen, *Food Works: A Vision to Improve New York's Food System* (New York: New York City Government, 2010), 3.

78. See New York Administrative Code, Title 16, Section 7(b). Adam claims, however, that the Supreme Court's 1988 ruling in *California v. Greenwood* permits scavenging on public property. See William Rathje and Cullen Murphy, *Rubbish! The Archaeology of Garbage* (Tucson: University of Arizona Press, 1992), 23.

79. Ted Botha, *Mongo: Adventures in Trash* (New York: Bloomsbury, 2004); Mitch Duneier, *Sidewalk* (New York: Farrar, Straus and Giroux, 1999).

80. According to Rachel Vaughn, one Kansas diver had been arrested, charged with burglary, paid hundreds in fines, and completed community service for dumpster diving. See "Talking Trash: Oral Histories of Food In/Security from the Margins of a Dumpster" (PhD diss., University of Kansas, 2011), 39.

81. Karen V. Fernandez, Amanda J. Brittain, and Sandra D. Bennett, "'Doing the Duck': Negotiating the Resistant-Consumer Identity," *European Journal of Marketing* 45, nos. 11–12 (2011): 1779–88.

82. Kelly, *Garbage*, 149.

83. "Intro to Freegan Philosophy," http://freegan.info/.

84. See, e.g., Herbert Marcuse, *One-Dimensional Man* (Boston: Beacon, 1964), 149.

85. David Graeber, *Possibilities: Essays on Hierarchy, Rebellion, and Desire* (Oakland, Calif.: AK Press, 2007), 395.

86. "Destructive Consumer Products, Boycotts, and 'Responsible Consumption,'" http://freegan.info/.

87. "Essential Points on Freeganism," http://freegan.info/.

88. See, e.g., Epstein, *Political Protest and Cultural Revolution*; Graeber, *Direct Action*; Juris, *Networking Futures*.

89. The working groups of freegan.info are constantly shifting and are often composed of just a single person. At the group's height in 2009, there were working groups for strategic planning, the bike workshop, films and forums, calendar preparation, media, the office, and the website.

90. "Essential Points on Freeganism," http://freegan.info/.

2. Diving In, Opting Out

1. See Guy Debord, *Society of the Spectacle* (Detroit, MI: Black and Red, 2000).
2. Bruce Grierson, *U-Turn: What If You Woke Up One Morning and Realized You Were Living the Wrong Life?* (New York: Bloomsbury, 2007).
3. Klaus Eder, "The Rise of Counter-Culture Movements against Modernity: Nature as a New Field of Class Struggle," *Theory, Culture & Society* 7, no. 4 (1990): 21–47; James Jasper and Dorothy Nelkin, *The Animal Rights Crusade: The Growth of a Moral Protest* (New York: Free Press, 1992); Claus Offe, "New Social Movements: Challenging the Boundaries of Institutional Politics," *Social Research* 52 (1985): 817–68.
4. Doug McAdam, "Recruitment to High-Risk Activism: The Case of Freedom Summer," *American Journal of Sociology* 92, no. 1 (1986): 64–90.
5. This finding parallels those of Kathleen Blee, *Inside Organized Racism* (Berkeley: University of California Press, 2002).
6. Frank Newport, "In U.S., 5% Consider Themselves Vegetarians," *Gallup,* July 26, 2012, http://www.gallup.com/.
7. Not coincidentally, one of Adam's favorite essays is Brian Dominick's pamphlet "Animal Liberation and Social Revolution," which publicized the term *veganarchy*—a marriage between anarchism and veganism.
8. Adam frequently mentioned a report from the United Nations Food and Agriculture Organization that found 18 percent of CO_2 equivalent greenhouse gases come from animal agriculture. See Henning Steinfeld et al., *Livestock's Long Shadow* (Rome: Food and Agricultural Organization, November 29, 2006). Livestock production is highly inefficient: feeding and raising animals takes up 80 percent of agricultural land but provides only 15 percent of total calories. See L. G. Horlings and T. K. Marsden, "Towards the Real Green Revolution? Exploring the Conceptual Dimensions of a New Ecological Modernisation of Agriculture That Could 'Feed the World,'" *Global Environmental Change* 21, no. 2 (2011): 449. As such, an animal-based diet places a far heavier strain on the environment than a plant-based one: to offer an example, meat takes twelve times as much water, calorie-for-calorie, as producing bread, sixty-four times as much as potatoes, and eighty-six times as much as tomatoes. See Peter Singer and Jim Mason, *The Way We Eat: Why Our Food Choices Matter* (New York: Rodale Books, 2006).
9. Edwards and Mercer, "Gleaning from Gluttony."
10. For the sake of simplicity, I use the terms *vegetarian movement* and *animal rights movement* interchangeably, although they are not the same thing.
11. Julia Twigg, "Food for Thought: Purity and Vegetarianism," *Religion* 9 (1979): 16.
12. Michael Fox, *Deep Vegetarianism* (Philadelphia: Temple University Press, 1999), 14.
13. Ulrike Heider, *Anarchism: Left, Right, and Green* (San Francisco: City Lights Books, 1994), 27.
14. Adrian Franklin, *Animals and Modern Cultures: A Sociology of Human-Animal Relationships in Modernity* (London: Sage, 1999), 186.

15. Jasper and Nelkin, *Animal Rights Crusade,* 41.

16. For criticisms of racism and sexism in the animal rights movement, see Bob Torres, *Making a Killing: The Political Economy of Animal Rights* (Edinburgh: AK Press, 2007).

17. Brian Lowe and Caryn Ginsberg, "Animal Rights as a Post-Citizenship Movement," *Society and Animals* 10, no. 2 (2002): 203–15.

18. Donna Mauer, *Vegetarianism: Movement or Moment* (Philadelphia: Temple University Press, 2002), 10.

19. He cited with particular horror a study that claimed more animal lives would be saved in total by eating grass-fed beef than switching to veganism: Steven L. Davis, "The Least Harm Principle May Require That Humans Consume a Diet Containing Large Herbivores, Not a Vegan Diet," *Journal of Agricultural and Environmental Ethics* 16, no. 4 (2003): 387–94.

20. Belasco, *Appetite for Change,* 111.

21. A. D. Beardsworth and E. T. Keil, "Contemporary Vegetarianism in the U.K.: Challenge and Incorporation?," *Appetite* 20, no. 3 (1993): 233.

22. Daniel Jaffee and Philip H. Howard, "Corporate Cooptation of Organic and Fair Trade Standards," *Agriculture and Human Values* 27, no. 4 (2010): 390.

23. Daniel Buck, Christina Getz, and Julie Guthman, "From Farm to Table: The Organic Vegetable Commodity Chain of Northern California," *Sociologia Ruralis* 37, no. 1 (1997): 3–20; Philip H. Howard, "Consolidation in the North American Organic Food Processing Sector, 1997 to 2007," *International Journal of Sociology of Agriculture and Food* 16, no. 1 (2009): 13–30.

24. Sally Eden, Christopher Bear, and Gordon Walker, "Mucky Carrots and Other Proxies: Problematising the Knowledge-Fix for Sustainable and Ethical Consumption," *Geoforum* 39, no. 2 (2008): 1051.

25. To offer one example: the "Animal Care Certified" label still permits chicken producers to starve hens for two weeks before they molt, give them a "meager" allowance of space that barely allows them to spread their wings, cut off beaks without anesthetic, and discard male chicks into a dumpster at birth (Singer and Mason, *Way We Eat,* 40).

26. Margaret Gray, *Labor and the Locavore: The Making of a Comprehensive Food Ethic* (Berkeley: University of California Press, 2013).

27. Luc Boltanski and Eve Chiapello, *The New Spirit of Capitalism* (London: Verso, 2005), 170.

28. For discussions of the rise of consumer activism, see Sophie Dubuisson-Quellier, *Ethical Consumption,* trans. Howard Scott (Halifax, NS: Fernwood Books, 2013); Jeffrey Haydu and David Kadanoff, "Casing Political Consumerism," *Mobilization* 15, no. 2 (2010): 159–77; Szasz, *Shopping Our Way to Safety.*

29. Mary Bernstein, "Identity Politics," *Annual Review of Sociology* 31, no. 1 (2005): 47–74; Ross Haenfler, Brett Johnson, and Ellis Jones, "Lifestyle Movements: Exploring the Intersection of Lifestyle and Social Movements," *Social Movement Studies* 11, no. 1 (2012): 1–20.

30. Gunderson, "Problems with the Defetishization Thesis," 110.

31. Numerous authors have also argued that modern consumer activism is fundamentally neoliberal activism. See Clive Barnett et al., "Consuming Ethics: Articulating the Subjects and Spaces of Ethical Consumption," *Antipode* 37, no. 1 (2005): 23–45; Josée Johnston, "The Citizen-Consumer Hybrid: Ideological Tensions and the Case of Whole Foods Market," *Theory and Society* 37, no. 3 (2008): 229–70; Daniel Jaffee, *Brewing Justice: Fair Trade Coffee, Sustainability, and Survival* (Berkeley: University of California Press, 2007).

32. MacBride, *Recycling Reconsidered*, 116.

33. Gunderson, "Problems with the Defetishization Thesis," 114.

34. Gidwani and Reddy, "Afterlives of 'Waste,'" 1633.

35. Jesse Goldstein, "Terra Economica: Waste and the Production of Enclosed Nature," *Antipode* 45, no. 2 (2013): 370.

36. His argument, he acknowledged, was drawn from William Cronon, *Changes in the Land: Indians, Colonists, and the Ecology of New England* (New York: Hill and Wang, 1983).

37. Private investors and international financial institutions have often justified "land grabs" and demands for privatization of state services in terms of "wasted" or "idle" resources. See Saturnino M. Borras and Jennifer C. Franco, "Global Land Grabbing and Trajectories of Agrarian Change: A Preliminary Analysis," *Journal of Agrarian Change* 12, no. 1 (2012): 45; and Michael Goldman, *Imperial Nature: The World Bank and Struggles for Social Justice in the Age of Globalization* (New Haven, Conn.: Yale University Press, 2005), 106, 235.

38. Marion Fourcade-Gourinchas and Sarah L. Babb, "The Rebirth of the Liberal Creed: Paths to Neoliberalism in Four Countries," *American Journal of Sociology* 108, no. 3 (2002): 535.

39. Richard Porter, *The Economics of Waste* (Washington, D.C.: Resources for the Future, 2002), 24.

40. Boltanski and Chiapello, *New Spirit of Capitalism*, 13.

41. Joel Makower, "Industrial Strength Solution," *Mother Jones*, June 2009, http://motherjones.com/.

42. Gille, *From the Cult of Waste*, 3.

43. According to neoliberal advocates, "The inefficiencies of government-provided goods and services would be replaced by the allegedly greater efficiencies of the competitive marketplace." See Lawrence Busch, "Can Fairy Tales Come True? The Surprising Story of Neoliberalism and World Agriculture," *Sociologia Ruralis* 50, no. 4 (2010): 334.

44. G. Scott Thomas, *The United States of Suburbia: How the Suburbs Took Control of America and What They Plan to Do with It* (Amherst, N.Y.: Prometheus, 1998), 162.

45. Jenny Gustavsson, Christel Cederberg, and Ulf Sonesson, *Global Food Losses and Food Waste* (Rome: UN Food and Agricultural Organization, May 16, 2011), 8; Amanda Keledjian et al., *Wasted Catch: Unsolved Problems in U.S. Fisheries* (Washington, D.C.: Oceana, March 2014).

46. Barbara McDonald, "'Once You Know Something, You Can't Not Know It': An Empirical Look at Becoming Vegan," *Society and Animals* 8, no. 1 (2000): 11.

47. Elizabeth Royte, *Garbage Land: On the Secret Trail of Trash* (New York: Little, Brown, 2005).

48. McAdam, "Recruitment to High-Risk Activism."

49. Jennifer Earl and Katrina Kimport, *Digitally Enabled Social Change: Activism in the Internet Age* (Cambridge, Mass.: MIT Press, 2011).

3. Waving the Banana in the Big Apple

1. Anon., "Extreme Happiness," 47.

2. Emily Donovan, "Day-to-Day Change Making: The Transformative Potential of Dumpster Diving" (senior thesis, Pomona College, 2012), 7.

3. For additional evidence on these stores' practices, see Bloom, *American Wasteland*, 155; and Stuart, *Waste*, 13.

4. See Graeber, *Direct Action*; and Katsiaficas, *Subversion of Politics*.

5. The abuses that go into coffee production and limits of "fair trade" as a solution to them are documented by Jaffee, *Brewing Justice*.

6. Direct analyses of grocery store garbage confirm that these items are the most commonly wasted. See Timothy W. Jones, *Using Contemporary Archaeology and Applied Anthropology to Understand Food Loss in the American Food System* (Tucson: University of Arizona, Bureau of Applied Research in Anthropology, 2004).

7. Steve Martinez, *The U.S. Food Marketing System: Recent Developments, 1997–2006*, Economic Research Report Number 42 (Washington, D.C.: U.S. Department of Agriculture, May 2007), 20.

8. Bloom, *American Wasteland*, 138.

9. Carlos Mena, B. Adenso-Diaz, and Oznur Yurt, "The Causes of Food Waste in the Supplier–Retailer Interface: Evidences from the UK and Spain," *Resources, Conservation, and Recycling* 55, no. 6 (2011): 652.

10. Jose B. Alvarez and Ryan C. Johnson, *Doug Rauch: Solving the American Food Paradox*, SSRN Scholarly Paper (Rochester, N.Y.: Social Science Research Network, December 7, 2011).

11. Martinez, *U.S. Food Marketing System*, 33.

12. Less than 20 percent of retail waste is a result of accidents. See Paola Garrone, Marco Melacini, and Alessandro Perego, "Opening the Black Box of Food Waste Reduction," *Food Policy* 46 (June 2014): 137.

13. Lyson and Raymer, "Stalking the Wily Multinational," 206.

14. General Accounting Office, *Food Waste: An Opportunity to Improve Resource Use* (Washington, D.C.: General Accounting Office, September 16, 1977), 46.

15. "Ideology of the Product," http://freegan.info/.

16. Nestle finds that 80 percent of the price of food is for labor, packaging, advertising, and other "value-adding" activities. See Nestle, *Food Politics: How the Food Industry Influences Nutrition and Health* (Berkeley: University of California Press, 2002), 17.

17. Todd Gitlin, *The Whole World Is Watching: Mass Media in the Making and Unmaking of the New Left* (Berkeley: University of California Press, 1981).

18. Graeber, *Direct Action,* 438.
19. Essig, "Fine Diving."
20. Juris, *Networking Futures*; Moore and Roberts, "Do-It-Yourself Mobilization."
21. Kelly Ernst, "A Revolution We Create Daily" (PhD diss., American University, 2009), 110.
22. In one survey, 67 percent of retailers cited liability reasons for not donating, while 17 percent blame regulations. See Food Waste Reduction Institute, *Analysis of U.S. Food Waste among Food Manufacturers, Retailers, and Wholesalers* (Washington, D.C.: Manufacturers Association and Food Marketing Institute, April 2013), 17. There are no liability reasons or government regulations that prevent donation, and a plethora of laws and tax incentives that encourage them to do so.
23. This duality of material and symbolic makes waste a "hybrid" object (Gille, "Actor Networks").
24. Marx, *Capital: Volume 1,* 595.
25. Max Weber, *The Protestant Ethic and the Spirit of Capitalism,* trans. Talcott Parsons (London: Routledge, 2001), 18.
26. See Marcel Mauss, *The Gift,* trans. Ian Cunnison (London: Cohen and West LTD, 1962); David Graeber, *Debt: The First 5,000 Years* (Brooklyn, N.Y.: Melvillehouse, 2011).
27. For further discussions of the need for a "moral" basis for capitalism, see Daniel Bell, *The Cultural Contradictions of Capitalism,* 20th anniv. ed. (New York: Basic Books, 1996); Boltanski and Chiapello, *New Spirit of Capitalism*; and Marion Fourcade and Kieran Healy, "Moral Views of Market Society," *Annual Review of Sociology* 33, no. 1 (2007): 285–311.
28. Weber, *Protestant Ethic,* 17.
29. Ibid., 104.
30. Zimring, *Cash for Your Trash,* 13–19; Benjamin Miller, *Fat of the Land* (New York: Four Walls Eight Windows, 2000), 40; Martin O'Brien, *A Crisis of Waste? Understanding the Rubbish Society* (New York: Routledge, 2008), 58–59.
31. Lauren Weber, *In CHEAP We Trust: The Story of a Misunderstood American Virtue* (New York: Little, Brown, 2009), chap. 3.
32. Quoted in Rogers, *Gone Tomorrow,* 109.
33. Quoted in Lizbeth Cohen, *A Consumers' Republic: The Politics of Mass Consumption in Postwar America* (New York: Vintage, 2003), 68.
34. J. R. McNeill and George Vrtis, "Thrift and Waste in American History," in *Thrift and Thriving in America,* ed. Joshua Yates and James Hunter (Oxford: Oxford University Press, 2011), 508–35.
35. Quoted in Cohen, *Consumers' Republic,* 121.
36. Sanitary napkins and paper cups are two examples developed by Strasser, *Waste and Want,* chap. 4.
37. Tim Cooper, "Slower Consumption Reflections on Product Life Spans and the 'Throwaway Society,'" *Journal of Industrial Ecology* 9, nos. 1–2 (2005): 57.
38. Vance Packard, *The Waste Makers* (New York: Pocket Books, 1960), 58.

39. Kelly, *Garbage*, 62.

40. Cohen, *Consumers' Republic*, 301.

41. Quoted in Packard, *Waste Makers*, 36.

42. Michael Pollan, *In Defense of Food: An Eater's Manifesto* (New York: Penguin, 2008); Pierre Chandon and Brian Wansink, "Does Food Marketing Need to Make Us Fat? A Review and Solutions," *Nutrition Reviews* 70, no. 10 (2012): 571–93.

43. Nestle, *Food Politics*.

44. Julie Guthman and Melanie DuPuis, "Embodying Neoliberalism: Economy, Culture, and the Politics of Fat," *Environment and Planning D: Society and Space* 24, no. 3 (2006): 427–48.

45. Nicky Gregson, Alan Metcalfe, and Louise Crewe, "Identity, Mobility, and the Throwaway Society," *Environment and Planning D: Society and Space* 25, no. 4 (2007): 682–700; Gilbert Harrell and Diane McConocha, "Personal Factors Related to Consumer Product Disposal Tendencies," *Journal of Consumer Affairs* 26, no. 2 (1992): 397–417; Valérie Guillard and Dominique Roux, "Macromarketing Issues on the Sidewalk: How 'Gleaners' and 'Disposers' (Re)Create a Sustainable Economy," *Journal of Macromarketing* 34, no. 3 (2014); Nina Brosius, Karen V. Fernandez, and Hélène Cherrier, "Reacquiring Consumer Waste: Treasure in Our Trash?," *Journal of Public Policy and Marketing* 32, no. 2 (2013): 286–301.

46. Linda Derksen and John Gartrell, "The Social Context of Recycling," *American Sociological Review* 58, no. 3 (1993): 434–42; Donna L. Lybecker, Mark K. McBeth, and Elizabeth Kusko, "Trash or Treasure: Recycling Narratives and Reducing Political Polarisation," *Environmental Politics* 22, no. 2 (2013): 312–32; Nelson Pichardo Almanzar, Heather Sullivan-Catlin, and Glenn Deane, "Is the Political Personal? Everyday Behaviors as Forms of Environmental Movement Participation," *Mobilization* 3, no. 2 (1998): 185–205.

47. MacBride, *Recycling Reconsidered*, 41.

48. Benedetta Cappellini and Elizabeth Parsons, "Practising Thrift at Dinnertime: Mealtime Leftovers, Sacrifice, and Family Membership," *Sociological Review* 60 (2012): 121–34; David Evans, "Beyond the Throwaway Society: Ordinary Domestic Practice and a Sociological Approach to Household Food Waste," *Sociology* 46, no. 1 (2011): 1–16; Matt Watson and Angela Meah, "Food, Waste, and Safety: Negotiating Conflicting Social Anxieties Into the Practices of Domestic Provisioning," *Sociological Review* 60 (2012): 102–20.

49. Susan Carpenter, "Food Waste Prompts Most Green Guilt, Survey Says," *Los Angeles Times*, August 15, 2012.

50. U.S. Environmental Protection Agency, *Municipal Solid Waste in the United States*; Bloom, *American Wasteland*, 187.

51. This is one of the main insights of "practice" theory; see Alan Warde, "Consumption and Theories of Practice," *Journal of Consumer Culture* 5, no. 2 (2005): 131–53.

52. De Coverly, O'Malley, and Patterson, "Hidden Mountain," 297.

53. Verena Winiwarter, "History of Waste," in *Waste in Ecological Economics,* ed. Katy Bisson and John Proops (Cheltenham, U.K.: Edward Elgar, 2002), 38–54.

54. Heather Chappells and Elizabeth Shove, "The Dustbin: A Study of Domestic Waste, Household Practices, and Utility Services," *International Planning Studies* 4, no. 2 (1999): 267–80; De Coverly, O'Malley, and Patterson, "Hidden Mountain"; Rathje and Murphy, *Rubbish!*

55. Nagle, *Picking Up,* 16.

56. Reno, "Your Trash Is Someone's Treasure," 37.

57. Strasser, *Waste and Want,* chap. 1.

58. Martin Melosi, *Garbage in the Cities: Refuse, Reform, and the Environment, 1880–1980* (College Station: Texas A&M University Press, 1981), 110.

59. Rogers, *Gone Tomorrow,* 61.

60. Boltanski and Chiapello, *New Spirit of Capitalism.*

61. Thorstein Veblen, *The Theory of the Leisure Class,* new ed. (Mineola, N.Y.: Dover Publications, 1994), 68.

62. Chase, *Tragedy of Waste.*

63. See also Baran and Sweezy, *Monopoly Capital.*

64. Marcuse, *One-Dimensional Man,* 49.

65. Department of Sanitation, *Annual Report* (New York: New York City Government, 2013).

66. Matthew Gandy, *Concrete and Clay: Reworking Nature in New York City* (Cambridge, Mass.: MIT Press, 2002), 190.

67. Stephen J. Mennell, Anne Murcott, and Anneke H. van Otterloo, *The Sociology of Food: Eating, Diet, and Culture,* 2nd ed. (London: Sage, 1992).

4. A New World Out of Waste

1. Jim Mason, *An Unnatural Order: Why We Are Destroying the Planet and Each Other* (New York: Lantern Books, 2005), 11.

2. I don't want to overstate freegans' collective agreement with these views. During Adam's diatribe, Quinn wandered off, returning only when—in his words—"the usual human extinction rant was over."

3. Gary Alan Fine, *Morel Tales: The Culture of Mushrooming* (Cambridge, Mass.: Harvard University Press, 1998), 34.

4. Roger Keil and Julie-Anne Boudreau, "Metropolis and Metabolics," in *In the Nature of Cities: Urban Political Ecology and the Politics of Urban Metabolism,* ed. Nik Heynen, Maria Kaika, and Erik Swyngedouw (Oxford: Routledge, 2006), 40–62; Nagle, *Picking Up,* 4.

5. Georg Simmel, "The Metropolis and Mental Life," in *Cities and Societies,* ed. Paul Hatt and Albert Reiss (Glencoe, Ill.: Free Press, 1957), 635–46.

6. Institution of Mechanical Engineers, *Global Food,* 23.

7. Estabrook, *Tomatoland,* 123.

8. David Pimentel, "Environmental and Social Implications of Waste in U.S. Agriculture and Food Sectors," *Journal of Agricultural and Environmental Ethics* 3, no. 1 (1990): 14.

9. Nestle quotes one food industry spokesperson as saying, "Food consumption is not supply driven, it is demand driven, and consumers are in the driver's seat" (*Food Politics,* 359).

10. Nagle, *Picking Up,* 49.

11. Szasz, *Shopping Our Way to Safety.*

12. Peter Jackson, "Food Stories: Consumption in an Age of Anxiety," *Cultural Geographies* 17, no. 2 (2010): 147–65; Watson and Meah, "Food, Waste, and Safety."

13. Richard Milne, "Arbiters of Waste: Date Labels, the Consumer, and Knowing Good, Safe Food," *Sociological Review* 60 (2012): 84–101.

14. Quoted in Emily Broad Leib and Dana Gunders, *The Dating Game* (New York: Natural Resources Defense Council, September 2013), 6, 19.

15. Brook Lyndhurst, *Consumer Insight: Date Labels and Storage Guidance* (Banbury, U.K.: Waste and Resources Action Program, May 2011), 35; see also Roni A. Neff, Marie L. Spiker, and Patricia L. Truant, "Wasted Food: U.S. Consumers' Reported Awareness, Attitudes, and Behaviors," *PLoS ONE* 10, no. 6 (2015): e0127881.

16. Leib and Gunders, *Dating Game,* 7–8.

17. Experts agree that these criteria are far more important than dates in determining safety (Leib and Gunders, *Dating Game*).

18. One exception came when Leia's partner, Tate, divulged to *Marie Claire* that he had gotten sick from eating day-old sushi. See Jay Goodwin, "She Lives Off What We Throw Away," *Marie Claire,* March 11, 2009, http://www.marieclaire.com/.

19. "Health and Safety Issues," http://freegan.info/.

20. Sarah Klein and Caroline DeWall, *Risky Meat* (Washington, D.C.: Center for Science in the Public Interest, 2013).

21. Nicole Eikenberry and Chery Smith, "Attitudes, Beliefs, and Prevalence of Dumpster Diving as a Means to Obtain Food by Midwestern, Low-Income, Urban Dwellers," *Agriculture and Human Values* 22, no. 2 (2005): 187–202.

22. Clark, "Raw and the Rotten," 22; Edwards and Mercer, "Gleaning from Gluttony," 389.

23. Mary Douglas, *Purity and Danger: An Analysis of the Concepts of Pollution and Taboo* (London: Routledge, 1966).

24. Valerie Curtis, Mícheál de Barra, and Robert Aunger, "Disgust as an Adaptive System for Disease Avoidance Behaviour," *Philosophical Transactions of the Royal Society* 366, no. 1563 (2011): 389–401.

25. Ryan Owens and Suzanne Yeo, "One Man's Trash Is Another Man's Dinner: Freegans Go Dumpster Diving for Unspoiled Food," *ABC News,* December 16, 2007.

26. See also Nguyen, Chen, and Mukherjee, "Reverse Stigma in the Freegan Community."

27. Gross, "Capitalism and Its Discontents," 62.

28. Marx, *Capital: Volume 1.*

29. Nigel Thrift, "A Capitalist Time Consciousness," in *The Sociology of Time,* ed. John Hassard (Houndmills, U.K.: Macmillan, 1990).

30. Lawrence Mishel, *Trends in U.S. Work Hours and Wages over 1979–2007,* Issue Brief No. 348 (Washington, D.C.: Economic Policy Institute, January 2013).

31. Alan Warde et al., "Changes in the Practice of Eating: A Comparative Analysis of Time-Use," *Acta Sociologica* 50, no. 4 (2007): 367.

32. John Thøgersen, "Wasteful Food Consumption: Trends in Food and Packaging Waste," *Scandinavian Journal of Management* 12, no. 3 (1996): 292.

33. JoAnn Jaffe and Michael Gertler, "Victual Vicissitudes: Consumer Deskilling and the (Gendered) Transformation of Food Systems," *Agriculture and Human Values* 23, no. 2 (2006): 143–62.

34. This point is documented in Kristofor Husted, "Supermarkets Waste Tons of Food as They Woo Shoppers," *NPR.org,* September 25, 2014, http://www.npr.org/.

35. Evans, "Beyond the Throwaway Society," 51.

36. Gay Hawkins, "The Performativity of Food Packaging: Market Devices, Waste Crisis, and Recycling," *Sociological Review* 60 (2012): 66–83.

37. Rathje and Murphy's "First principle of food waste" from their archaeological forays into America's dump is that "the more repetitive the diet, the less waste" (*Rubbish!,* 62).

38. Ernst, "Revolution We Create Daily," 86.

39. Emily Sullivan, "The Youth Mystique: Downward Mobility and Emerging Adulthood" (undergraduate thesis, Princeton University, 2011), 46.

40. Donovan, "Day-to-Day Change Making," 19; More, "Dumpster Dinners," 19.

41. See Graeber, *Fragments*; and Mauss, *Gift.*

42. "Home Page," http://rrfm-nyc.blogspot.com/.

43. Nik Heynen et al., *Neoliberal Environments: False Promises and Unnatural Consequences* (London: Routledge, 2007).

44. Anon., "Extreme Happiness," 55; see also Graeber, *Debt,* chap. 5; Richard White and Colin Williams, "The Pervasive Nature of Heterodox Economic Spaces at a Time of Neoliberal Crisis: Towards a 'Postneoliberal' Anarchist Future," *Antipode* 44, no. 5 (2012): 1625–44.

45. John Bohstedt, *The Politics of Provisions: Food Riots, Moral Economy, and Market Transition in England, c. 1550–1850* (Surrey, U.K.: Ashgate, 2010).

46. Michael Goldman and Rachel Schurman, "Closing the 'Great Divide': New Social Theory on Society and Nature," *Annual Review of Sociology* 26 (2000): 564; William Cronon, ed., *Uncommon Ground* (New York: W. W. Norton, 1996), 34.

47. Bisson and Proops show how "waste" in the form of excess energy is necessary to any mode of production (*Waste in Ecological Economics* [Cheltenham, U.K.: Edward Elgar, 2002]).

48. For sociological discussions of the social construction of nature, see Michael Bell, *Childerley: Nature and Morality in a Country Village* (Chicago: University of Chicago Press, 1994); and William R. Freudenburg, Scott Frickel, and Robert Gramling, "Beyond the Nature/Society Divide: Learning to Think about a Mountain," *Sociological Forum* 10, no. 3 (1995): 361–92.

49. As O'Brien observes, "It is the circumstances, not the material itself, that determine whether or not said material is to be treated as waste" ("A

'Lasting Transformation' of Capitalist Surplus: From Food Stocks to Feedstocks," *Sociological Review* 60 [2012]: 199).

50. Appadurai, "Introduction."

5. The Ultimate Boycott?

1. Elizabeth L. Cline, *Overdressed: The Shockingly High Cost of Cheap Fashion* (New York: Portfolio, 2012).

2. Borealis Center, *Environmental Trends and Climate Impacts: Findings from the U.S. Book Industry* (New York: Book Industry Study Group, 2008), 31.

3. Paper Project, *Environmental Impacts of the Magazine Industry and Recommendations for Improvement* (Washington, D.C.: Independent Press Association, May 2001).

4. "Home Page," http://freegan.info/.

5. Neil Smith, *The New Urban Frontier: Gentrification and the Revanchist City* (New York: Routledge, 1996), 216.

6. Graeber, *Direct Action*, 266.

7. John Leland, "With Advocates' Help, Squatters Call Foreclosures Home," *New York Times*, April 10, 2009.

8. Of course, Adam himself was living in the Surrealestate basement. Quinn lovingly called him "the basement troll," adding, "He knows, you can quote me on that."

9. Moon Wha Lee, *Housing and Vacancy Survey* (New York: Department of Housing Preservation and Development, 2011), 351, http://www.nyc.gov/.

10. Right to the City, *People without Homes and Homes without People: A Count of Vacant Condos in Select NYC Neighborhoods* (New York: New York City Chapter of the Right to the City Alliance, 2010).

11. "Home Page," http://freegan.info/.

12. Ibid.

13. Emily Darrell, "Leftovers: A Search for the Freegan Ideal" (master's thesis, University of Montana, 2009), 32.

14. U.S. Environmental Protection Agency, *Electronics Waste Management in the United States through 2009* (Washington, D.C.: Office of Resource Conservation and Recovery, May 2011).

15. Ibid.

16. Mark Sundeen, *The Man Who Quit Money* (New York: Penguin, 2012).

17. Epstein, *Political Protest and Cultural Revolution*; Mary Grigsby, *Buying Time and Getting By: The Voluntary Simplicity Movement* (Albany: State University of New York Press, 2004); Paul Lichterman, *The Search for Political Community: American Activists Reinventing Commitment* (Cambridge: Cambridge University Press, 1996).

18. See Ben Fincham, "'Generally Speaking People Are in It for the Cycling and the Beer': Bicycle Couriers, Subculture, and Enjoyment," *Sociological Review* 55, no. 2 (2007): 189–202.

19. Occupy Wall Street also moved into a public–private atrium "provided" by Deutsche Bank after it was evicted from Zuccotti Park.

20. Don Mitchell, *The Right to the City: Social Justice and the Fight for Public Space* (New York: Guilford, 2003).

21. Karen Schmelzkopf, "Urban Community Gardens as Contested Space," *Geographical Review* 85, no. 3 (1995): 364–81; Sarah Maslin Nir and Jiha Ham, "Fighting a McDonald's in Queens for the Right to Sit. And Sit. And Sit," *New York Times*, January 14, 2014.

22. Edwards and Mercer, "Gleaning from Gluttony," 282.

23. For recycling and environmentalism, see Stewart Barr, "Factors Influencing Environmental Attitudes and Behaviors A U.K. Case Study of Household Waste Management," *Environment and Behavior* 39, no. 4 (2007): 435–73; Lori M. Hunter, Alison Hatch, and Aaron Johnson, "Cross-National Gender Variation in Environmental Behaviors," *Social Science Quarterly* 85, no. 3 (2004): 677–94; Caroline J. Oates and Seonaidh McDonald, "Recycling and the Domestic Division of Labour: Is Green Pink or Blue?," *Sociology* 40, no. 3 (2006): 417–33.

24. See Lichterman, *Search for Political Community*, chap. 5.

25. Brannen, *Food Works*, 3.

26. Other interviewees from locations as varied as San Francisco and Athens, Greece, likewise confirmed that the economic downturn had led to a surge in dumpster diving.

27. Ernst, "Revolution We Create Daily," 123.

28. This is consistent with the findings of other studies on freegans. See Carolsfeld and Erikson, "Beyond Desperation"; and Edwards and Mercer, "Gleaning from Gluttony." Two people of color denied my request for interviews, which is itself revealing and cause for reflection.

29. David Pellow, *Resisting Global Toxics* (Cambridge, Mass.: MIT Press, 2007), 98.

30. Julie Guthman, "Bringing Good Food to Others: Investigating the Subjects of Alternative Food Practice," *Cultural Geographies* 15, no. 4 (2008): 435.

31. Lindsey Dillon, "Race, Waste, and Space: Brownfield Redevelopment and Environmental Justice at the Hunters Point Shipyard," *Antipode* 45, no. 5 (2014): 2.

32. Quoted in Corman, "Getting Their Hands Dirty," 46.

33. Ibid.

34. David Pellow, *Garbage Wars: The Struggle for Environmental Justice in Chicago* (Cambridge, Mass.: MIT Press, 2004); Julie Sze, *Noxious New York: The Racial Politics of Urban Health and Environmental Justice* (Cambridge, Mass.: MIT Press, 2006).

35. Gandy, *Concrete and Clay*.

36. For a discussion of the largely undocumented and invisible place of industrial by-products in the overall waste stream, see MacBride, *Recycling Reconsidered*, chap. 3.

37. Kyle Crowder and Liam Downey, "Interneighborhood Migration, Race, and Environmental Hazards: Modeling Microlevel Processes of Environmental Inequality," *American Journal of Sociology* 115, no. 4 (2010): 1110–49; Don Grant et al., "Bringing the Polluters Back In: Environmental Inequality and

the Organization of Chemical Production," *American Sociological Review* 75, no. 4 (2010): 479–504.

38. Ernst, "Revolution We Create Daily," 108.
39. W. E. B. Du Bois, *Black Reconstruction in America* (Oxford: Oxford University Press, 1936); Charles Post, *The American Road to Capitalism* (Chicago: Haymarket Books, 2012).
40. Peter King, "Customary Rights and Women's Earnings: The Importance of Gleaning to the Rural Labouring Poor, 1750–1850," *Economic History Review* 44, no. 3 (1991): 474.
41. Peter King, "Legal Change, Customary Right, and Social Conflict in Late Eighteenth-Century England: The Origins of the Great Gleaning Case of 1788," *Law and History Review* 10, no. 1 (1992): 1–31.
42. James C. Scott, *Weapons of the Weak: Everyday Forms of Peasant Resistance* (New Haven, Conn.: Yale University Press, 1985), 118.
43. Martin Medina, *The World's Scavengers: Salvaging for Sustainable Consumption and Production* (New York: Altamira, 2007), 35.
44. Zimring, *Cash for Your Trash*, 79.
45. Teresa Gowan, *Hobos, Hustlers, and Backsliders: Homeless in San Francisco* (Minneapolis: University of Minnesota Press, 2010), 151; see also Duneier, *Sidewalk*; Jeff Ferrell, *Empire of Scrounge: Inside the Urban Underground of Dumpster Diving, Trash Picking, and Street Scavenging* (New York: New York University Press, 2006).
46. I could be wrong: 19 percent of a survey of four hundred low-income residents of Minneapolis claimed to have eaten from a dumpster at some point (Eikenberry and Smith, "Attitudes, Beliefs, and Prevalence of Dumpster Diving").
47. Anon, "Extreme Happiness," 48.
48. See Ferrell, *Empire of Scrounge*; and Gowan, *Hobos, Hustlers, and Backsliders*.
49. Duneier, *Sidewalk*, 84.
50. See Bloom, *American Wasteland*, 258.
51. Henderson, "'Free' Food"; Poppendieck, *Sweet Charity?*
52. Sarbjit Nahal, Valery Lucas-Leclin, and Julie Dolie, *No Time to Waste—Global Waste Primer* (London: Bank of America–Merrill Lynch, April 2013), 1.
53. Harriet Bulkeley, Matt Watson, and Ray Hudson, "Modes of Governing Municipal Waste," *Environment and Planning A* 39, no. 11 (2007): 2733–53; Davies, *Geographies of Garbage Governance*; G. Honor Fagan, "Waste Management and Its Contestation in the Republic of Ireland," *Capitalism Nature Socialism* 15, no. 1 (2004): 83–102.
54. Germà Bel and Mildred Warner, "Does Privatization of Solid Waste and Water Services Reduce Costs? A Review of Empirical Studies," *Resources, Conservation, and Recycling* 52, no. 12 (2008): 1337–48.
55. Medina, *World's Scavengers*.
56. William K. Rashbaum, "N.Y.C. Sanitation Officials Puzzled over Missing Appliances," *New York Times*, December 14, 2010.
57. Robert Lange, "Stealing Recycling's Future," *Recycling Review*, February 2012, 29.

58. See Grigsby, *Buying Time and Getting By*; Nicole Shepherd, "Anarcho-Environmentalists: Ascetics of Late Modernity," *Journal of Contemporary Ethnography* 31, no. 2 (2002): 135–57.
59. Anon., "Extreme Happiness," 37.
60. Corman, "Getting Their Hands Dirty," 33.
61. Abbott, "Problem of Excess."
62. Jake Halpern, "The Freegan Establishment," *New York Times,* June 4, 2010.
63. Carolsfeld and Erikson, "Beyond Desperation," 259.
64. "Freegan Visions," freegan.info.
65. See also Clark, "Raw and the Rotten."

6. Backlash, Conflict, and Decline

1. Amin Ghaziani and Delia Baldassarri, "Cultural Anchors and the Organization of Differences," *American Sociological Review* 76, no. 2 (2011): 179–206.
2. When one freegan contacted Dunkin' Donuts about its waste, for example, the response was that "it is left to the discretion of the individual owner/franchisee of each restaurant whether or not food is donated at the end of the day."
3. Anon., *Evasion,* 73.
4. Ibid., 251.
5. *Dive!* (dir. Jeremy Seifert, 2010).
6. Stores often also claim that they are concerned that divers will resell items or return them to the store for cash—practices that I've never observed among freegans, but which do seem to be part of the overall dumpster-diving landscape.
7. Nguyen, Chen, and Mukherjee, "Reverse Stigma in the Freegan Community."
8. Jim Dwyer, "A Clothing Clearance Where More Than Just the Prices Have Been Slashed," *New York Times,* January 6, 2010.
9. David Giles, "Dumpster-Divers and the Smoothies of Wrath," *FoodAnthropology,* January 6, 2012, http://foodanthro.com/.
10. Katja de Vries and Sebastian Abrahamsson, "Dumpsters, Muffins, Waste, and Law," *Discard Studies,* March 27, 2012, http://discardstudies.wordpress.com/; Christian Goutorbe, "Hérault: Des glaneurs de poubelles au tribunal," *La Depeche,* February 4, 2015; Murray Wardrop, "Woman in Court for Taking 'Waste' Food from Tesco Bins," *Telegraph,* June 1, 2011; Amelia Gentleman, "Three Charged with Stealing Food from Skip behind Iceland Supermarket," *Guardian,* January 28, 2014.
11. Stuart, *Waste,* 39.
12. Food Waste Reduction Alliance, *Analysis of U.S. Food Waste,* 16.
13. Quoted in Stuart, *Waste,* 10.
14. Ibid., 210.
15. Thirty-five percent of global food losses in 2009 happened at the consumer level. See Brian Lipinski et al., "Reducing Food Loss and Waste" (working paper, World Resources Institute, Washington, D.C., June 2013), 8.
16. Institution of Mechanical Engineers, *Global Food,* 18.

17. Surveys showed that such offers played a role in 30 percent of decisions to waste food in households, and the most frequently wasted items—like yogurt, salads, or juices—were among the most likely to have promotional offers. See WRAP, *Investigation into the Possible Impact of Promotions on Food Waste* (Banbury, UK: Waste and Resources Action Program, December 2011). See also Geremy Farr-Wharton, Marcus Foth, and Jaz Hee-Jeong Choi, "Identifying Factors That Promote Consumer Behaviours Causing Expired Domestic Food Waste," *Journal of Consumer Behaviour* 13, no. 6 (2014): 397.

18. Evans, "Beyond the Throwaway Society"; Brian Wansink, "Abandoned Products and Consumer Waste: How Did That Get into the Pantry?," *Choices* 16, no. 2 (2001): 46.

19. Helén Williams et al., "Reasons for Household Food Waste with Special Attention to Packaging," *Journal of Cleaner Production* 24 (March 2012): 141–48.

20. Packard, *Waste Makers*, 38.

21. In 2009, for example, a Whole Foods employee in New York was fired for taking a tuna sandwich designated for disposal. See Jennifer Lee, "Fired over a Tuna Sandwich, and Fighting Back," *New York Times*, March 16, 2009, http://cityroom.blogs.nytimes.com/.

22. Stephen Kurutz, "Not Buying It," *New York Times*, June 21, 2007, http://www.nytimes.com/.

23. Halpern, "Freegan Establishment."

24. Gitlin, *Whole World Is Watching*, 121.

25. Reshma Kirpalani, "Freeganism: Dumpster Diving to Buck the Spending Trend," *ABC News*, August 8, 2011.

26. Three thousand Americans die each year from *purchased* food. See Centers for Disease Control and Prevention, "Estimates of Foodborne Illness," 2011, http://www.cdc.gov/.

27. Sarumathi Jayaraman, *Behind the Kitchen Door* (Ithaca, NY: Cornell University Press, 2013), 44.

28. Giles, "Mass Conspiracy to Feed People"; Nik Heynen, "Cooking Up Non-Violent Civil-Disobedient Direct Action for the Hungry: 'Food Not Bombs' and the Resurgence of Radical Democracy in the U.S.," *Urban Studies* 47, no. 6 (2010): 1225–40; Max Liboiron, "Tactics of Waste, Dirt, and Discard in the Occupy Movement," *Social Movement Studies* 11, nos. 3–4 (2012): 393–401; Parson, "Ungovernable Force."

29. Anne Kadet, "Free, but Not Always Easy," *Wall Street Journal*, August 31, 2012.

30. Kate Storey, "She Loves 'Ew!' York," *New York Post*, October 16, 2012.

31. Gitlin, *Whole World Is Watching*.

32. Halpern, "Freegan Establishment."

33. Benji and Kaylan, "Dumpster Dive," 2.

34. Although certainly not because of freegan.info, foraging (and hunting) in city parks has had enough of an impact that the city has moved to ban it. See Lisa W. Foderaro, "New York Moves to Stop Foraging in City's Parks," *New York Times*, July 29, 2011.

35. See Nina Eliasoph, *Avoiding Politics: How Americans Produce Apathy in Every-day Life* (Cambridge: Cambridge University Press, 1998).
36. Clark, "Raw and the Rotten"; Gross, "Capitalism and Its Discontents"; Rachel Shteir, *The Steal: A Cultural History of Shoplifting* (New York: Penguin, 2012), chap. 4.
37. After he left the group, Adam openly endorsed shoplifting, arguing, "We shouldn't ask 'is it ethical to shoplift'? Rather we should ask, 'is it ethical to buy?'" He then proceeded to lay out some guidelines for shoplifting: take only necessities (not luxury items), don't resell items, and target major corporations (Shteir, *Steal*).
38. The quick demise of another freegan project in Boston—the "Gleaner's Kitchen"—confirms the unwillingness of most landlords to play host to prefigurative projects, particularly those that blatantly violate health codes. See Jon Christian, "The Gleaners' Kitchen: The Freegan Revolution Will Not Be Kickstarted," *Boston Magazine*, March 18, 2014, http://www.bostonmagazine.com/.
39. His account is consistent with Ruth Milkman, Stephanie Luce, and Penny Lewis, *Changing the Subject: A Bottom-Up Account of Occupy Wall Street in New York City* (New York: City University of New York, 2013).
40. See also Liboiron, "Tactics of Waste, Dirt, and Discard," 400.
41. Ibid., 397. Adam, as usual playing Cassandra, told me that Occupy was actually exceptionally wasteful with the resources showered on it.

Conclusion

1. Or, if you ask Tim Barry, Fine Foods Market.
2. Kai Erikson, *Everything in Its Path: Destruction of Community in the Buffalo Creek Flood* (New York: Simon and Schuster, 1978).
3. Stacy St. Clair and Todd Lighty, "Chicago Man Charged with Taking Part in Anonymous Hacking," *Chicago Tribune*, March 7, 2012.
4. Gabriel Hetland and Jeff Goodwin, "The Strange Disappearance of Capitalism from Social Movement Studies," in *Marxism and Social Movements*, ed. Colin Barker et al. (Leiden, Netherlands: Brill, 2013), 83–102.
5. Boltanski and Chiapello, *New Spirit of Capitalism*, 170.
6. I am heavily influenced by Burawoy's assertion that "third wave" countermovements to commodification will center on land and nature ("From Polanyi to Pollyanna").
7. Joshua Yates, "Disputing Abundance," in *Thrift and Thriving in America*, ed. Joshua Yates and James Hunter (Oxford: Oxford University Press, 2011), 536–69; John Vail, "Decommodification and Egalitarian Political Economy," *Politics and Society* 38, no. 3 (2010): 310–46.
8. Anon., "Extreme Happiness," 70.
9. Sidney Tarrow, *Power in Movement*, 3rd ed. (Cambridge: Cambridge University Press, 2011), 98.
10. See Erik Olin Wright, *Envisioning Real Utopias* (London: Verso, 2010), chap. 10.

11. Voss and Williams, "Local in the Global"; Elizabeth Bennett et al., "Disavowing Politics: Civic Engagement in an Era of Political Skepticism," *American Journal of Sociology* 119, no. 2 (2013): 518–48.

12. Juris, *Networking Futures*; Lauren Langman, "From Virtual Public Spheres to Global Justice: A Critical Theory of Internetworked Social Movements," *Sociological Theory* 23, no. 1 (2005): 42–74; Joshua Sbicca and Robert Perdue, "Protest through Presence: Spatial Citizenship and Identity Formation in Contestations of Neoliberal Crises," *Social Movement Studies* 13, no. 3 (2013): 309–27.

13. Buzby et al., "Value of Retail- and Consumer-Level Fruit and Vegetable Losses," 508.

14. Buzby, Wells, and Hyman, *Estimated Amount, Value, and Calories*, iii.

15. USDA Office of Communications, "USDA and EPA Join with Private Sector, Charitable Organizations to Set Nation's First Food Waste Reduction Goals," Press Release (press release, U.S. Department of Agriculture, Washington, D.C., September 16, 2015), http://content.govdelivery.com/accounts/USDAOC/bulletins/11a2c78.

16. Marie Mourad, "France Moves towards a National Policy against Food Waste" (National Resources Defense Council, Washington, D.C., September 2015); Matteo Vittuari et al., "Review of EU Legislation and Policies with Implications on Food Waste" (FUSIONS EU, Bologna, Italy, June 15, 2015).

17. Melissa Breyer, "Seven Surprising Things Pope Francis Has Done in His First 100 Days," *MNN—Mother Nature Network*, June 8, 2013, http://www.mnn.com/earth-matters/politics/stories/7-surprising-things-pope-francis-has-done-in-his-first-100-days.

18. M. Kummu et al., "Lost Food, Wasted Resources: Global Food Supply Chain Losses and Their Impacts on Freshwater, Cropland, and Fertiliser Use," *Science of the Total Environment* 438 (2012): 485.

19. Food and Agricultural Organization, *Food Wastage Footprint* (Paris: United Nations, 2013), http://www.fao.org/.

20. World Bank, "Food Prices Decline but Remain High" (news release, World Bank, Washington, D.C., November 26, 2013), http://www.worldbank.org/.

21. H. Charles J. Godfray et al., "Food Security: The Challenge of Feeding Nine Billion People," *Science* 327, no. 5967 (2010): 812–18.

22. Edwin Amenta and Michael Young, "Making an Impact," in *How Social Movements Matter*, ed. Marco Giugni, Doug McAdam, and Charles Tilly (Minneapolis: University of Minnesota Press, 1999), 22–41; Rachel Schurman and William A. Munro, *Fighting for the Future of Food: Activists versus Agribusiness in the Struggle over Biotechnology* (Minneapolis: University of Minnesota Press, 2010).

23. Jon Agnone, "Amplifying Public Opinion: The Policy Impact of the U.S. Environmental Movement," *Social Forces* 85, no. 4 (2007): 1593–620.

24. Evans et al. conclude that freeganism, alongside the 2008 economic crisis, government antiwaste policies, and the broader growth of the environmental movement, led to recent initiatives to combat food waste ("Brief Pre-History of Food Waste").

25. Stuart, *Waste,* 294.
26. Bloom, *American Wasteland,* 11, 28.
27. Mena, Adenso-Diaz, and Yurt, "Causes of Food Waste," 648.
28. Christopher Hope, "Jamie Oliver and Nigella Lawson Should Tell People How to Use Up Scraps in Their Cookbooks, Says Cabinet Minister," *Telegraph,* December 11, 2012.
29. USDA Office of Communications, "USDA and EPA Join with Private Sector."
30. Think.Eat.Save, "About the Campaign," United Nations Environmental Program, 2013, http://www.thinkeatsave.org/index.php/about.
31. T. E. Quested et al., "Spaghetti Soup: The Complex World of Food Waste Behaviours," *Resources, Conservation and Recycling* 79 (2013): 45.
32. Anna Bernstad, "Household Food Waste Separation Behavior and the Importance of Convenience," *Waste Management* 34, no. 7 (2014): 1317–23; Ann Carlson, "Recycling Norms," *California Law Review* 89, no. 5 (2001): 1231–300; Derksen and Gartrell, "Social Context of Recycling"; David Evans, "Blaming the Consumer—Once Again: The Social and Material Contexts of Everyday Food Waste Practices in Some English Households," *Critical Public Health* 21, no. 4 (2011): 429–40; Geremy Farr-Wharton, Marcus Foth, and Jaz Hee-Jeong Choi, "Identifying Factors That Promote Consumer Behaviours Causing Expired Domestic Food Waste," *Journal of Consumer Behaviour* 13, no. 6 (2014): 393–402; Karen Refsgaard and Kristin Magnussen, "Household Behaviour and Attitudes with Respect to Recycling Food Waste—Experiences from Focus Groups," *Journal of Environmental Management* 90, no. 2 (2009): 760–71.
33. Stuart, *Waste,* 206.
34. Tom Quested, Robert Ingle, and Andrew Parry, *Household Food and Drink Waste in the United Kingdom 2012* (Banbury, U.K.: Waste and Resources Action Program, November 2013).
35. Stuart, *Waste,* 190.
36. The mission statement of the USDA, for example, continues to include "to promote [i.e., increase] agriculture production," even as it participates in initiatives to reduce food waste. See U.S. Department of Agriculture, "Mission Statement," April 15, 2014, www.usda.gov.
37. Stuart, *Waste,* xx.
38. General Accounting Office, *Food Waste,* 44.
39. Jonathan Bloom, "Something to Shoot For: US Sets Food Waste Reduction Goal," *Wasted Food,* September 16, 2015, http://www.wastedfood.com/2015/09/16/something-to-shoot-for-us-sets-food-waste-reduction-goal/.
40. Ugo Gentilini, "Banking on Food: The State of Food Banks in High-Income Countries," *IDS Working Papers,* no. 415 (2013).
41. Jane L. Midgley, "The Logics of Surplus Food Redistribution," *Journal of Environmental Planning and Management* 57, no. 12 (2014): 872–1892; Poppendieck, *Sweet Charity?*; Valerie Tarasuk and Joan M. Eakin, "Food Assistance through 'Surplus' Food: Insights from an Ethnographic Study of Food Bank Work," *Agriculture and Human Values* 22, no. 2 (2005): 177–86.

42. Ed Bolen, Dorothy Rosenbaum, and Stacy Dean, *Summary of the 2014 Farm Bill Nutrition Title* (Washington, D.C.: Center on Budget and Policy Priorities, February 2014).

43. Bloom quotes one food bank manager saying that she throws out 50 percent of donations (*American Wasteland,* 49).

44. Buzby, Wells, and Hyman, *Estimated Amount, Value, and Calories,* 20.

45. Mourad, "Food Waste Inspiration."

46. Adam Przeworski demonstrates how redistributing wasted food to the poor would lower productivity and profits throughout a capitalist economy. See Przeworski, "Could We Feed Everyone? The Irrationality of Capitalism and the Infeasibility of Socialism," *Politics and Society* 19, no. 1 (1991): 32.

47. Griffin, Sobal, and Lyson, "Analysis of a Community Food Waste Stream," 79.

48. Philip McMichael, "The Land Grab and Corporate Food Regime Restructuring," *Journal of Peasant Studies* 39, nos. 3–4 (2012): 681–701.

49. O'Brien, "'Lasting Transformation' of Capitalist Surplus."

50. As Gille sagely observes, "profit-oriented incineration does not so much eliminate wastes as produces them" (*From the Cult of Waste,* 170).

51. Sven Lundie and Gregory M. Peters, "Life Cycle Assessment of Food Waste Management Options," *Journal of Cleaner Production,* Environmental Assessments and Waste Management, 13, no. 3 (2005): 275–86; Effie Papargyropoulou et al., "The Food Waste Hierarchy as a Framework for the Management of Food Surplus and Food Waste," *Journal of Cleaner Production* 76 (2014): 106–15.

52. Bloom, *American Wasteland,* 307.

53. U.S. Environmental Protection Agency, *Municipal Solid Waste in the United States.*

54. Rhodes Yepsen, "Residential Food Waste Collection in the U.S.," *BioCycle* 53, no. 1 (2015): 23–33.

55. Even the recycling rate itself may be vastly overstated. See Rob Van Haaren, Nickolas Themelis, and Nora Goldstein, "The State of Garbage in America," *BioCycle* 51, no. 10 (2010): 16–23.

56. One study, for example, found that composting food made respondents feel as though they were "doing their bit" and thus did not need to engage in further environmental action. See Alan Metcalfe et al., "Food Waste Bins: Bridging Infrastructures and Practices," *Sociological Review* 60 (2012): 135–55.

57. MacBride, *Recycling Reconsidered,* 6.

58. "PAC Board Approves the PAC Food Waste Initiative," Packaging Consortium, December 5, 2013, http://www.pac.ca/.

59. Bloom, *American Wasteland,* 24.

60. Fair Labor Association, *Independent Investigation of Apple Supplier, Foxconn* (Washington, D.C.: Fair Labor Association, March 29, 2012); Edward Wyatt, "Use of 'Conflict Minerals' Gets More Scrutiny," *New York Times,* May 19, 2012.

61. International Labor Organization, *Bangladesh: Seeking Better Employment Conditions for Better Socioeconomic Outcomes* (Geneva, Switzerland: International Institution for Labor Studies, 2013).

62. Brad Plumer, "What Trash Can Tell Us about the U.S. Economy," *WonkBlog*, August 20, 2012, http://www.washingtonpost.com/.

Index

Abbott, Andrew, 239n51

abject capital, 238n36; abject land capital, 240n63

Abrahamsson, Sebastian, 258n10

activism: around food, xii; basic flaws in mainstream, 72; biographical availability for, 56; environmental, 43–44, 77, 171–72; frustration and disillusionment with prior, 76; importance of Internet in activist recruitment, 77; neoliberal, 248n31; political, 6–7; searching for activist fit, 55–56, 72–76; transformation of mainstream American, since 1960s, 68. *See also* anarchist movements; anticapitalism; consumer activism; Food Not Bombs; freegan.info; freeganism; radicalization

Adenso-Diaz, B., 249n9

advertising to encourage consumer profligacy, 110

African Americans: freeganism and, 170–71. *See also* racism

age: appeal of freegan.info by, 167

AGM. *See* antiglobalization movement

Agnone, Jon, 261n23

agribusiness, international: conglomerates dominating, 2; factory farming, 7; farm subsidies to, 36–37; food waste across food supply chain and, 191–92; "green check mark," using food waste reductions as way to get, 227; Mexican small-scale farmers uprooted by, 1; "organic," "vegan," or "fair-trade" product lines owned by, 66; post–World War II promotion of waste and abundance, 110

Agricultural Adjustment Act of 1933, 35–36

agriculture: animal, inefficiency of, 236n18, 246n8; continued growth as primary imperative of capitalist, 36; crops ploughed under, 37–38; decommodification of surplus, during Great Depression, 36; farmland used to grow wasted food, 221; farm subsidies, 36–37, 110, 235n1; kilocalories per person per day produced in United States, 38; overproduction by start of twentieth century, 35–36; total global food supply per person per day, 224

alienation, freeganism and feelings of, 162–67; from friends and families, 165–66, 184; from other nonfreegan activists, 166

Al Jazeera, 195

Almanzar, Nelson Pichardo, 251n46

Alvarez, Jose B., 249n10

Amenta, Edwin, 261n22

AM New York (broadsheet), 187

Alex V. Barnard, an avid dumpster diver and food justice activist, is a doctoral student in sociology at the University of California, Berkeley.